LIVING BY THE SWORD

LIVING BY THE SWORD

WEAPONS AND
MATERIAL CULTURE
IN FRANCE AND
BRITAIN, 600–1600

KRISTEN B. NEUSCHEL

CORNELL UNIVERSITY PRESS
Ithaca and London

First published 2020 by Cornell University Press

Printed in the United States of America

Library of Congress Cataloging-in-Publication Data

Names: Neuschel, Kristen Brooke, 1951– author.
Title: Living by the sword : weapons and material culture
 in France and Britain, 600–1600 / Kristen B. Neuschel.
Description: Ithaca, [New York] : Cornell University Press,
 2020. | Includes bibliographical references and index.
Identifiers: LCCN 2020003683 (print) | LCCN 2020003684
 (ebook) | ISBN 9781501753336 (hardcover) |
 ISBN 9781501752124 (paperback) | ISBN 9781501752131
 (ebook) | ISBN 9781501752148 (pdf)
Subjects: LCSH: Swords—France—History. | Swords—Social
 aspects—France—History. | Swords—Great Britain—
 History. | Swords—Social aspects—Great Britain—History.
Classification: LCC U856.E85 N48 2020 (print) |
 LCC U856.E85 (ebook) |DDC 306.2/709410902—dc23
LC record available at https://lccn.loc.gov/2020003683
LC ebook record available at https://lccn.loc.gov/2020003684

For Alan, Jesse, and Rachel

❧ Contents

🍂 ILLUSTRATIONS

Color Plates

❧ PREFACE AND ACKNOWLEDGMENTS

I wrote this book to solve a problem the archives handed me regarding the material culture of warrior life in sixteenth-century Europe. It was possible that swords could be imagined, almost simultaneously, as workaday weapons, as jewel-like accessories, *and* as quasi-mythic objects from a distant and heroic past. Certainly, it was possible, but *how?* What might we need to know about elites' material circumstances, their dependence on swords in practice and in imagination, and so on? How do we set aside our own myths regarding swords, and our condescending assumptions about past actors' credulousness?

To answer the questions the documents posed, I began by looking at the life of swords in a more remote time, the early Middle Ages, and worked forward. As a consequence, this book is grounded in my own archival findings, particularly for the late medieval period through about 1600, but also depends on scholarship—of archaeologists, historians, scholars of literature—for earlier periods. Texts, from literature to lists, are how we get at swords and their meaning.

I consider evidence of swords in use and imagination in both Britain and France across about one thousand years of time. Thus, I march through historical periods often kept separate by scholars. I also cross and recross a number of disciplinary subfields including political and social history as well as military history, the history of literature, and, of course, material culture studies. My hope is that, in pursuing my own questions, I have opened useful windows for others in these various fields, without frustrating those who expect a more conventionally bounded investigation.

This book has matured over many years and has incurred profound debts along the way. All writing, perhaps especially scholarly writing, is done in community and for a particular community. I have been extremely lucky that my writing community included first readers Jehangir Malegam, Kristin L. Huffman, and Clare Woods—without whose expertise and inspiration this project would not have come to completion. I am likewise grateful to many other colleagues, whom I also count as friends. Chief among them is Ann

Marie Rasmussen, whose breadth of historical vision and humane approach to academic work were equally invaluable. Both Elinor Accampo and Ann-Louise Shapiro blazed trails for me with their own, quite different, work, and supported me with their counsel at crucial junctures. I thank Ruth Morse for sharing both her unpublished research and her learned perspectives on medieval texts and Stefan Collini for his writerly advice and for the example of his scholarly voice. My colleague and fellow early-modernist John Martin has offered steady encouragement and a refreshingly omnivorous curiosity about my subject. Also in Duke's History Department, I thank Jamie Hardy for taking care of the many administrative tasks that supported my research. I am also indebted to many former colleagues in Duke's Thompson Writing Program for their wisdom about the writing process. Among them, I thank above all Melissa Pascoe for her strategic intelligence and her generous help of many varieties.

I have been fortunate to have enjoyed the support of Emily Andrew, senior editor at Cornell University Press. I also thank Alexis Siemon, Karen Laun, and Martyn Beeny at CUP for their expertise and efficiency. I thank as well the anonymous readers who evaluated the manuscript; their conscientious reviews were invaluable, and made *Living by the Sword* a better book. Of course, all shortcomings and any remaining errors are my own.

I have dedicated this book to my husband and fellow historian Alan Williams and to my children and fellow writers Jesse and Rachel Williams. They have always understood the importance to me of this project, as well as of writing more generally. Without that understanding, and their patience and cheerleading, nothing would have come from my dive into the archives.

Note on Translations and Spelling

Translations are my own unless otherwise indicated. I have not modernized the spelling found in documents, including labels or titles of the documents, and have not inserted accent marks where modern French expects them. I have retained, however, the modernized spelling found in certain editions of documents.

LIVING BY THE SWORD

Introduction
What Do Swords Mean?

Every now and then, a historian enjoys an "Aha!" encounter, a moment when one fragment of data begins to gleam like a morsel of gold at the bottom of a pan of sand. I had such an experience a few years ago when reviewing my notes on a household inventory compiled for one French nobleman's heirs. Inventories are common enough in sixteenth-century record keeping but are precious sources because they capture not just things but also an event—a death, a journey—that necessitated a record of the belongings. So it was with the 1525 inventory of "movables" of the French aristocrat René d'Anjou, Sire de Mézières. In his case, the occasion was his death, as well as a journey that some of his belongings had taken afterward. I had been studying this inventory for a project on chateau furnishings and had noticed the presence of René's armor, his "harnois de guerre" packed tidily in a trunk, as well as his horse's armor nearby, all in a single room of his residence. I had, at first, assumed the room to have been René's own; after all, a good deal of his clothing was also stored there, along with other personal effects, in several other trunks of various descriptions.

The "Aha!" moment came when, reviewing my notes, I realized that there were no beds in the room. Indeed, there was no furniture at all in this room except a trestle table and a buffet. Even the kitchen in such a chateau, I knew, would have had beds (in the plural). So, this was not René's room, but a poorly turned out dining chamber or, more likely, a multipurpose

1

great hall.[1] I then guessed that René's armor and almost everything else in the room must simply have been deposited there together after having been brought home after his death, earlier that year, in the Italian wars between the French crown and the Hapsburgs. In other words, everything in those trunks had likely gone with René to the war in Italy. The inventory had preserved the material culture of aristocratic military life in an extraordinary way.

The list of René's belongings was typically punctilious and literal, enumerating every article found in every trunk. First, each piece of René's armor was named individually, beginning with the breastplate and backplate, the helmet, pieces for the shoulders, arms, and so on down to the armored shoes and the spurs. The pieces protecting the shoulders and upper arms, as well as the greaves (shin coverings), sabatons (shoes) and spurs were all gilded. The fact that René went to war with a complete suit of armor did not surprise me. Mounted men-at-arms generally wore full body armor at this point; it had been continuously developed since the fourteenth century to protect against missile fire from infantry—from longbows, crossbows, or harquebuses—and it was now at what would be its historical peak of development. Since the makers of the inventory also carefully noted the decorative embellishment of the pieces, I knew that René's armor served as protection but also functioned as a form of luxurious display. Thus, it could serve for battle or for tournament.

The inventory went on to record René's clothing and other personal effects with equal attention to detail. The trunks held cloaks "for riding," and several other cloaks made of taffeta, or of velvet, lined with this or that expensive fur. René had also packed seven doublets, each identified by its fabric—velvet, satin, taffeta—and by its trimmings in silver and gold. Tucked in among the clothes rested an inlaid mirror. René had also taken four hunting horns with him, one of them beautifully worked in silver with an image of St. Hubert, the patron of hunters. Protected together in a box were his private seal, some important papers, one piece of jewelry, and a silver reliquary in the form of a cross. Intermingled with these accoutrements were a few bladed weapons. Some, like René's armor, speak of splendor as well as function. Amid the clothes in one trunk, for example, lay two daggers with velvet sheaths and two poignards (a popular kind of dagger with a thin, tapered blade); one poignard, the list notes, has a tassel—a fashion of the time. In another coffer is an old single-edged sword, called a *braquemart*, decorated with a gilded hilt.

René's elegant clothes, his hand mirror, his papers and seal in their wooden box, his beautifully worked small weapons, all attest to the fact

WHAT DO SWORDS MEAN?

that traveling abroad for war did not detach an aristocrat from the routines of life: he would dress the part, participate in the usual pleasures, including riding out to the hunt; he would correspond with secretaries, attend to property and to his own appearance. Indeed, for the purposes of daily life, the tableware included in the trunks seems deficient. René had only a few pewter vessels and a solitary silver spoon, which suggests that more valuable pieces may have been pawned or sold as his need for funds dictated.[2]

After these full accounts of René's elegant accoutrements, I was surprised by meager descriptions of his battle weapons. The presence of "two swords" is simply recorded—as is that of his battle flags: "two large banners," says the inventory, "and one small one." Why are these battle flags not more fully depicted? And why are the most important items of all, we might think— his battle swords—described so cursorily? His armor is so fully depicted, but his usable weapons are not. Is there some significance, in other words, not merely to the individual items he carries but also to the way they are described?

I knew to consider the primary purpose of the inventory: the need to fully identify each article, in order to keep track of it. Perhaps it was felt that the usable swords could not be mistaken for anything else and therefore did not need a detailed description. The hangings meant to accompany René's camp bed may also have been treated in this way; they are noted but not described, though even the camp bed itself and his chamber pot are recorded with their leather cases, while the only one of the swords' scabbards is mentioned. Or perhaps, somehow, the cursory descriptions are ironic evidence of the swords' and battle flags' overriding importance, although the literal nature of most inventories weighs against this reading. And some of René's weapons, such as the poignards, resemble elegant clothing in both their luxurious qualities and in how those properties are reported in the document. It is striking that the distinguishing features of the swords—on their hilts, particularly—are not mentioned at all, though the braquemart is at least cursorily described, as having a gilded hilt. Why did the braquemart accompany René on campaign? Perhaps its decoration suggests it is a showpiece or an heirloom. Meanwhile, René's other swords do not seem to carry added value; they are not decorated or beautiful, old or new, family heirloom or treasured gift. They are simply "arming swords" (*epées d'armes*), meaning battle-worthy blades, in the eyes of the inventory maker. One of the two is distinguished from the other by its velvet scabbard, but that is all we learn about them.

The intriguing data as well as the missing information in this inventory started me on an investigation of the material culture of warrior life, above all of the significance of swords, that has resulted in this book. Immediately, I encountered two other lists of belongings that complicated the questions I would carry into further research. The first of these was another inventory from the same stash of family papers. It appeared to document a dramatic change in the life of swords over the course of the sixteenth century. In this inventory, all of the nobleman's swords have become like René's decorated daggers or poignards: they resemble clothing in their abundance and their luxuriousness. Notably, they are described in some detail, their decorative attributes obviously important.

The nobleman in question, François de Bourbon-Montpensier, had married René's granddaughter and namesake, Renée d'Anjou, in 1572. In this list, made in 1576, each of François's swords is paired with its own poignard. Each set has a matching sword belt and sheaths, which are always noted and sometimes depicted in great detail. One set, for example, consisted of "one sword, with its poignard, of Damascus steel, with sheath and belt of velvet"; another pair is described as both gilded and worked with silver, with belt and sheaths of velvet, but covered also with a leather case.[3]

This list was created to keep track of effects sent from Paris for safekeeping to the same family chateau, Saint-Fargeau, where René's belongings had been returned some fifty years earlier, while François himself traveled to England on a diplomatic mission. I could imagine the impressive garments François must have taken to Queen Elizabeth's court, yet he had left to be shepherded to Saint-Fargeau no less than twelve splendid doublets and thirteen pairs of hose. There are five sword-and-dagger "sets" recorded in the inventory, too. All, like the doublets and hose, were considered superfluous for the mission, to be sent home for safekeeping, though they had nonetheless figured among François's furnishings while in Paris. How many sword "sets" did he have, in total? Many more than five, since he must have taken some with him abroad. So, perhaps the question posed by the earlier inventory had been answered, I mused: swords are described when their decoration is what distinguishes them, when they have become an indispensable article of clothing, often matched with outfits.

Did these two lists of belongings from the chateau at Mézières tidily document a transformation in the lives of swords? This mutation of swords—from broadsword to rapier, battle sword to civilian sword—is well known, in its outlines. A gentleman would no more go out in public without his sword-and-dagger set, in the later sixteenth century, than without his shirt, so we believe. These swords were longer, more delicate, than battle swords. Their swept hilts could carry ornamentation of great finesse. They had become masculine jewelry, a luxury technology for display, in the words of one modern curator.[4]

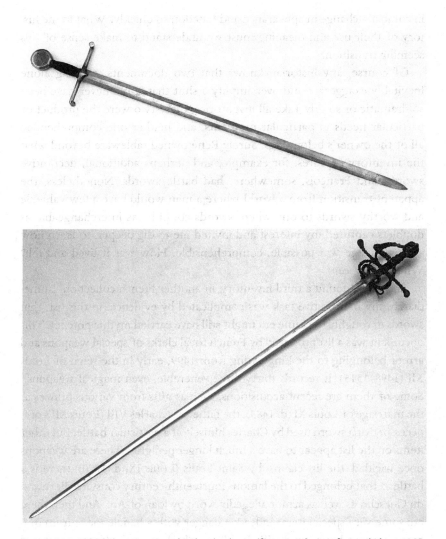

FIGURE I.1. Sixteenth-century swords. The simple cruciform sword, manufactured about 1500, could have been like one of those carried by René d'Anjou early in the century; the narrower blade with an elaborate, gilded hilt was made in Italy around 1570 and would have been a highly coveted possession by a great nobleman such as François de Bourbon-Montpensier. © RMN-Grand Palais / Art Resource, NY.

Yet if the sword was the most symbolically potent of all of a warrior's weapons, as most scholars of material culture and aristocratic life believe, and perhaps the most potent of all his belongings, we should pause to look at this change in the design and use of swords more closely. How could an object so important, with such symbolic valence—not to mention usefulness in combat—change in appearance and function so quickly? What in the history of their use and meaning must we understand to make sense of this seeming transition?

Of course, any historian knows that two documents standing alone inevitably exaggerate and oversimplify a shift that could never have been so dramatic or so tidy. Like all inventories, these two were the product of particular needs in particular moments, and neither one comprehended all of the owner's belongings. Surely René owned tableware beyond what the inventory captures, for example, and perhaps additional, decorative swords; and François, somewhere, had battle swords. Nonetheless, the apparent transition from a world where a man would have a few valuable and worthy swords to one where swords could be as interchangeable as doublets captured my interest and invited me to dig deeper, to learn how such a change was possible, comprehensible. How was it lived and felt? What did it *mean*?

And then I found a third inventory, in another French collection. Immediately, my interpretive task was complicated by evidence, in this list, that swords in roughly the same era might still have carried mythic potency. This document was a list produced by French royal clerks of special weapons and armor belonging to the king dating from 1499, early in the reign of Louis XII (1498–1515). It records thirty-three venerable, even magical weapons.[5] Some of them are recent acquisitions, such as gifts from various princes at the marriage of Louis XI (d. 1483), the father of Charles VIII (Louis XII's predecessor), or a sword used by Charles himself at a particular battle. But other items on the list appear to have a much longer pedigree. There are weapons once wielded, the list claims, by Saint Louis (Louis IX, d. 1270); there is a battle ax that belonged to the famous fourteenth-century constable Bertrand du Guesclin as well as armor allegedly worn by Joan of Arc. And then there are some very special items indeed: a dagger with a handle made from unicorn (horn or bone, unspecified) called "Charlemagne's dagger"; a sword with a long pommel, "the giant's sword," which had been taken in battle on the Île de la Cité (the island in Paris where Notre Dame is sited) by "a king of France"; and, grandest of all, a sword with an iron grip fashioned like a key that had belonged to Lancelot du Lac, called—it is added helpfully—the "fairy sword."

Like all inventories, this list must have been drawn up for a particular occasion—actually two occasions, since the document we have is a copy of a lost original.[6] Like other lists, this one varies somewhat in the level of detail from object to object. Throughout, though, the juxtaposition of its dutiful, almost mundane, structure to the extraordinary objects catalogued was arresting and fascinating. The supposedly mythical objects—swords won off a giant or belonging to a fictional hero like Lancelot—were recorded methodically along with newer items, whose provenance was more certain. What was the author of the document actually looking at when he described Lancelot's sword? In other words, beyond the question of why these objects were documented is the more basic question of what these objects were, why they were assembled to begin with, and when they were saved. When was the sword that slew the giant "saved"? Or "discovered"? What impulse moved Charles VIII to set aside a symbolically potent sword? Was Charles, in his own mind, following a tradition? And what was the purpose of this collection; what was its life beyond this list?

Most important for my investigation was the question of whether this inventory is only intelligible if one assumes that swords were still regarded in reverent terms, as repositories of myth, or even as enchanted objects, as late as the turn of the sixteenth century. If so, does that mean that the "decline of magic" occurred in weapons so quickly that, within two generations, swords could be treated instead like other objects of conspicuous consumption, as François's 1576 inventory suggests? In other words, this list of mythic weapons underscored my earlier musings about the experience of a profound transformation. If swords can still be imagined or portrayed as individually powerful, as mythic objects, how then can they be reimagined, demoted, in effect, to mere ornament? A gulf between swords as enchanted objects and swords as (even) deadly jewelry may require accounting for some kind of fundamental change.

On the other hand, the seeming tensions among these three documents might also reflect a false impression of what the lists actually reveal, whether separately or together. Inventories were more events than comprehensive records, so the differences between René's and his grandson-in-law's effects, for example, might primarily reflect greater disposable wealth of François's generation, and the increasing expectation of conspicuous consumption and display felt by all would-be courtiers and their princes. In addition, the fairy or the giant's sword in the 1499 document may have resembled, in function, the gilded sword René carried all the way to Italy rather than leave at home; they all might have been souvenirs, as that term is used by some scholars of material culture: memory aids to a past that can be remembered but not relived.[7] Thus, perhaps there is actually very little tension between and among these documents, and they all, together, tell a different story, one of continuity rather than rupture, in which swords played practical and symbolic roles that we have not yet discerned or delineated. The history of the role of swords in warrior culture needed a fresh interpretation, I concluded, before these different, coincidental skeins of value and meaning could be disentangled.

Historians of warfare have argued that the rise of gunpowder weapons was dramatic, in fact traumatic for elite warriors, but have not asked as much about the mutations of swords. A number of scholars have also studied the prescriptive literature about swordsmanship and dueling, which began to proliferate in the sixteenth century after the spread of print technology. Few, however, have examined material culture. Here I will present evidence about swords in the possession of aristocrats and more humble fighters, as well as royalty, found in records generated by their households or from contemporary observers. I will scrutinize the practical and symbolic uses of swords as weapons, as gifts, as markers of authority, and as talismans of identity. The swords in use by the sixteenth century—whether wielded in battle, worn almost as jewelry, or saved as memorabilia—had deep pasts. Lancelot's sword would neither have been saved nor recorded, nor the record in turn copied, if it did not carry at least an imagined past with it. Thus, I will set the stage for the world of swords around 1500 with an investigation of swords in use and in imagination in the medieval world.

My goal has been to rethink what we believe we know about swords, to defamiliarize them in order to see them in their premodern contexts more clearly and more fully. I have sought to examine swords afresh, but have been mindful from the beginning that part of what makes swords appear as known quantities, with obvious significance, is our present fascination with them, which my own interest in the topic reflected. In all societies (not just in "primitive" ones where certain objects may be invested with enormous power), objects have agency simply by the fact that human beings have relationships with them, have expectations of them. To put it another way, things have desires.[8] Swords are characterized in these terms with almost banal frequency, as I was reminded at an exhibition of fencing practices at a London museum where a historical weapons expert displayed modern-built facsimiles of arrows, armor, bows, and swords. The broadsword he handed me, he assured me, was the right weight (and far lighter than we commonly think). But, he added, "you can tell the difference between a real sword and a fake—you pick up a real sword and it's alive. It wants to kill somebody."[9] Our fascination with objects reflects our own expectations, our participation in relationships with objects in the present. Objects have a historical existence in that we must always set them in the context—of use, of other objects, of texts and images and other symbolic possibilities—they inhabited. That context always includes our own lens, our own gaze and our imagined needs, in our present day. Our own longings, however, should not be projected onto men and women of the past.

As I travel, here, through several centuries' worth of swords and their uses, I draw on the research of archaeologists, historians, and literary scholars concerning specific artifacts and texts. However, my study is also grounded in recent theoretical work of anthropologists and archaeologists regarding material culture in general and the kinds of analytical challenges it poses. Much of that work asks us to consider how the things human beings create become, in turn, active agents in their lives, including in our lives in the here and now. We find it easy to dwell on the impact of artifacts we label technology, in fact we tend to exaggerate their impact and overlook the conservative ways humans have tended to adopt new technologies. But all the goods people have created, bought, seized, and preserved have had a role in shaping their culture—not just materially, but also mentally. Objects are not merely the product of thought, they become in turn shapers of thought and of feeling. Things, especially certain things, are useful tools to think with, to shape thought, habits, behavior—culture, in short. In this way, objects are like texts: they are out in the world, detached from the producer, gaining and giving meaning in action in the human lifeworld.[10]

The analogy with texts can go only so far, however, because objects are not wholly the same as language in how they function as conceptual tools. Unlike with language, the relationship between a material signifier (say, a grave) and whatever is signified (say, ancestors) is not wholly arbitrary. It is in part because material culture is not wholly arbitrary as a symbolic system, that it has a unique power to shape human thought and perception. Objects do not merely reflect prior thoughts, they can help make ideas and practices possible. Large multiple-grave tombs, for example, could both reflect an enhanced sense of community and help foster—even launch—a new or redefined sense of the community that constructed them.[11]

Material objects help us think, imagine, mourn, and celebrate precisely because they are not empty vessels waiting to convey meaning derived elsewhere. The meaning you can make with an object always depends in part on the perceived properties of the object.[12] On the one hand, this means they are less useful for complex, abstract thinking than is language. On the other hand, they remain flexible conceptual tools; we have many examples of humans repurposing objects to meet new conceptual or symbolic needs. Objects never mean just one thing; their meaning is capable of being reworked in different contexts, and thus can be ambiguous, multivalent, at any one moment. They carry and express tension, in other words. Swords can break and also keep the peace.[13] So, although it is inevitable that we want to know what objects "mean," we should concentrate instead on *how* they mean: how they suggest ways of thinking; how they draw human attention; how they do conceptual and symbolic work on humans' behalf.[14] How, in a sense, objects are actors, in the present and in various pasts.

The "present," our world of relationships with objects, includes the conventional scholarly question of what is our evidence? What possibilities and limitations are embedded in it, and in our use of it? By foregrounding these surviving lists of belongings, and the conditions under which they were made, I draw attention to the power of these records themselves, not just the objects they name. These records of belongings are neither neutral nor haphazard, but they are arbitrary. They are events as well as records and they preserve certain features of the objects and not others. Thus, they add to rather than subtract from the problem of "survival" in ways that anticipate later museum collections. As scholars of material culture point out, gathering artifacts in a museum creates a supercategory of objects that is a distortion of what "was" in the original culture.[15] So, while inventories document swords for our use now, they also distort our vision of the past. Records of swords also shaped the way swords and other objects were valued in their day, as well as by intervening generations. How things are recorded, described, and fixed in record keeping for certain audiences at certain moments is part of the work the objects did then and do now in the world.

The inventories that permit us to document what aristocrats, gentry, and even more common folk owned at a particular time are late developments: the earliest surviving household accounts are from the thirteenth century, but inventories of this kind do not survive in any significant number before the fifteenth century. The fact that these documents do not proliferate until after 1400 not only means that we lack evidence about earlier periods; it also means that we must be especially careful to take the documentation of belongings into account as we evaluate the importance of the items captured in them. In other words, the documents that survive from the end of the Middle Ages are not merely a window that enables us to see what we cannot see as well for earlier periods. Rather, the documentation itself is part of the story of the importance of these objects in the lives of their owners. Inventorying objects is a way not only to document one's prior acts of consumption; it is also, in itself, a systematic act of consumption.

In addition, documents are things too. All information requires human energy and all of it has a physical embodiment, in a human body, on paper, in microchips. Indeed, I will argue that it is misleading to imagine that, at any time, the world of goods was separate from the world of information and of texts, one physically embodied, the other not. First, some texts were also, in the most obvious sense, objects: they were pieces of parchments or books. Second, objects could contain or anchor texts in other ways: for example, they were used (as they still are) as "memory pegs," to preserve stories about people and events.[16] Also, objects could take meaning partly from their relationship to a text—a biblical story, a myth—that was part of its users' or viewers' repertoire, such as the Bayeux Tapestry's references to the story of Roland, or the fairy sword's reference to the character Lancelot.[17] The textual world warriors inhabited, I argue, collaborated with artifacts to help fashion the meanings of those objects.

If swords or any other object could take and give meaning in connection with stories or with texts of any sort, they also did so in the context of other objects—including other weapons, clothes, jewels, household furnishings, religious paraphernalia, even buildings. In this study, I situate swords in the material contexts to which they originally belonged: environments in which a variety of goods was used to symbolize and display both identity and status. Through the Middle Ages, as the European economy expanded, the sheer amount as well as the variety of goods that aristocrats, and even middling nobles and gentry, could collect and value likewise expanded. What could a sword mean to an aristocrat in the late Middle Ages, amid all his other luxurious belongings? Did the growth of conspicuous consumption, the growth in collecting and fetishizing many objects, diminish the symbolic valence of that preeminent object, a warrior's sword? Did swords perhaps become just one more category of goods to assemble in quantity, such as the sword-and-dagger pairs in François's collection seem to be? Excess and variety accomplished political work, yet swords still conveyed distinct messages, I will argue. We should not respond to the riot of objects captured in an inventory as though we are staring at too many pairs of shoes on the floor of a closet.

One problem we face in trying to tease out the value of things to their contemporaries is that the study of material culture is one of the domains where historians have stressed a premodern-modern divide in European history. Scholars of the "military revolution," for example, focus on the ripple effects of gunpowder weapons on warrior identity as well as on states and economies by means of changes in the nature of battle and the composition of armies. The precise effects of these changes on the warring classes, and the timing and the mechanism of those effects are widely debated, as are the salient features of the wider "revolution" itself, but the changing technology of weaponry and fortification is implicated in every recent interpretation.[18] Scholars interested in the emergence of modern forms of identity, the modern "self," also have anchored much of their thinking in changes they see both in the objects surrounding early modern elites and in elites' relationships to objects. One object in particular, the printed book, has received concentrated attention. Interaction with a wider range of texts helped foster the interiority of the self, a self that is detached from others and capable of new kinds of self-reflection and emotional privacy. But attention has also fallen on the early modern world of goods as a whole: the expansion of European-dominated trade and the growth of consumption within Europe. The proliferation of goods, many scholars have argued, created new symbolic means to display power, to mark the distance between self and other (particularly colonized peoples or heretical "others"), and to imagine a relationship of mastery between the subject and the object, the self and the world.[19] More goods, in short, helped pave the way to modernity.

Yet we have also acknowledged of late that the whole notion of mastery of the physical world is a story, a cultural artifact itself. The industrial-age conceit that we are masters of the physical world is an illusion. It is a narrative about modernity; it is not what constitutes modernity in the sense of contemporary history, whatever is happening in the present moment. It is certainly not a true description of our relationship to the world of things. Thus now, as we inhabit what some call a "postmodern" position, we are better placed than our immediate forebears to appreciate the power and agency of objects. For example, the fact that we are today surrounded by objects, even expensive ones, which are nonetheless ephemeral and disposable enables us to see wastage or loss as part of the life of an object.[20] We are more attuned to use as well as deliberate waste of objects and how we interact with them, and thus no longer think that objects passively carry our identity, but rather work with us to fashion our sense of self. We also are better able to see, compared to prior generations of interpreters, the role of power relations in constructing the value and agency of objects.

But our postmodern position still rests on the assumption of a firm premodern-modern divide, and thus makes it difficult for us to interrogate our own attachments to things. Our position does not exempt us from the pull of things—the reciprocal desires of objects and of ourselves particular to our own context. For example, as many scholars have recently noted, it is no coincidence that we have become particularly fascinated by material culture—the presence and use and value of *things*—now that we are immersed much of the time in virtual or digital reality. Our interest in the world of the tangible is in part a nostalgic reflex for the lost premodern world where things, we suppose, were more durable, where "reality" always had a physical embodiment, and where the meaning of things, we imagine, was straightforward and anchored in a three-dimensional object or fellow human you could see and touch. We can compensate for our nostalgia by inquiring about the work that reflex is doing in its own present. We still, however, need to uncover our implicit bias toward a notion of rupture with the past, which is propped up by an assumption of a premodern-modern divide.

When it comes to analyzing the significance of swords in the past, our attachments, and the reasons for them, are particularly effective at clouding our vision. Modern interpreters, such as we still are in many ways, often make the mistake of thinking the meaning of objects stays the same across time—failing to remember that it is we in the present (as well as others, in past "presents") who imagine that continuity for our own purposes.

A parallel move, which also implicates how we assess swords, is a resolute bracketing-off of superstition about or reverence for objects in a premodern past. This actually amounts to a kind of hypernostalgia for a long-ago time when special objects (and maybe special creatures) inhabited the earth. In both cases, that of imagined continuity or of rupture, we are outside time and absolved of the need to explain change through time. Moreover, when we seek to contain magical properties of things in a primitive, non-modern past, we only expose our own fascination with them. Our fetishizing of superstition and magical properties of objects occurs in the present, in response to our own felt needs.[21] We cannot deem belief in magical swords to be a relic of the premodern past and also call a sword "alive." And yet we do. What constitutes magic—the unexplained, the marvelous—has a history too, and we are particularly blind to our own present fascinations.

With objects like swords, there are additional reasons for our nostalgic attachment. Material survivals from the past are enticing because of the promise of physical encounter. We are embodied persons and objects generate a more instinctive, more profound response than does any abstract description of the past carried out in words. We have a much more immediate sense of contact with a past that is nonetheless out of reach. Indeed, the sight of a sword, a shoe, or any object that also exists in a modern form, can incite not merely a false recognition, but also longing, even mourning, for a world that remains literally and figuratively untouchable.[22] We will encounter, here, other highly valued objects, such as shields or coats of mail, which are treated with much care, as are swords, in aristocrats' wills, for example, but hold much less power to provoke longing in us in the present. This point was borne out recently by a televised feature about a team of archaeologists working at a previously unknown Roman site in Britain. The lead archaeologist discussed several finds, including an unusual and very fine fragment of armor, but the entire feature was edited so that the display of a found sword—dull and rusted though it was—ended the interview. The journalist or editor assumed interest and a sense of recognition of this object in the audience.

We are also fascinated with surviving swords because we do not control the technology that produced them. Sword blades from the migration age (roughly the fourth century) until the fourteenth century were forged by metal smiths from iron and the small amounts of steel that could be produced by contemporary smelting processes, which did not change markedly in western Europe until the years after about 1300. Hand-forging meant that each sword was a unique combination of low- and high-carbon iron (steel), and of variations on techniques to create a workable blade: hard enough, but not brittle, with a durable sharp edge. The individual qualities of each sword depended on the specific characteristics of the metal available, as well as on the processes the smith used; quenching and tempering to improve the toughness of the blade were an art, not a science, in part because their effects on the metal depended on the amount of carbon in the blade, which could not be precisely controlled or even determined. Contemporary written "recipes" for making steel reveal the experimental nature of the work. And, as with much premodern technology, we today cannot always understand the process the written sources are describing, nor can we always tell precisely by what techniques a particular surviving sword was made, which stokes our wonderment in the present.[23] One eminent historian of swords reveals the allure of the handcrafted sword when she claims, "no single object among the possessions of modern man may be compared to it."[24]

This inability to understand how an object, such as a sword, comes into being is one reason why we are enchanted with new technology in our own day, and why we fail to recognize our response as enchantment. The late anthropologist Alfred Gell argued that we think of art objects as a form of technology, perhaps the highest form of technology, because we cannot ourselves reproduce the object; the way of its making is mysterious. Enchantment, he continues, is "immanent in all kinds of technical activity," by which he means that wherever we cannot fully see or understand how an object, especially a beautiful one, came into being, we will be enchanted by it. "Enchantment" means that these objects exert a special kind of power and fascination. They are objects of desire, which we cannot fulfill. It is not that we cannot own them (if we had enough money); it is that we cannot explain them, render them transparent.

"The resistance which they offer, and which creates and sustains this desire," Gell says, "is . . . the difficulty I have in mentally encompassing their coming-into-being as objects in the world accessible to me by a technical process which, since it transcends my understanding, I am forced to construe as magical." Gell points out that our culture thinks of art and technology as polar opposites, one is "beautiful," the product of creativity, and the other merely technical, "dull and mechanical" in its origins.[25] But, he argues, we seek to contain the power of art over us by means of aesthetics, by trying to fetishize and decipher its beauty, whereas the power of the object over us remains not one of aesthetics, but what he calls the enchantment of technology, of the coming-into-being of the object by means we cannot execute ourselves, hence enchantment applies to both "art" and "technology."

Gell's notion of aesthetic experience or enchantment resembles what another scholar, Hans Gumbrecht, calls "presence effect." It is an immanent, immersive experience which, in the contemporary world, can occur in the presence of a wondrous object—like the Roman sword displayed in the televised segment mentioned above—or an image or sound; it might be the momentary witness of the elegant body of an athlete poised impossibly on tiptoe to catch a football; it might occur in listening to a performance of a Mozart aria; it might be in the startling sight of a bolt of lightning as we thrum along an interstate highway. In such "moments of intensity," Gumbrecht argues, we let go of our interpretive impulse, our modern desire to be observers driven to make the world make sense all the time. The interpretive habit of mind, deeply ingrained in our culture since at least the seventeenth century, is of no use to us in such moments, in fact would impede the (magical) sense of "presence," a sense of being wholly present, outside of time. Our desire for presence, Gumbrecht argues, is as strong as our desire to understand and interpret the world; the two dispositions are in tension.[26] In fact, the more we need to interpret, to analyze, the world, the greater our felt need for moments of "presence."

Our enchantment with swords in our own day is particularly powerful because it contains all of these elements I have discussed here: a desire for a connection to the past; a simultaneous and conflicting desire to contain the mysterious and irrational in a remote past (to which our nostalgia then gives us access); an unwillingness to understand our own fascination in the present as both a kind of nostalgia and an instance of enchantment and, occasionally, via film or performance, especially, an experience of "presence." We are not wholly blind to our fascination with old objects like swords, but we believe the wonder is inherent in the object, not also in ourselves. The sensation that a sword is alive is as much our work as it is the sword's.

To historicize the meaning of swords, that is, to re-create in any measure contemporaries' encounters with them across the centuries, we need to situate them not only in the dense field of other prestige objects that surrounded them but also in the context of the interpretive strategies and categories of experience available to their human owners. In other words, we must historicize the notions of enchantment, of presence, and of the perceived qualities of swords within their lifeworlds to discern, insofar as we can, how warrior men responded to and valued them. At a minimum, we must try to unearth simply what objects were there, over time, in warriors' hands: the number and kinds of swords men owned; what else they collected and valued; and how these conditions changed over generations.

Medieval and early modern people were enormously sophisticated interpreters and consumers of symbolic materials.[27] Especially after about 1100 CE, coats of arms, personal mottoes (whether inscribed on a shield, on a garment, in some other image, or spoken aloud), signature emblems on badges or banners, the rich iconography associated with saints, all were circulating and continually mutating. As property relations and mechanisms of government became more complex and impersonal, artifacts such as wax seals became necessary to stand in for the author of a document, and coats of arms or other such signs likewise stood in for the lord in locations where he could not actually be. Encounter with these representations of lordly power were more experiences of recognition, of presence, than an encounter with a political symbol, say, would afford today.

Presence of another kind was an effect of the way an artifact participated in the power of the divine—the prototype being the Eucharist, where Christ's body and blood ritually reappeared in mundane things. Kings tried hard to associate themselves with sacred power in their symbolic trappings, as in the case of the French kings, who displayed a banner claiming the sacred aura of St. Denis. Yet the transcendent power of an artifact, even of a saint's relic, diminished over time; it had to be reintroduced into the community and thus into living memory every three generations or so in order to retain its potency. The same was true of the allure of an iconic sword. The potency of such a sword came from its reputation, from the feats it had accomplished, or from its ability to share in and convey the exalted persona of its owner. All the way through the Middle Ages, into the sixteenth century, a sword's power came from its function, its aesthetic character, but also from its connection to the body of the man who wielded it and the deeds it had helped him accomplish. It had to be actively remembered in some way to remain effectual.

As in our own eyes, the attraction did not reside solely in the sword, but also in the user or beholder. Their uses of objects, including swords, occurred in the context of the arbitrary foundations of their power. Warrior men fought, at times literally, to claim a place in a hierarchy of privileged actors, whose status depended in part on continually staging their claim to that status. Their privilege, in short, had to be continually performed to be safeguarded.[28] Display, liberality, and competitive gift-giving were the routine experience of both objects and their users. Neither swords nor any other single kind of object would stand alone, to dominate on that stage, since all belongings were part of an economy not of consumption, as we would understand it, but of excess. But simple excess was also not enough. An elite warrior's goods, like the arbitrary nature of his power, had to exist in a hierarchy of value, which he could not only appreciate, but also help create. If an elite man performed his claim to power by means of the stuff around him, then he also had the power to create iconic objects, to invest a particular iteration of a sword, for example, with added value, by means of its artistry, its ancestry, its remembered accomplishments—with enhanced identity, in effect. Simultaneously, he could "read" and interpret the various registers of meaning he encountered in other weapons, coats of arms, clothing, and so on. When a sword passed from one man to another, identity was conveyed with it—in the sense of a unique, identifiable status, but the human interpreters would attach nuances of meaning.

These capacities are not well understood if imagined as the product either of distanced "interpretation" or of a mesmerizing presence, a singularity that cuts through the routine experience of the world. The need for presence, in the ordinary sense of that word, was simply a fact of life in medieval and early modern warrior culture. Investment in coats of arms, signature devices on clothing, and the like represented the need to project one's presence beyond one's body in the moment. Swords could carry the experience of a man, convey his identity and an attachment to it, because they were associated with his body. They were encountered by others on his body and conveyed from one body, from one set of hands, to another, when bequeathed. And yet they were still weapons and products of technical craft both rare and highly valued. Their special magnetism, for contemporaries, came from this combining of intimacy, incipient violence, and control of prized materiel—all of them, separately, qualities that marked warrior men's privilege.

I believe our own fetishizing of the past, and of objects like the sword, to be part of the story of what appears to "happen" with regard to swords and their significance over time. The material record speaks of change, and profound change at that, but we need a more nuanced understanding than one that locates an undifferentiated enchantment working through time, or a sense of "presence" that would apply to a largely oral culture in the past as well as to ours, inundated as we are by digital texts and ephemeral belongings. A sixteenth-century rapier may be masculine jewelry, but it is nonetheless vital to the wearer's persona; we must adjust our gaze to see the power residing in such an object. I will argue that swords safeguarded warrior identity through the early phases of the so-called military revolution—the transformation of battles and armies by gunpowder weapons—because they already had a long history as required identity markers, and had long been central yet insufficient to the task on their own. In fact, nostalgia for a time when swords were rare, singular, and magically potent can be discerned as early as the tenth century, and perhaps before.

But we have to presume that tenth-century nostalgia was not doing the same work as our nostalgia now. Nor should we assume that objects had agency, behaved as much like actors as like things, in the same ways over time. On the one hand, many would argue that we have never been "modern"; we have always lived in a world where objects have had various kinds of power over us, were in some ways subjects like us, whether or not we were able to acknowledge it. On the other hand, vastly different material conditions over time mean that *how* objects mean and the possible experiences of presence could change dramatically. The context around swords which changed over time included, of course, other goods, but also various kinds of texts, some embodied, some not—wills, household accounts, treasury lists, but also stories, oral and written. In what follows, I will stress the way oral culture, especially in the early medieval centuries, shaped the imagined capacities of swords and other objects. In predominantly oral cultures, objects typically have enhanced power because they are essential for memory and because human identity in face-to-face cultures is relational, in which circulating objects play a role in constituting each person. Thus, objects in turn carry human attributes. Swords, in early medieval practice and texts, while helpful for remembrance of a person, also carried emotional memory, such as feuding, from one generation to another.

By the time we get to the High Middle Ages, economic expansion and political consolidation produced both a wider array of goods to mark status and a greater necessity to deploy them. Inflation, of a sort, was diminishing swords' power. Though now essential, swords were already insufficient as markers of status. As mythic swords—like Lancelot's—make their first appearance in collections of actual objects as well as in literature, they immediately have competition from other worthy objects, such as a holy lance from Christ's crucifixion. At the same time, written histories of peoples and families begin to supplement heirlooms as carriers of memory; and, in the rich corpus of chivalric tales, warriors' repertoire of behavior and of emotional range expands, without the same dependence on artifacts.

The fourteenth century marks a watershed—perhaps the most significant one—in the material culture of European elites. Enough steel could now be produced to fashion plate armor. Swords changed shape somewhat to adapt to their new uses against this defensive weapon. At the same time, styles of clothing changed dramatically, which led to an exaggeration of gender difference in garments. In many ways, the well-turned-out Renaissance man and his sword-as-jewelry began here. This is the era, moreover, when records of belongings begin to be kept in earnest. Documentation is a kind of virtual collecting which encourages further collecting, further proliferation and assembling of goods, by its very existence. A fifteenth-century aristocrat devoted huge resources to gathering and maintaining and tracking goods of all sorts, and to carefully deploying them for effect—down to which tapestry cushions to use for an outing on his river barge, and how to refurbish them when they got wet on the excursion. By the sixteenth century, royal collections of weapons are open for view, one of the era's collections of marvels on display. These collections overawed contemporaries with the sheer number of weapons, and they also fed nostalgia; armor or weapons belonging to great men of the past were included next to mounds of contemporary swords and crossbows. The 1499 list of French royal weapons is one such collection.

It might seem tempting to see in these developments a straightforward progression from early centuries of relatively few prestige goods, where each object had an outsize presence in human life, to later periods where things, in their greater number, became mere commodities, and swords only objects of nostalgia and no longer in any way "enchanted" in the present. Such a view is our own nostalgia speaking. Enchantment is the product of the resistance of an object to our understanding, to routine gestures of interpretation. While swords could be virtually mass-produced by the sixteenth century, high-quality swords still were signature possessions; and elegant dress swords, meanwhile, partook of enchantment too, partly because they were works of art deploying new skill in metalwork and because they were, after all, still swords. They were newly powerful and compelling precisely because they were both jewelry and weapon, and the expertise required of swordplay with these new weapons protected their allure.

I will argue that material culture did not simply reflect changes in aristocratic identity originating elsewhere, but also helped set in motion those changes; in short, changing artifacts and their uses enabled, not merely expressed, some of the dramatic shifts we seem to see in aristocratic culture at the end of the Middle Ages. Beginning around 1200, swords are essential for elite warrior status. But as soon as they become essential, they are no longer enough, so that they become the object of myth. Even earlier, when not all warriors used them, swords were already the focus of and vehicles for nostalgia. Medieval aristocrats had already had a crisis of swords, in other words, long before the supposed "military revolution." Swords were the central myth of warrior identity, always smaller in life than they were in stories, and it is in that role that they go forward in time to underwrite dramatic change in warrior identity and behavior both off and on the battlefield. When the British army debated the precise dimensions of their officers' swords on the eve of World War I, it was not a laughable exercise. It may seem to us simply one of the most absurd (among many) preoccupations of armies and leaders on the eve of a war of unprecedented scope and ferocity. Their task was not absurd, however; swords had been adapted for personal adornment and defense, as well as for battle, many times before, and swords were never only about fighting.

I suggest that the "modernization" of warfare and of warrior identity was a profoundly cultural process, as well as being a political, social, economic, and technological one. Swords provide a particularly useful vantage point on the problem of culture and warfare because they were preeminent weapons which always carried both instrumental and symbolic value. They enable us to see, and were a means for their owners of claiming, profound continuity in warrior identity over time. I argue that their "value" in their owners' eyes highlighted the arbitrary character of warrior identity. Like gender roles in most societies, warrior identity is continually refashioned to appear timeless, natural, and without internal contradiction. Warrior identity at the end of the Middle Ages appeared well anchored in the past yet was in fact capable of rapid mutation and adaptation to new forms of fighting and new inflections of identity. It had changed already, over the course of the Middle Ages; in fact, major transformations in the props for warrior identity were complete before gunpowder weapons dramatically reshaped the battlefield. In short, I argue for a partial reversal of the common sequence of causation, whereby technological changes forced cultural adaptation. I contend that cultural constructions of warrior identity and selfhood underwrote the changing face of warfare.

Hence, this book sweeps through about one thousand years of western European history, which I will consider in recognizable, if contested, chronological chunks. Its arguments are grounded in primary evidence from the period 1300–1600 and built, as well, on the work of specialists in archaeological and written sources from prior centuries. In order to evaluate surviving evidence about swords, I weave together the work of scholars of material culture from the migration age forward with that of historians of aristocratic culture, military and political history, and that of scholars of literature. Many of their arguments, particularly regarding earlier periods, are necessarily based on small numbers of artifacts or texts, and represent controversial positions within their subfields. In other areas—chivalric literature, for example—a robust body of scholarship exists which I try to draw on strategically, though hardly comprehensively, for my purposes here.

Though French documents launched this study, the evidence I consider here comes from both British and French archives. Of course, specific political, social, and economic circumstances are a vital part of the context that informs interpretation both of documents and of artifacts, but my goal is not to understand those different national institutions or political trajectories better in and of themselves. I examine these two warrior cultures deliberately because they were historically intertwined—indeed virtually identical for a time following the Norman Conquest of 1066. In addition, examining two "national" contexts side by side helps avoid the nostalgia and the narrative fixity inherent in national myths. The discussions in the chapters to follow are thematically as well as chronologically organized and, at times, will rely more heavily on British evidence, while, at others, I privilege French examples. Each chapter opens, as did this introduction, with a vignette from source material that points the way to the interpretive questions that follow.

The reader will also notice that I sometimes diverge from a focus on swords altogether in order to consider the wider material context. Swords were simultaneously utilitarian weapons and products of craft mystery, treasured mementoes, and characters of literary imagination. Their symbolic as well as their practical use changed over time as circumstances changed around them. In the early Middle Ages, for example, they were surrounded by other prestige goods produced by craftsmen highly skilled in manufacture of fine, portable metalwork. Swords could be considered, then, as the epitome of both weaponry and art. After about 1300, with improvements in metallurgy, plate armor developed; at times, records of body armor almost eclipse traces of swords. Thus, I widen and narrow my focus periodically to consider the broad context that helped construct the life and significance of swords over time. I will consider the development of luxury industries and the growing array of prestige objects in elite hands, the changing technology of sword production and of the material conditions of warfare, the elaboration of literary traditions, imaginary worlds, and documentary practices. So, I will come and go from actual swords themselves the better, ultimately, to keep them in view.

While I move through centuries and across borders and plumb material culture in broad terms, I will nonetheless remain close to the ground. My argument is not based on any claim of having compiled a definitive quantity of evidence but rather on having taken a rich sample of evidence seriously: what lists of things can tell us about the life of things; the power of single examples of texts or images, carefully read or scrutinized. Scholars of material culture warn us not to make quick leaps away from objects to look instead at "society," as though we are afraid of gazing too long, perhaps afraid of our own tendency to fetishize things. When the object gets left behind too quickly, it is easily reduced to a one-dimensional symbol. We think we know already what it must mean, how it functioned in its day. The danger of this kind of reductive thinking is what moves scholars to talk about how things meant, not what they meant, including both contemporaries' interpretive contexts and experiences of what we (who are far removed from their face-to-face performative society) call "presence."[29] And it is vital to keep the play of meaning open, in motion, if we are to account for change. The relationship between material culture and culture more generally is complex; change does not come from hidden ideas somehow imagined without objects, or fixed meanings of objects that we did not know were there.[30]

There is an additional complication I must signal here, one having to do with the cast of characters—beyond swords, themselves actors in the drama. Part of the story of the significance of swords is how widely they were dispersed among fighting men as time went on. Men for whom swords were a vital accoutrement ranged from great princes, to lesser aristocrats, down to more modest fighters poised to climb the social and political scale by means of military skill and opportunism. No single term encompasses them all—from an aristocrat who was a courtier, even a royal prince, as well as a warrior, down to a mercenary who hoped to eventually be less a warrior and more a secure landholder if he lived to enjoy his fruits. And on down below that to simple fighters of very modest stature who wielded a sword when they could get hold of one. The catchall term "noble" can be used for many French elites but does not apply in the same way to English warriors, where nobility was a narrower category and did not carry legal privilege in the same way it did in France. "Knight" was also a specific term, since not all men who functioned as knights (our shorthand for medieval warrior) were in fact formally dubbed knights, as the costs of assuming that distinction grew over time. So, I will use a variety of terms as I describe these historical actors: "elites," "fighters," and, where appropriate, magnate, aristocrat, noble, gentry, mercenary, fighter, and so on. I use "warrior" as the generic term to identify my subject, when speaking generally or when the precise status is not clear or is not known.

I end this book, in the conclusion, with further reflection on some of the work swords accomplish in our present. In the case of the United States in the twenty-first century, swords can elevate their wearers, whether in life or in memoriam, to the status of honorable warrior, an identity which can then override more controversial attributes. It is when we see that symbolic heft in the context of other objects and claims—for example, Robert E. Lee's sword on display, now, in tension with Jim Crow–era celebrations of the Confederacy—that we can appreciate anew the weight swords bear in our imaginations and the importance of historicizing our imaginative and interpretive reach.

🍂 CHAPTER 1

Swords and Oral Culture in the Early Middle Ages

In a pathbreaking 1936 essay, J. R. R. Tolkien set scholarship on *Beowulf* on a new course when he argued that the poem should be considered as a piece of literature and not simply mined for data about the migration-era societies it purportedly depicts. The poem, Tolkien asserted, does not describe actual societies but rather is an "echo of an echo," a rendering of a long-gone world many generations later. Whatever historical meaning there is to be had, he argues, is found in the poem as a piece of literature, in the emotions, the longings, the grief, evoked by the story *as it is being told.* Hence, we should not dismiss the dragon, who guards the buried hoard near the end of the tale, because we believe it to be a commonplace—its meaning obvious as evidence of a medieval imaginary we think we know already. Whatever we may think we know, Tolkien cautions, there are actually very few dragons in literature of this epoch. Like any important character, this one merits attention. We must ask: what is this dragon (and other dragons mentioned in the tale) doing here, what does it *mean*? We should set aside assumptions and condescension and, instead, should listen, really listen, to this echo.[1]

Tolkien's breakthrough was to recognize *Beowulf* as literature before scholarly work on oral culture made it easier to see the structure of storytelling and use of language peculiar to oral traditions and thus to expand our definition of what constitutes "literature." The barriers to appreciating the work as art, in Tolkien's day, included the fragmented structure of the story, which contained many digressions or interruptions of other tales, such as the story of Ingeld, the best known of these sidebars. Subsequent scholarship about *Beowulf* has not allowed all of Tolkien's perspectives to stand, such as his view that the poem was composed in the age of Bede, meaning roughly the first half of the eighth century.[2] The consensus now is that the composition of the poem is more recent, much closer to the date of the extant manuscript (ca. 1000) than Tolkien thought. In fact, recent scholars have suggested, the only poem we really have is the one preserved in the British Library, the product of a poet or poets and his (perhaps) later interpreters, including the two scribes who edited, amended, and produced the actual text that we do have.[3] Thus we have an interpretive problem that amplifies Tolkien's original point: if the poem is an echo, why was a scribe determined to preserve it, "hear it," so many centuries after the events it purports to describe, and what vision of the past was the poet creating?

Here, I will in turn echo Tolkien's plea regarding the dragon as I consider evidence of swords from the early medieval past. Unlike Tolkien and his dragon, we have remains of actual swords from the early medieval centuries with us in the present, and evidence of how they were saved, exchanged, buried, and memorialized, sometimes in documentary traces. Swords were expensive, high-prestige weapons. We do not know precisely how rare swords were among fighting men, though we know that some warriors fought only with the less expensive spear. We also know that, along with spears, other kinds of cutting blades such as long knives or seaxes, wide single-bladed weapons, were also common. But much of the story of how swords were valued lies, as with the dragon, in what we can retrieve of their users' imaginations, and of the symbolic world of which swords were a part. Material evidence, documents, and stories must all be weighed together.

Yet neither material remains nor textual evidence is transparent to our gaze. Interpretation can be difficult partly for technical reasons: for example, the task of making philological comparisons within a small body of surviving sources to prise meaning from a unique text, as *Beowulf* is. In addition, as disciplinary protocols and interpretive stances have changed over time—dramatically, in some cases—evidence has been lost. Archaeologists practicing a century ago had unearthed artifacts with ambitious methods we now regard as reckless. They also brought rigid notions about sex and gender with them to their sites, and did not consider jewelry (such as brooches) to be worn by men. Often, evidence from these sites was not preserved in ways to make reinterpretation by later investigators possible, thus we may never know the full range of grave goods in many cases.[4]

Much of the interpretive challenge we face, however, is inherent in any effort to make sense of fragmentary evidence. The limited surviving evidence from the early medieval centuries means that the bits we do have must help build a basic narrative of the period, but which then, in turn, becomes the context in which we interpret each piece of evidence. With works of literature, this circularity means we interpret it in relationship to its context, which it illuminates, and only after conjecturing when it was written. In addition, the richest sources, like *Beowulf*, are relatively late—the ninth or tenth centuries or even later—and most scholars find it irresistible to extrapolate backward from them.

Narratives of medieval history, moreover, tend to be weighed down with the burden of accounting for origins, with seeing eventual nation-states or national cultures or "peoples" in artifacts or texts from the fifth or eighth or tenth century.[5] Rich texts like *Beowulf* or *The Song of Roland* are virtual national monuments, certainly national myths.[6] One scholar describes the investment modern English readers have in *Beowulf*: "we view and re-view [it] over years, even over generations, with something like the care we give our own personal pasts, and what those will mean for our future."[7] In other words, we inevitably respond to these tales not only as myth, but as our own myth, and do not easily recognize when we are conflating our myths with ones the texts advance. When encountering swords in documents or poems or in images or within graves, we experience familiarity instead of a sense of rift with the past.[8]

In what follows, I will sketch the history of the manufacture of early medieval swords, then discuss evidence of those swords' symbolic lives revealed by archaeological finds, namely grave goods and our reconstruction of rituals that accompanied their deposit. Then I consider written evidence of swords, particularly in early wills that record both the bequeathing but also the prior circulation of a sword among allies and kin. Finally, I turn to literature, to *Beowulf* and its near-contemporary, *The Battle of Maldon*, to explore the roles those poems ascribe to warriors' (and monsters') swords. We cannot rigidly separate these different sorts of evidence; all are frustratingly incomplete, and one genre allows us to pose interpretive questions of others. In addition, the world of fiction—to the degree these poems are fictional—inevitably responded to and added its imaginative weight to the possibilities of human experience, including the significance of swords to the men who wielded them.

Early medieval literature is filled with references to the aesthetic qualities and the mysterious origin of swords and their constituent parts, as well as to their power to strike fear, to wound, and to kill. The uncanny properties of blades alone spurred much poetic effort: a blade was lightning bright, deadly, unpredictable; or the rippling marks produced by the smith's hammer were imagined (borrowing from another craft) as woven silk, or as rushing water or writhing serpents. The making of the blade could even supply an image for the very work of the warrior: in one poem, fighting men are described as "war-smiths."[9] Spears and axes as well as defensive weapons like helmets and chain mail are also celebrated, but swords are clearly at the center of the linguistic imagination of early medieval warriors. Literary sources evoke an aesthetic appreciation of swords along with a sense of their utility as weapons and their power, as actors in their own right, to create memory and myth. These different meanings would not have been experienced as entirely separate. The ways in which they shaded into each other can be traced in literature but also by examining how swords were manufactured, used, and exchanged in early medieval society.

Europeans of this era could not have imagined a distinction between objects of beauty and those of powerful technology like swords. Both were the products of individual craft labor, and "art objects" in such geographically mobile peoples always connoted accessible wealth and generally consisted of fine metalwork; gold armbands, jewels, drinking vessels, helms, and weapons could all be rewards for loyal service as well as representations of a leader's power. Not surprisingly, many memorable swords of which we have any trace from this era were *both* objects of art and weapons at the same time.[10] The best blades, however elaborately decorated, were most effective as weapons precisely because they were artful: individually crafted from unique materials by a smith skilled in metalworking techniques and able to improve and innovate.

It is likely that high-quality sword blades (as opposed to wholly iron-made low-quality blades) were initially produced in relatively few locations and traded across distances.[11] Some of the finest steel blades, probably produced at one site on the Baltic coast, wound up as far away as modern Ireland, in the wake of Norse settlement. They can be identified by the inscription "Ulfberht"—seemingly the Germanic name of the smith. The early blades with this inscription were made from steel produced by a more expensive method than was used in Europe, thus no doubt procured via Norse trade in the Volga basin from Iran, Central Asia, or India. But the swords bearing this mark were produced over about three hundred years, long after the trade of Asian steel was cut off. Such was the reputation of these blades that subsequent generations of craftsmen traded on the identity of the original maker, even though they produced blades of decidedly lower quality. Well-made

European blades were traded across borders, too, to the east as well, in violation of proscriptions, such as in Charlemagne's capitularies, which are no doubt evidence of that very trade.[12]

The most skilled European smiths twisted small bits of steely iron produced by their smelting process together with pieces of inferior iron, then forged them together with other like bundles of mixed carbon contents to form a blade with adequate steel distributed in it. Steel edges were sometimes also welded on. Known as "pattern-welded" blades, when finished, they were distinguished by a wavy pattern or water-like ripples that appeared on the surface of the metal, somewhat like the so-called "damascene" blades made from Iranian or Indian iron. Modern artisans have estimated that a pattern-welded blade took some two hundred hours of work time to complete.[13] Well-made blades and great smiths inspired much lore, which we can glimpse in surviving texts. For example, in a laudatory poem about the battle of Brunanburh, a Saxon victory over Vikings and Scots in 937, the swords wielded by the Saxons are referred to by a particular finishing technique (being milled down in a particular way after forging) that would have produced superior weapons.[14] The technology of producing fine blades was rare, and it was celebrated.

But swords did not consist merely of blades; they were then, and remained, composite artifacts. Indeed, just as blades varied, one from another, so did the other components of swords: the hilt, made up of guard, grip, and pommel, and the scabbard and sword belt, and all of their fasteners. The designs, especially of hilts, relied on local craftsmen with expertise in other metal and jewel-working skills. The sword in the famous ship burial at Sutton Hoo in Essex, England (ca. 625), for example, was decorated with gold and cloisonné, with garnets inset into both concave and convex surfaces, while a surviving piece from about 250 years later, known as the Abingdon sword, has an hilt of engraved silver mounts depicting the four evangelists; the engraving is set off by inlayed niello (a black sulfide of silver), the work of a master silversmith.[15] Scabbards, too, had metal fittings, which required one kind of expertise, but also used wood, leather, sheepskin, and cloth. A fine sword and its accoutrements, in other words, was the product of a number of different craftspeople and their specialized skills; the wonder of a great sword in its day lay in the blade, whose construction was the most unaccountable, but also in the combination of expertise and artistry that produced both the whole and each of the parts. Those combinations could be reworked, a worthy blade given a new hilt or scabbard, for example. Swords circulated as both new and remade objects.

PLATE 1. The artistry of Sutton Hoo artifacts. The partially reconstructed sword hilt (approx. 6.5 cm. x 9.5 cm.) and the buckle from the sword belt (7.3 cm. x 2.3 cm.) found in the Sutton Hoo ship burial. Both buckle and sword hilt are decorated with gold and garnet cloisonné. © The Trustees of the British Museum. All rights reserved.

So as swords themselves changed when a new hilt was attached to an old blade, or a new scabbard created for an existing sword, they also changed hands, through gift, inheritance, burial, and conquest. The biggest mistake we can make, standing at a distance as we do from this thicket of imagery around swords, is to see swords as static objects of reverence rather than in motion in the warrior lifeworld, alive because they changed materially and also by means of their "lives" in different human hands. Even swords deposited in graves had lives and afterlives, and their significance must be interpreted, not assumed.

Grave goods, including swords, other weapons of all kinds, jewelry, and clothing, have been found at burial sites in what is now France and England (as well as Germany and the Low Countries) dating from more or less a four-hundred-year span, from the end of the fourth century, when Roman power began to withdraw from northern Europe, to about 700 CE. In most locales, the deposition of grave goods tailed off in the eighth century, not because elites had embraced Christianity, which mostly happened earlier, but because relatively more settled political conditions called for new kinds of rituals and sites for burial, which now became closely associated with church buildings. Inhumations with goods slowly were deemphasized relative to the sacred spaces built aboveground.[16]

Furnished inhumations were not the typical practice in Roman communities, so the very existence of such cemeteries in western Europe seemed a kind of identity marker for "barbarian" peoples to early twentieth-century archaeologists, whose methodology led them to interpret particular styles of artifacts as evidence of specific "cultures." The movement of peoples from east to west across Europe in the migration age, in their eyes, could be traced through archaeological finds. One lingering outcome of this kind of thinking has been the assumption that the presence of a sword "meant" a warrior who had been buried with his weapon.[17] Other weapons found in graves, by similar logic, also signaled warrior burials. So, sword or ax or knife were straightforward markers of status or function, and nothing more.

Historians have revised these interpretations by establishing the contingent, porous nature of barbarian groups and their long-standing interactions with Roman power. Together with recent archaeologists, they have reinterpreted data from a number of grave sites to demonstrate that the point of weapons deposits in graves was equally contingent—that is, closely related to immediate political conditions on the ground. We now believe that swords, weapons, and other goods were selected and placed in individual graves deliberately, for a reason, not merely reflexively because they were the belongings of the dead person.

First, it is clear that swords were *less* common in graves than they would have been in actual use by living fighters. Indeed, fewer than one-quarter of all the *cemeteries* on the northern continent that have been excavated to date contain any sword burial at all. Of those that do, more than three-quarters have only one or two swords in the entire site.[18] Data from pagan Saxon cemeteries in England, surveyed in 1989, reveal that 18 percent of all inhumations with goods (including about 47 percent of identifiable males) have weapons, but only one in ten of these weapons burials includes a sword.[19] Swords, therefore, were placed in a small minority of male graves; most graves of fighting men are not marked by a sword deposit.

In addition to swords, and often separately from them, graves included accoutrements associated with swords: baldrics (sword belts) and scabbards. The latter rarely were deposited without swords themselves, but sword belts were often found alone. Belt buckles displayed the artistry of metalworkers and survived in the ground when leather and cloth of the belt itself disintegrated. Other items sometimes present in male graves included brooches to fasten cloaks, which, like the fasteners for baldrics, were among the most valued accoutrements of the era. Other weapons, in varying combinations, make up the majority of weapons in graves and included spears, shields, bows and arrows, knives of various dimensions, as well as axes. Interestingly, these weapons were often not deposited in usable combinations—spears buried without shields and bows without arrows, or vice versa. When complete "sets" of fighting gear have been found, they sometimes appear in graves of children. Thus, even when the bodies of warrior-age men are found accompanied by weapons in likely combinations, we know, in the light of this wider sample of graves, not to regard the items simply as transparent markers of warrior identity but rather as symbols in need of interpretation.

Many scholars agree that grave goods were used to create, reestablish, echo, or fix the identity of a once-living person in the minds of the community, and to do so in ways that permitted appropriate mourning that would then construct the memory of that person. Precisely what identity, or cluster of personal attributes, were being claimed by the use of different objects is more difficult to establish. The rhythm of weapons burials can, when we can determine it, be an important piece of the puzzle—that is, when weapons burials happened, vis-à-vis other events or political and social circumstances. Deposits of weapons in graves of Angles and Saxons in southern England, for example, may reflect a particular rhythm with regard to the progress of their invasion and settlement of the island. When the dating of grave sites is compared with what we know of the actual progress of conquest and migration northward after 495, it appears that more weapons may have been interred during times of relative peace, that is, *between* periods of expansion, than in phases of active conflict. One historian argues that these burials during (at least relative) peacetime were a form of intentional myth-making, an effort to keep the heroic ideology of conquest alive, by ritual means, by generations of warriors who did not themselves do the conquering.[20] We also have at least one example of a Viking sword likely kept only for display by a member of a settled Norse farming community. The blade had been deliberately broken before being interred, in its scabbard, next to a man's remains. It was not some ancestor's battle sword but a very low-quality blade with a nicely decorated hilt, the scabbard also decorative but not adequate to protect a sword in actual use. So, the sword was some kind of remembrance of past achievements, even though it could not have taken part in them.[21]

But it is rare that we know much at all about the chronology of burials vis-à-vis other events.[22] We can be confident only that weapons, especially swords, were, in the words of one historian, "part of a discourse about new forms of power." In the shifting social, economic, and political circumstances as Roman power waned, families sought to claim localized status by means of a burial. Weapons, in these burials, carried wider symbolic possibilities than mere conquest or a claim to violence. When we find axes, it is possible that not conquest but land-clearing—the creation and maintenance of arable land—was symbolized. In short, an individual's power to control agricultural production was being articulated and celebrated. Bows and arrows as well as spears could have represented another symbolic claim to control of land: the prerogative of hunting.[23] In many cases, as we have seen, bows or arrows or spears were not usable weapons in that they are deposited alone; or, also commonly, they were not actual weapons at all but purpose-made symbolic weapons—for example, beautifully crafted but unusably small arrows and bows, or axes made from precious metals, useless for cutting. The claims, whatever they were precisely, were not made in the abstract but on the occasion of one individual's burial: the creation of an ancestor who could be remembered for these attributes, and thus a family whose identity in the community could be carried forward from the event in these terms.

The burial process itself was important in every case of a furnished grave, but our fascination with swords in the present makes it particularly necessary to dwell on it. The recovered swords we now see displayed in museums, or in glossy illustrations in books and on websites, were not only rarely deposited in graves but, when placed there, *disappeared from view* for contemporaries, once a burial was complete. The dead person could be remembered afterward because this event became a memory and the memory, in turn, was kept alive by retelling the tale of the burial as well as, in many cases, by visiting or viewing land forms marking the grave. A number of the best-fur-nished graves in migration-era cemeteries were clearly in well-demarcated sites such as mounds that could be recognized by kin and communities for at least a generation afterward. But to interpret the meaning of a sword burial (or any burial with grave goods), we have to first imagine the grave as a burial ritual conducted before the mound was afterward made. The body, with its various adornments, was first staged; the point of the inclusion of objects is that they be seen first, in a staged tableau, so that they could be remem-bered appropriately. The grave site kept memory alive not simply because the mound existed but also because, demarcated in some way, it functioned as a mnemonic device to help the community recall the event, "the perfor-mance," of the burial.

An emphatic example of a burial tableau, one used by archaeologists to comparatively interpret more modest graves, is the ship burial at Sutton Hoo in East Anglia (Sussex, England). This is a grave mound of a Saxon lord, ca. 625, who was buried with splendid weapons and armor, jeweled clasps for his clothing, a purse (filled with coins, from several different mints), pots, tableware, even a lyre. The wide provenance of the objects—from England but also modern Scandinavia, France, Italy, Turkey, and Syria—as well as the style of the accoutrements suggests that an imperial identity was fashioned by this burial, that this Saxon prince—perhaps a local king, Raedwald—was presented to his people, in death, as an heir to Roman authority, either as a partner or as a rival to the Frankish princes across the Channel.[24] Whatever he had actually achieved in life, in death Raedwald's kin and community made a dramatic political claim by making him into an august ancestor or dynastic founder in this way.

The armor and weapons in the grave are clearly not ones he would have used in life. Enough survives of the helmet, for example, for us to know it had never been worn; the sheer number of spears in the grave represents a cache of weapons, the promise of arming supporters, rather than his own supply. The sword was also pristine, and both its hilt and its scabbard were embellished with gold and cut garnets. All of the goods had been deliber-ately chosen and carefully arranged within a chamber built on the deck of a ship, which had been positioned in a huge burial pit. Individual articles were arranged with a view to how they would be seen from above by living witnesses at the burial. The entire process of digging the pit, dragging the purpose-built ship into place from the nearby estuary, and assembling and displaying the grave goods took days to accomplish, and the labor of many members of the community. The building of the grave must have happened in stages: the placing of some objects, then the body, then the closing of the coffin, followed by the addition of more objects to the tableau. Archaeologists imagine that the goods carefully arrayed on and around the coffin left enough space for observers to walk among them.[25]

With the body, in the outsize coffin, were robes, cloaks, shoes, buckles, toiletries, a fur hat, a down pillow, a cup and bowl and, most interesting for our purposes, a coat of mail carefully laid on a folded cloth: Raedwald's personal effects, researchers have surmised. The helmet, the sword, and the sword belt were displayed on top of the large coffin only after it was closed. First, two yellow cloaks covered the surface, then, in a very deliberate sequential arrangement were a large silver platter (from Constantinople) with a burnt offering of food, drinking bottles and drinking horns, then further along, between two spears laid along the edges of the coffin as though standing guard, the sword, scabbard, and baldric, along with the purse and its coins. Finally, at the western end of the coffin, rested the helmet but also silver bowls and spoons, gaming pieces, and a collar with a bell, perhaps for a pet. This was a statesman's regalia.[26] It not only included ceremonial sword and helmet but also dishes for feasts: Raedwald is both lord and host. This identity is echoed in some of the other objects propped against the walls of the chamber. Spears and shield lie to the side of the coffin, with many other objects such as a huge iron cauldron, the lyre, against the side of the chamber, but also tools for repairing the ship itself. This lord with imperial pretensions is also a host at a lively court, and he is also a seafarer.

Once the site was complete, one archaeologist imagines, the community filed past in a long procession to view the scene laid out in the grave one final time before the mounded earth covered all. Afterward, the large mound would call the event to memory but the memory would have to be orally conveyed and, to do that, we must imagine that the entire burial process was constructed at the time and remembered later in formulaic, thus memorable, oral narrative—in short, as a poem, more precisely a lament or elegy.[27] And, it is important to note: Raedwald himself was no longer visible in this last viewing, but all these objects, speaking loudly about his stature and capacities, were. The sword, but also the lyre and cloaks, and helmet and everything else, were good to grieve with, to make an appropriate end for a leader, and to seal his memory in these capacious terms. Raedwald's claim to lordship, perhaps an imperially tinged kingship, rested on the impressive accoutrements, deliberately chosen and arranged.

There are a mere handful of discovered sites of richness comparable to Sutton Hoo, but they can help us imagine the significance of the more plentiful, though still rare, burials with swords or, sometimes, sword belts. Many of the less elaborate sword graves in Merovingian territory were sited in distinctive ways: at the edge of a cemetery, under a mound of some kind, often surrounded by a few other burials deliberately grouped around it, the entire ensemble oriented or organized differently than the rest of the site. These burials reflect planning, and signify the decision to perform a claim about the dead individual and his kin and their relationship to the community that could then reverberate afterward. The burials were not merely a claim to warrior status—which many could claim but did not signal with a sword burial—but to something more. Just as hunting gear or axes may have demonstrated or laid claim to the use of land, a sword could mean a claim to local authority, a status as a local protector, a successful strong man whose still-living community wanted to fix that identity for themselves and their descendants. Swords were chosen at a given moment to make a claim of a distinctive social or political status in the context of particular local tensions in the unsettled political landscape. Like hagiographies that survive from the era, one scholar suggests, it is difficult to be sure of "facts" in such a rhetorical act but such sites did their work for survivors, in part, in the same way the tombs of saints did as regions became Christian: as the creation of a member of the community of the dead, which could provide models for, and, more importantly, patrons or protectors for the living.[28]

A sword grave thus often denoted not a just a warrior, but a protector, a node in an emerging and shifting network of power in the post-Roman world. The sword was not a marker of warrior identity, pure and simple, but of lordship. While this assertion can only be conjecture, it explains more of the evidence than do earlier, simplistic equations of swords with warrior identity. It assumes that people were capable of making decisions of some subtlety in matters of symbol and ritual, and it allows for the evolving political conditions on the ground. A rare burial like Sutton Hoo enables us see what a particularly striking "lord" could have added to his identity with other goods: weapons and armor but also regalia such as brooches, and goods that stage hospitality such as tableware, cooking pots, a musical instrument. Lordship on Raedwald's scale was successful lordship in part because of its plural attributes: protection but also generosity, conviviality, grandeur and, with his shipwright tools, competence.

The example of Sutton Hoo, with its carefully gathered wonders, also reminds us to consider where the individual swords in the sword graves came from. The sword chosen for a grave had to be a particular sword, not just *a* sword, to accomplish its symbolic mission. Sometimes it was crafted for the occasion, sometimes chosen for the role. In either case, it was deliberately removed from circulation. Just as an imperial-like identity was sketched for Raedwald by objects of wide-ranging origin, so too was the lordly character of a man buried with a sword shaped in part by the provenance of the sword, by the associations the family and community could attach to it, and its situation alongside other goods. In Raedwald's case, the sword itself was more treasure than weapon, and certainly not an heirloom, but some of the other objects such as the silver bowls were clearly gifts. In many cases, archaeologists can determine that buried swords had been used, sometimes over generations, before entering a grave.[29] A sword removed from circulation carried the associations of that circulation with it; that is, it had once been part of a network of gift-giving, family alliance, perhaps even a prestigious gift from a still more powerful leader, such as a "king" like the occupant of Sutton Hoo. Indeed, there is some evidence that sword burials in northern Gaul appeared with greater frequency over time, which may have reflected gifts from the more powerful regional notables to less powerful associates.[30]

For the most part, we can only indirectly glimpse the networks of affiliation and gift-giving that may have preceded a weapons burial. Speculation about what networks of exchange looked like all derive from texts that postdate this period, from the eighth century and later—mostly wills that document such networks or literature that celebrates them. We can glimpse in these sources a world where swords are given to worthy retainers, and by warriors to their lords upon death (which then are recirculated); weapons are lent to peers, retainers and relations, then reclaimed and gifted again. Coats of mail, hunting horns, golden torques, belts circulate too.[31]

The earliest surviving wills in England, dating from the ninth century, embody concepts of inheritance and gift-giving that must already have been well established. The will of the Anglo-Saxon king Ethelred's eldest son, Aethelstan, for example, dating from the years around 1015, tells us much about the circulation of prestige goods as it makes bequests. Aethelstan's will deliberately reveals prior exchanges of lands and goods, partly in order to identify their origin and their worth as his to bestow. To the church where he will be buried, he grants several pieces of land he had received by gift or purchase, and a sword with a silver hilt and a gold armband and belt made by one Wulfric. His bequests to his father and eldest brother are particularly noteworthy for the evidence of the networks of gift exchange that they reveal. His father the king gets various estates. But he also receives a sword belonging to Ulfcytel, an important East Anglian lord (perhaps Aethelstan's brother-in-law) still active when this will was written, ca. 1014, and a coat of mail that is currently in yet another magnate's hands. This hauberk (as mail garments were called) had been gifted and now will be reclaimed to be regifted. Meanwhile, Aethelstan's brother, Edmund, is granted the sword that belonged to the Mercian king Offa (d. 796), along with another blade (described as a blade not a sword) and yet another sword and a silver-coated trumpet. Aethelstan wills a further five swords, including one to his chaplain, which "belonged to Withar," and another to a servant, which is "the sword which he gave me," thus a gift returned.[32]

The number of weapons disbursed in this will is extraordinary, but the evidence of circulation, captured here, is not. It is from wills such as this one where a large number of swords are gifted and from stories, especially *Beowulf*, that scholars have found enough examples of exchange to suggest that goods carried value not only, or even primarily, because of their inherent worth as precious objects but because of the relationships that their exchange created. Offa's sword is the obvious example. The sword may not have belonged to Offa, but it must have been old and of a design that seemed plausible for such an origin.[33] The heir to the throne, in this will, passes on to his brother, the next heir, this weapon that proves their affinity to the legendary king. The ancestry of weapons, in other words, constitutes their significance; they embody relationships and therefore help establish the identity of the person who holds them for a time. Interestingly, the monsters in *Beowulf*, including the dragon as well as the dreaded Grendel and his mother, violate these norms: they hoard treasure, and unlike great warriors, they have no intention of sharing out their goods. They allow it to molder and rust, rather than circulate usefully.[34] Both goods and people were composite entities, constructed, literally, by more than one person in the case of swords, and accumulated their identities through relationships. A person in such a society came into being, we believe, by means of these exchanges of gifts, rewards, and bequests; a warrior's worth, the nexus of relationships he represented, continued to exist after death only as long as he was remembered in his death and through some of the goods that had passed through his hands.[35] The individual needed to continue in the world through the objects, including swords, he had owned or used for a time, and which remained in circulation after he was gone.

Sword burials, though "loud" evidence that claims our attention, represent a rare decision to remove a sword from this world of circulating goods. However symbolically freighted that staged burial, it represented only *one* use of *one* object associated with the person and created one set of attributes to be associated with a man in death.[36] It is not surprising, therefore, that scholars have emphasized that the meaning of such a burial must have been closely tied to context, to the power dynamics in play at that moment; the interment was a carefully choreographed political event. A buried sword meant a warrior but especially a leader, or a lesser notable connected with other powerful men, perhaps in the ambit of a king. His value and his connections were perpetuated by means of other goods, which we cannot now see. Perhaps a baldric, with its jeweled buckle, circulated for a sword left behind, or vice versa. Perhaps additional swords, knives, or spears remained in heirs' or followers' hands. Perhaps a brooch, or that rarest of items, a hauberk (a coat of mail), remained behind to distinguish or protect the heir. We must imagine other strongly ritualized moments of exchange in this life-world, such as weapons or adornments bestowed before a battle, at a birth, or at a celebratory feast.[37] The life of objects did not end when one warrior died and grief at a death in this society was centered on and experienced by means of objects.

The laments performed at and after Raedwald's burial would likely have mentioned individual objects in the grave and how each one triggered grief and memory—a "veritable cacophony of sound," suggests one archaeologist.[38] The specific content of any such elegies—how exactly the ornamented sword was regretted, for instance—remained in the oral story world of contemporaries and their descendants and are lost to us except as their residue appears in later narratives, some of which were captured in writing. To say more about the circulation of swords, their value to their owners, and their symbolic heft in the early medieval lifeworld, we will leave evidence of furnished burials behind and move forward in time to the ninth century and beyond, when dependence on written records expanded.

Here I will consider swords captured in written records, especially a wider sampling of wills, before turning to depictions in imaginative literature. Surviving artifacts remain part of the evidence to weigh as we move forward in time, however. Weapons were no longer interred with human remains but still were saved by various ritual means and were buried in hoards for later use. Weapons hoards still, today, come to light quite unexpectedly. In 2009, for example, a man wielding a metal detector in a farm field in the English Midlands located one of the largest caches of medieval metalwork ever discovered. Some 3,500 objects were eventually unearthed there, almost all gold and silver fittings of swords and other war gear. More than ninety separate sword pommels alone emerged, including some pommel designs never before recorded, as well as more than two hundred pieces of hilt fittings of various sorts—reminders, both, of the composite and changeable nature of swords.

The estimated dates for this material range from the seventh through the ninth centuries, when this region constituted the kingdom of Mercia. Thus, some of the artifacts in the Staffordshire hoard, as it is called, might be almost contemporaneous with the Sutton Hoo material. These gold and silver objects, however, were buried for safekeeping and never afterward retrieved. In the words of one of the first scholars to assess it, the hoard represented "bling for the warrior companions of a king."[39] So, although some of the material may have been contemporaneous with Raedwald's burial, this hoard points forward to the period after furnished burials when political units were consolidating; rulers collected and disposed of increasing numbers of goods and could arm and reward numerous retainers with weapons whose fittings displayed their preferment. Hard on the heels of these growing collections were written records that documented and regulated their dispersal.

In Anglo-Saxon England, the ability of rulers to arm their followers became institutionalized as the custom of "heriot," which literally means war gear, and referred to swords and other equipment received from a lord, to be returned to him upon death. By the early eleventh century, the practice had been regularized in written law with specific expectations for the value of war gear and coin returned to the king upon the death of men of different social classes: so many horses, swords, worth so much, counted for an earl and so on down the hierarchy—the specific items given to the king at a death less and less likely to have actually come from him in the first place.

One will from shortly before the Norman Conquest lists grants of land in great detail but the heriot to his lord (an intermediate lord, not the king) is just enumerated: "as my heriot [I grant] a helmet and a coat of mail and a horse with a harness and a sword and a spear."[40] The earl Aelfgar's will, one century earlier, from the 950s, begins with a similar, businesslike list: "I grant to my lord two swords with sheaths and two armlets, each of fifty mancuses of gold, and three stallions and three shields and three spears." But the will goes on to record a prior gift; when Aelfgar had returned to the king a truly spectacular sword that the prior king (Edmund, d. 946) had bestowed on him, he had been promised that he could make his will and, by implication, its provisions be respected. This sword alone was worth 120 mancuses of gold, and, the will is precise, had four pounds of silver on its sheath: a truly spectacular weapon, no doubt presented to Aelfgar because his daughter had married King Edmund.[41]

This deliberate return of a sword, documented here, reflects the way high-prestige goods helped accomplish personal relationships and transfer status. After his death, this special sword bestowed the authority and charisma of King Edmund and carried the king's honoring of Aelfgar into the aged earl's distribution of his own property. It is the kind of transaction, in other words, we might call on to imagine what might have occurred in earlier centuries from which only burials survive. But over time more of these goods became concentrated—as was perhaps the case in the Staffordshire hoard—in the hands of great lords and kings.[42] As we approach the year 1000, the trail of documents and literary sources grows too, if not as thick on the ground as we might like. A handful of wills do survive from earlier centuries when grave depositions were still practiced, though mostly they date from the eighth century and later, when weapons burials had ceased.[43] Still, they are rare, and more often include landed estates than movable wealth. Through those that survive, we can glimpse the way some objects were deliberately bequeathed to maintain the individual's and family's status, rather as gift-giving may have operated before. We can also note how weapons are put into the hands of the Church. The sword that might have been buried with the man in earlier times is now presented to the Church itself, perhaps a local monastic foundation, while the man's body, alone in a grave, is a symbol of humility. But now some exchanges of weapons generated a written record, and their significance was shaped by those records.

In considering a will, or any other record, we must keep in mind both its purpose and its effects. Written wills in the early Middle Ages were produced only in the most elite families and were thus instances of displaying as well as safeguarding that status. They were a means of advertising the distinction they also protected. Even when they mention specific goods—swords, jewels, and the like—they never record or bequeath all of a great lord's or lady's belongings. Some goods, such as bequests to the poor, would have been shared out in person in advance of a death. Nonetheless, wills shaped humans' relationships to the objects named in them. First, the memory of a particular sword, a particular gift, could now rely partially on a document, not just on the tale of an event cued by a feature in the landscape, and not just on the continued exchange of goods that the document captures in some measure. When goods are no longer usually in burials, the attention of the community is shifted, partly by means of writing, from the moment of burial and its memory in narrative to posterity: the care of memory shifts to descendants and to the Church (by whose hands many of the wills were copied).[44]

In addition, a written will amplified the power of the testator as a source of wealth and prestige. Positional goods like swords—goods with both practical and status value—were always bestowed deliberately and strategically, and this very measured and purposeful dispersal served to make it clear who still had the wealth, even as objects were given into circulation. The existence of a list in a will increased the tension in this instance of what one scholar calls "keeping while giving" because both the named items and the fact of the document itself displayed in new ways the lord's power to gather treasure and award it by choice.[45] A will, in other words, was a list that enabled the heirs and witnesses to apprehend the gifted goods anew as a *collection*, and the power to both create and disburse it, even though the document mentioned only a tiny portion of what constituted a dying warrior's belongings.

For that reason, and because it inhabited a list, the status value of any single sword named in a will was heightened. Swords in many Anglo-Saxon wills, such as Aelfgar's, are routinely enumerated as heriot, as though we are staring at a pile of goods of so much value due the lord. These swords are items on the pile, not special by virtue of their attachment, their prior affiliations. These brisk lists are what make the fuller descriptions of particular swords stand out. The sword from King Edmund returned to the new king to seal a promise gains part of its value from that context, from the way it is singled out in the will itself. Great swords, insofar as wills make them visible, were singular objects *because* they did not stand alone. Some of their added value came from being distinguished as special in a world of more routine exchanges, including of other swords, and some from the sheer fact of being singled out for mention, for description, in the will.

We must also take note of what is accomplished in the way wills group personal effects: what is listed, what is not, how the named items are organized into categories. The testators at this elite level were deeply familiar with and reliant on clerical help. Thus, they knew the power of writing to give renewed importance to objects described in lists.[46] A document in a monastery, they knew, recorded their gift to that house of some high-prestige good, and thus embodied, for the future, the connection that that gift represented. In a will, they could shape the way their heirs and the larger audience of the will perceived their bequests.

One ninth-century will, from a Carolingian count and his wife, is particularly illuminating because the organization of the bequests allows us to see swords purposefully grouped and associated with other objects. Eberhard, count of Friuli, and Gisela, his wife, make bequests of land, but also name various belongings to be dispersed among their four sons and three daughters. The four sons, two in the lay world and two in clerical orders, get two or three swords apiece. What is interesting, though, is that the swords are grouped with other accoutrements: bequeathed with the swords are one or more sword belts for each son, plus knives and spurs (and, in the slimmest lot, cash). For the eldest son, Unroth, every one of these items—sword, knife, spurs, belt—is described as "golden" or "gold-decorated." For him and for his brother in lay life, there are tunics embroidered in gold and, for him alone, also a golden cloak and a golden buckle. Unroth was thus given a complete set of golden regalia. By means of this precise list, the count of Friuli brings into being the official dress of his heir.

In the next century, the sword belt became the official symbol of comital authority in the empire. For now, it was an indispensable part of a somewhat flexible menu of accoutrements of rule. A contemporary commentator observed that "belts heavy with golden strap-fittings and gem-encrusted knives, exquisite garments and heels weighed down with spurs" were the secular ornaments that churchmen were supposed to shun.[47] Swords had a role, too, in displays of rule. His biographer, Einhard, is careful to assure his reader that Charlemagne always wore a sword, usually one with a gold or silver hilt, thus implying he had more than one from which he could choose on any given day. On feast days or to greet ambassadors, Einhard continues, the king carried a jeweled sword and, though his clothes were usually variations on the modest Frankish dress of his day, on special occasions he wore embroidered garments, shoes with a golden buckle and a bejeweled diadem: his embellished sword a necessary but not sufficient display on such occasions.[48]

Note, however, that in Eberhard and Gisela's will, all four sons, lay or clerical, received swords, though spurs and embroidered garments were given only to the two brothers in lay life. The will goes on to distribute tableware— cups, silver spoons, large vessels for containing drink—and liturgical goods "from our chapel," such as reliquaries.[49] The two younger sons, destined for careers in the Church, get a share of the feasting tableware. Likewise, all the sons, whether lay or cleric, receive reliquaries and other sacred objects, some of which originally came from the Carolingian court. These objects came to the family as gifts and probably were conveyed onward to ally the family with various religious foundations. Like the swords, tableware and liturgical objects are imagined as symbolically necessary to all male members of the family, not because they will all be fighters, but because they all must have the means to command authority in their respective communities.

The will also names books, which are distributed fairly evenly among sons as well as daughters. But among the personal equipment bequeathed is a separate category that, for our purposes, is particularly intriguing. It is armor. Here there is virtually no distinction among the four sons. Each of them receives a coat of mail, and in most cases a helmet, some arm guards and greaves, though only the eldest son and, interestingly, one of his clerical brothers, an abbot, receives a complete set of equipment. (It is not surprising that clerics would receive this defensive weapon and its accessories, since they could participate in battle, though were not supposed to shed blood.) Mail was extremely costly, so we have stark evidence here of the family's resources. Indeed, hauberks were so valuable a defensive weapon that their possession was regulated by the Carolingian state; trade in them was restricted, lest they fall into enemy hands. Along with spears and shields, edicts specified, hauberks were considered weapons, not to be worn or carried routinely, lest feuding or other violence result. Swords, on the other hand, were required markers of status, and were not so prohibited. Count Eberhard and Countess Gisela's will reflects, also in writing, this division between swords on the one hand and other weapons. While armor is considered necessary even for clerics, as markers of authority, swords are not grouped with it, or with other weapons in an abstract category like "military equipment," or even "weapon." The sword, here, is close to the lifeworld of how elite men went through their lives; it is a weapon but it is also a claim to the status the weapon reflects. And it is depicted as such in writing. It is the status claimed and also performed.

In fact, the single copy of the will that survives is an incomplete one from an eleventh-century cartulary, from the monastery where one of the sons had ruled as abbot two centuries before. In that context, the will constituted a record of that son's possible endowments of the monastery, as there would have been pressure, by that time, for the institution to consider the abbot's property as its own.[50] The scholars who have imagined burials remembered as poems, or who have compared sword burials to hagiographies, reflect this interdependence of material and textual evidence. The visible act of giving, repeated into the future by the document, like the remembered act of burying, helps endow the gift with its power to fix the identity of the lord and associate others with it. But now the balance has begun to shift, and the power of writing shapes how weapons are used, represented, and imagined.

Thus, these wills reinforce what we now recognize in the earlier grave deposits: a chosen sword is a necessary marker of lordship, the more so when that lord is a king, or would be one. But it is not sufficient. Other belongings must continue to circulate after a burial or be gifted in a will, or in life, as we can glimpse in wills such as Aethelstan's. Swords are not alone, and they are rarely left to stand alone as an emblem of lordship or, especially, kingship. Rather, swords are part of increasingly calibrated paraphernalia that writing can advertise.

Making the evidence of graves speak led us to reach forward to later written sources for interpretive help, and to momentarily set aside the fact that written evidence shapes as well as reports conditions on the ground. Literature, meanwhile, whether written or oral, shapes the world for dramatic purposes. Yet compelling evidence about swords, evidence used by most interpreters of this period, lies also in seemingly "fictional" accounts. In this final section, I will discuss two Anglo-Saxon poems that survive in written texts, in part by means of the scholarship that has grown up around them. Both texts date from around 1000 CE. The first is a poem fragment that memorializes one battle, between Saxons and Vikings, at Maldon in 991. The second is the epic *Beowulf. The Battle of Maldon* offers a detailed narrative of the fight in which the use of weapons is described in some detail. We naturally approach such a narrative with questions about swords: how were they used, remarked upon? Is it possible to discern, through a commemorative poem, how swords were valued in the "real world" of everyday? Or, as with wills, how did this version shape or even determine how swords were valued? With *Beowulf*, the questions include how we interpret the subject matter—tales about the sixth century—since we cannot know when the poem was composed, nor its relationship to a prior cache of oral tales. Its relationship to context, in short, is obscure. In both cases, in fact, we find ourselves wrestling simultaneously with text, context, and artifacts.

The fragment of 325 lines that constitutes what we know as the poem *The Battle of Maldon* survived until the eighteenth century, when it was destroyed in the fire that also damaged the sole surviving manuscript of *Beowulf*. All modern commentary on *Maldon* is based on a transcription executed in about 1724, and published in 1726. The battle itself, mentioned in one version of the Anglo-Saxon Chronicle and in other sources, probably took place in 991 near the settlement of Maldon in the estuary of the Blackwater River in modern Essex. Though swords do not figure prominently in the poem, their brief mention is highly suggestive. But to understand why, we first need to examine the poem's overall focus and its historical roots.

The poem recounts a battle between Saxons, led by the ealdorman (earl) Byrhtnoth, and a raiding party of Danes. The royal mint at Maldon no doubt had attracted the Scandinavians who had gone "a-viking" and had recently sacked Ipswich to the north. The Danes win at Maldon, the poet tells us, in part because of the treachery and cowardice of some of the earl's men, as well as because the earl was himself foolhardy. But while he tells about both betrayal and overweening pride, the poet is also quite specific about how the fighting actually played out.

The battle, as he relates it, opens as an archery and spear-throwing duel between the two armies standing at a distance from each other; after this initial phase, the armies fight in closer quarters. Byrhtnoth's dangerous pride or sense of honor led him to allow the Vikings across a narrow causeway to face him on his chosen ground. The fight continues, by the Saxons, from behind their shield wall and is almost entirely accomplished with spears. The Saxon force falters when Byrhtnoth's horse, ridden by a traitor, is spotted in retreat, recognizable from its trappings. The discipline and coherence so essential for the success of the shield wall is lost when more cowards flee the battle, while warriors holding their ground wonder if their leader has abandoned them.

There is virtually no mention of swordplay in the poem. The exceptions include one reference to Byrhtnoth wielding his sword in self-defense after being wounded by an enemy spear and a second reference to Edward, one of his thegns, who avenges the death of one of Byrhtnoth's kinsmen with his sword. In one further instance, Edward draws his "broad and gleaming" sword when an enemy tries to steal precious goods from the fallen Byrhtnoth's body—not merely to protect the hero's gold-hilted sword, lying on the ground next to him, but also his gold armbands and rings.

How we imagine the relationship between this text and its context affects the meaning we can draw from these depictions of swords. Historian Nicholas Brooks concludes that we should accept that the poet knew what he was doing with this rendering of the battle; spears, while more common than swords, were nonetheless an elite weapon, and had swordplay dominated the battle, the poet surely would not have missed the chance to describe action with such dramatic possibilities. Significant, for Brooks, is the fact that the poet does not describe any armor, whether helmet or hauberk, worn by the English, though he depicts the Danes wearing mail. Evidence of heriots in English wills, Brooks argues, suggests that mail armor and helmets were still relatively rare in Saxon England at this time. Thus, it makes sense to imagine the English fighting behind a shield wall with spears in 991; they needed to keep their better-protected foes at a distance. Brooks goes on to suggest that this familiarity with tactics argues for an early composition of the poem, before the English would have been better armed, like their opponents (which was mandated—so many helmets and hauberks per unit of land—by the early eleventh century). "The later the date we assign to the poem, the less relevant its message would have been," Brooks concludes; the emotional power of the poem's evocation of heroic ideals of loyalty and bravery would have swayed its elite audience whatever the circumstances, but the pathos of their hopeless confrontation with better-armed troops would have been muted if heard by an audience even one generation later.[51]

Other scholars disagree with Brooks's suggested early date for *Maldon*. Comparison with other texts of its approximate date, particularly the various versions of the Anglo-Saxon Chronicle, leads another scholar, George Clark, to argue that the poem is much more crafted fiction than accurate description, at least as far as the known history of Danish raids is concerned. The poem presents the face-off at Maldon in isolation from other Viking raids that the chronicles also mention; the three named traitors (one of whom rides the hero's horse away) recall another trio identified in chronicles as having fled the site of another confrontation with Danes much farther north, at Bamborough; thus, three fleeing men are a familiar trope. The setting for the battle, though likely accurate, since the audience would have known the topography, is nonetheless ideal for staging a doomed encounter; Byrhtnoth allows the Vikings to cross a narrow causeway onto the mainland to face his army fairly. A later battle against the Danes, in 1014, occurred in similar circumstances. In short, Maldon was an early episode in a conflict that would last another twenty years and more, but it is celebrated in the poem as an iconic moment of tragic heroism—the perfect way to celebrate the Saxons in their eventual loss to the Dane Canute, who claims the English throne in 1016. The poem creates a lost age, which it appears to report via one example: "the poem's subject is the beginning of that heroic age whose close the poem announces."[52]

The poem celebrates heroism but, Clark argues, in the interests of accommodation. Imagining themselves as heroes makes accepting Danish rule more palatable—that is, possible without loss of honor. Doomed heroism is a fictional trope that stands out as such in this text the more we envision its world as one in motion politically and ethnically. In the current moment, after decades of open borders within Europe, we can acknowledge ethnic diversity as a constant feature of the European past and that these regions must have been, at the time, culturally, linguistically, and ethnically fluid. Hence, we are less interested in interpreting conflict as "national" struggles.

Both scholars' perspectives, in my view, should be deployed to make sense of the appearance of swords in *Maldon*. Poems in a still largely oral culture conveyed information for their publics, in addition to celebrating and lamenting. Thus, it is appropriate to think that, in Brooks's words, the poet knew what he was doing when he described a battle in which swords were rare. At the same time, the narrative device of doomed heroism is a key to interpreting the mentions of swords that do occur. Two of the references to swords in the poem occur together in one moment of the action: when the thegn, Edward, draws his gleaming sword to protect the fallen earl's body, as well as Byrhtnoth's ornamented sword, armbands, and rings. We are thus invited to gaze, in our mind's eye, at the earl's wealth, at his insignia of rank, lying with him on the ground. His rank has also been displayed, in another scene, by his horse's trappings, which his retinue recognize, and tragically assume he has fled the battle.[53] Taken together, some have argued, these goods might be construed as standing in symbolically as the earl's heriot payment, which means we are being invited to think of Byrhtnoth as the doomed loyal servant of the king.[54] More important, I think, is that it is the sword and other regalia of the earl that are doing the work of expressing shock and grief. We are asked to imagine the sword on the ground, to see the contrast between its shining, gold hilt and the earth, and that of the gold accoutrements and the lifeless body. The thegn protects his leader's body from desecration and his identity, embodied in the goods, from attack. The loss of this noble hero is expressed in the image of these vital belongings abandoned, even defenseless. It is quite possible, in fact, that the poet understated the amount of swordplay in his telling of the tale in order to highlight the tragic irony of the gold-hilted sword that is good for nothing. This is a version of history where heroic deeds give way to a more complex present day. A sword is good to lament with, and to be a focus for nostalgia.

Some of these same points have been advanced about the long epic text, *Beowulf*: that it laments heroes of days gone by, and often uses swords to do that "work."[55] In fact, a danger in mining *Beowulf* for evidence of prior practices, such as the circulation of prestige goods, lies not only in the late date of the manuscript but also in the fact that the tale appears to be consciously backward looking; it is an evocation of a time not like the poet's present. The appearance of many swords and other objects gifted, wielded, and regretted in the tale must be evaluated in this context, that of what the story is trying to accomplish.

Beowulf, like *The Battle of Maldon*, is both a singular text and a singular object. It is an Old English poem of 3,182 lines that survives in one damaged copy in the British Library, part of a codex that includes other tales about monsters. There is considerable agreement among scholars about the age of the manuscript itself, based on an analysis of the script and on clues in the other texts in the codex: it dates from the reign of the English king Ethelred the Unready, who reigned between 978 and 1016 (when he was succeeded by the Dane Canute), thus contemporaneous with *The Battle of Maldon*.

Where debate has focused energetically is on when the poem was actually composed. Here, the singularity of the text is especially problematic, since it is difficult to date vocabulary and syntax when a poem preserves the only use of particular words or expressions *anywhere* in the surviving corpus of Anglo-Saxon texts and when the "rules" for meter and orthography and so on, depend so heavily on the very text we hope to analyze.[56] It is true that some features of the poem suggest an early date of composition. Any reader familiar with the kinds of formulae characteristic of oral composition can notice these characteristics in *Beowulf* and thus presume that the poem preserves orally circulating material—hence we could assume the poem was composed as early as the late seventh century. (Since it is impossible to overlook the Christian overtones in the poem, it cannot be dated earlier than the firm establishment of Christianity in Britain in the 600s.) Any interpretation of the poem must work with the residue of oral culture present in it.

Another argument for an early composition is the equally obvious fact that the action of the poem takes place almost entirely in modern day Denmark and Sweden. A number of scholars have argued that the poem must thus have been composed before Norsemen conquered swaths of English territory in the ninth century. This is a version of the same argument we encountered regarding the *Battle of Maldon*. How else could the English celebrate such a heroic past, if they were fighting tooth and nail against it in their present? Recent scholars point out, in this case as well, that we have plenty of evidence and imaginative scope for thinking of England in the late ninth and early tenth centuries as a polyglot world, not without political tensions and outright violence but nonetheless one where Danes were a familiar part of the landscape.[57] Even if the Danes were perceived as a dire threat, the tale could serve a purpose that had very little to do with immediate political circumstances. The purpose, in the minds of the monks who copied it, or the family that commissioned it, may have been to contain thrilling stories of monsters and heroes in a safe, remote past.[58]

Debates about the date of *Beowulf*'s composition are not mere technicalities; they reflect interpretive stances that have direct bearing on how we assess the text—for our purposes, how we evaluate the significance of objects described in the poem, especially the swords singled out by the poet. *Beowulf* is often cited as evidence of the circulation of goods that are both works of art and easily movable wealth.[59] Is the circulation of swords, arm rings, and the like in *Beowulf* a description of a familiar, then-current process, or a nostalgic vision of a world of loyal retainers and free gifts? What kind of work do swords accomplish in the poet's vision of the past?

There are several swords of note in the poem: Hrunting, given to Beowulf by another warrior at Hrothgar's court after his hand-to-hand combat with Grendel, as he sets off to hunt Grendel's mother; the giant's sword Beowulf finds in Grendel's mother's lair; and, at the end of the poem, a sword wielded by Wiglaf, Beowulf's young retainer, which kills the dragon when Beowulf's own sword, Naegling, could not. There are many other references to swords, to swordplay, as well as to other weapons such as knives and spears, to mail armor and shields. In fact, as several scholars have noted, Beowulf is about monsters but it is also about feuds, and it is about *stuff*.[60] When Beowulf is about to leap into the water for the climactic battle with Grendel's mother, he pauses to distribute his gear and treasure in case he should not return. He asks Hrothgar to "act like a father to me," as he had promised, which meant taking care of Beowulf's "young company," but especially sending all of the gifts Hrothgar had given Beowulf home to Beowulf's uncle, king Hygelac. "Let the lord of the Geats [Hygelac] gaze on that gold . . . and see that I found a ring-giver of rare magnificence and enjoyed the good of his generosity," he says (lines 1484–87). Earlier, when about to fight Grendel, Beowulf pleads, do not lament overlong if I die, but do send my body armor back to my home.

Indeed, all these things, this stuff, are also narrative devices by which the story moves forward. For example, when Hrothgar, whose mead hall Beowulf has rid of the monster, bestows a golden torque on him in gratitude, the poet uses the object as a moment to reflect on what will happen in the future, when Beowulf's own king and uncle, Hygelac, will lose the torque, and other treasures, in a failed raid.[61] Not only do we watch objects being gifted and exchanged throughout the story, to reward and to sustain relationships, but the poet assumes our attention on them and uses them as connective tissue to describe the future or remind us of the past.

When a people meet disaster, it is imagined partly in these material terms, which is why Hrothgar's gift to Beowulf can provide a symbolic link to another king's demise later. Toward the end of the poem, an old warrior contemplates treasures, the hoard later guarded by the dragon. He has placed these heirlooms "with deliberate care" in a new barrow, because "death had come and taken" all his people. His own joy in these treasures will be brief, but he has carried into the barrow all the golden wares "worth preserving." He addresses the barrow:

"Now, earth, hold what earls once held
and heroes can no more . . .
. . . My own people
have been ruined in war; one by one
they went down to death, looked their last
on sweet life in the hall. I am left with nobody
to bear a sword or to burnish plated goblets,
put a sheen on a cup. The companies have departed.
The hard helmet, hasped with gold,
will be stripped of its hoops; and the helmet-shiner
who should polish the metal of the war-mask sleeps;
the coat of mail that came through all fights,
through shield-collapse and cut of sword,
decays with the warrior. Nor may webbed mail
range far and wide on the warlord's back

beside his mustered troops. No trembling harp,
no tuned timber, no tumbling hawk
swerving through the hall, no swift horse
pawing the courtyard. Pillage and slaughter
have emptied the earth of entire peoples."
And so he mourned as he moved about the world. (lines 2247–67)

When people vanish, their treasures remain, abandoned, deprived of human touch: the mail, which came through all fights like a true war companion, does not range far and wide on a man's back but decays, the war mask is abandoned by the sleeping helmet shiner. There is no life in the hall either, no sound, no movement from warriors' other companions: hawk and horse and harp. The lone survivor, bereft of his fellows—whom, we note, he describes in terms of their attention to these objects—gives the treasure that remains into the earth's care. It is not just that men are dead, it is that relationships with their treasures have been broken. Part of the tragedy for this last survivor is that the objects themselves are orphaned, that the rightful care and distribution of goods will not take place.

The poet also imagines that his characters believe that swords, shields, and the like have the power to evoke memory, that individual objects can carry specific memories and can therefore incite human action. When Beowulf relates his exploits once back home, for example, he publicly remembers King Hrothgar's daughter, whom he has met, who was betrothed to "heal old wounds." But Beowulf imagines the planned marriage will not work to end the feuding, since "the spear is prompt to retaliate . . . no matter how admirable the bride may be." Beowulf goes on to imagine the bridal feast where the guests of one tribe glimpse their own heirlooms in the hands of their enemies; the objects awaken memories of the earlier fight in which the treasures were lost. Indeed, as Beowulf imagines it, an old spearman will speak in exactly these terms, goading his fellows,

> "Now, my friend, don't you recognize your father's sword, his favorite weapon, the one he wore . . . on that fateful day? . . . and now here's a son of one or other of those same killers coming through our hall . . . mouthing boasts and rigged in armor that is by right yours."
> (lines 2047–56)

Peace will not last between these two peoples, Beowulf predicts.

Swords and spears and armor work as gifts to cement relationships not merely because they represent wealth but because they symbolically convey the identity of the giver, and, in this case, of those from whom they were won in an ambush. They work as trophies precisely because they carry something of the individual who lost them, but, more than that, they can demand, even take, revenge. This embedded identity is one reason why they work as characters; they can drive the story forward, prompt humans to reflect on other stories or drive them to other acts.

These moments in the text appear to readers today as digressions. We find ourselves wondering why Beowulf interrupts his triumphal speech back home with this drawn-out, grim prediction. Though we now appreciate the interlace structure of the story, we do so in a scholarly or intellectual way. We cannot appreciate the way in which these references would have reverberated with meaning for a medieval audience. Accustomed to oral narratives and deeply skilled in listening, they would have easily recognized the significance of objects, and could have followed *them*, characters in the story, without getting lost or losing interest.[62] The power of objects to drive human action would have been far greater for contemporaries than for us, and their attention would be more readily captured by high-value objects like torques, armor, weapons.

The very language of the poem reflects this conflation of people and things. The Anglo-Saxon word "laf," for example, an heirloom or something or someone left behind, can refer to a survivor, such as a widow, but also a remnant or relic, such as a sword passed down. This kind of cluster of meaning makes it hard for modern scholars even to determine whether a sword or a person is being referred to at some points in the text—an example of the interpretive difficulties that the small amount of surviving poetry presents.[63] Perhaps contemporaries knew what was meant, or perhaps these contested passages allowed for an ambiguity about persons and weapons that contemporaries found both comprehensible and congenial.

Some of the notable swords in the tale carry individual histories that the poet shares with us, including those that carry evil intention or the enhanced power that evil can confer: the result of having been used to murder, or having been crafted for some dark purpose. The worthy retainer Wiglaf's sword, which comes to Beowulf's aid against the dragon at the end of the tale, had been used in the past to commit a fratricidal murder. The poet pauses in his story again, while the dragon threatens the two men, to share with his audience this backstory regarding Wiglaf's sword. It is the dark power inherent in the blade that enables it to pierce the dragon's body when the hero's own sword could not. After Beowulf's death, Wiglaf eulogizes him but, once again, the speech is filled with significant "digressions." Wiglaf shames the retainers who did not help in the fight with the dragon, laments Beowulf's death and sets out how he will be remembered, but also returns to the subject of the blood feud, in which his own sword had once participated. He retraces some of the fighting in his sword's past, and the implications for the future are clear: with the childless Beowulf's death, the kingdom will once again be engulfed in feuding, and the sword is the bridge between the two worlds.

This is a pre-Christian world imagined by a Christian poet where there is no knowledge of the peace and good order that a Christian high king could ensure. Feuds are endemic, and the warriors' stuff, especially weapons and above all, swords, helps perpetuate them. All of this is very subtly conveyed by the poet. Swords are not simply weapons, nor are they impersonal instruments of doom, but are entities with histories; their individual pasts are used to create the dark mood of the poem, the knowledge that feuding will not be ended. Swords, like men, can be powerful and yet act rashly, unwisely, out of pride or anger or revenge, and leave that mixed legacy to the next generation.[64]

Above all, swords are not miraculously powerful in the hands of heroes. They are actors in the drama and, like men, they can let us down. Interestingly, Beowulf, a renowned warrior, has trouble using swords successfully against the monsters. His trusty sword fails him against the dragon. Earlier, since no sword seems to affect Grendel, Beowulf proposes to kill the monster with his bare hands, and does so. When it comes time to face Grendel's mother, Beowulf uses a "rare and ancient" sword that has "never failed the hand of anyone who had hefted it in battle," a gift from the boastful warrior Unferth, who recognizes Beowulf's superior worth. But when facing the "tarn-hag" even the "fabulous powers of that heirloom" fail. Swords can be both as fearsome and as unreliable as humans can be. Even the great and powerful ones have their limits, and meet their doom. Great swords are not available to solve problems magically.

Except one, if only for a single use. Beowulf finds another great weapon in the mother's lair, after he flings Unferth's useless sword aside. In the hoard, underwater, Beowulf spies an ancient heirloom, "from the days of the giants," a sword so formidable that only the hero Beowulf could even lift it. And with this weapon, he beheads the dreadful beast-mother of Grendel. Then, when Beowulf uses the weapon also to behead Grendel's corpse— which has been lying in the mother's underwater lair—the "scalding blood . . . of the poisonous fiend" causes the blade to melt, "wilt[ing] into gory icicles to slather and thaw." Only the bejeweled hilt remains.

After this, the hilt stays at the center of our attention for a time. Beowulf swims back to the surface carrying only the trophy of Grendel's head and the remnant hilt. His retainers, waiting by the lake, quickly help him out of his helmet and chain mail, wondrous protectors because he has been able to survive underwater while wearing them. Then his retainers manage to bear Grendel's head back to the mead hall, where all assembled stare at it in awe. The inevitable celebratory speeches then begin. Beowulf tells of finding this sword, which "the Lord of Men allowed [him] to behold," and of the melting of the blade, and then goes on to assure the assembled company that at last they are truly safe from the monsters that have been preying on them. The hilt is presented to King Hrothgar, and here we have a moment, like some of the "digressions," where the action of the narrative pauses to focus on one object and the story it prompts. The poet's audience is invited to imagine that they too are in the audience in Hrothgar's mead hall, watching the king now stare at the hilt, which holds a cryptic message written in runes.

This moment has also riveted scholarly attention. Some scholars argue that Hrothgar reads the message on the hilt, while others note the poet's ambiguity about the actual reading and argue that we are meant to understand that the king is fascinated but cannot make out the strange writing. They point out that the king's *scop*, his court poet and rune-reader (understood to be a counselor), has been deliberately killed by Grendel's mother, and is no longer available to decipher the message. Nonetheless, the story, whether read or only gazed upon by Hrothgar, is briefly encapsulated by the poet; the runes refer to the origins of the sword in the days of giants. Whether they argue that Hrothgar can make out this story or not, scholars agree that the vocabulary in this part of the tale, virtually unique in the poem as well as in the corpus of Anglo-Saxon literature, guarantees that the audience would have understood that it refers to a deep past, that can be captured and barely rendered in stories that its audience, in the poet's day, can understand.[65]

The whole scene around the hilt is too highly dramatized for the object to be a mere curiosity, in any case. In some ways, the presence of the hilt and the action around it constitute the hinge of the entire tale. It is a dense moment of storytelling, in which the deep past is described but not, unusually, copiously renarrated. In just eleven lines, the poet efficiently relates that the runes tell of "how war first came into the world and [how] a great flood destroyed the race of giants." And how Almighty God, the Christian god of the poet, caused the great deluge that swept the giants away. Finally, the poet mentions, these runes "stating and recording for whom the sword was first made" were "correctly inscribed." And then, abruptly, the focus returns to Hrothgar, who begins again to praise Beowulf.

This moment operates as the hinge of the tale because it accomplishes so much in the poet's hands. It is an example of how Christian literates invented the idea of the myth of runes and their magic, as part of their vision of a mythic past.[66] It is also an example of how stories can contain, in the sense of domesticate, stories about monstrous creatures and outsize events, precisely as happens in greater compass throughout the poem. This episode is the hinge of the story above all because it reflects on storytelling itself; it is about language and tale-telling, about writing and communication and about the role of stuff in conveying history and constructing memory. The very brevity of the scene assumes both the power of writing, for the audiences in and of the poem, to contain and convey the past, and that of singular objects to evoke it. Most significant for our purposes is the fact that it is a sword hilt that forms the bridge linking three worlds: the remote past, the "present" of Beowulf, and the poet's own present.

The object itself would have been familiar. In the ninth and tenth centuries, runes were known to be a pre-Christian form of writing, and a sword decorated with runes a common enough relic of Scandinavian forebears. The poet was also drawing on his audience's understanding that the message on a written document might be less important than possession of the document. In the early days of charters, the thing was the guarantee of whatever the words conveyed.[67] The meaning of the rune-covered hilt also must have

FIGURE 1.1.   A blade incised with runes. A long single-edged weapon, this tenth-century seax is inscribed in runes with the name Beagnoth (perhaps its creator) as well as with the complete runic alphabet along one side of its blade. © The Trustees of the British Museum. All rights reserved.

resided in the linguistic relationship of writing to swordplay. The word for writing in Old English, in the sense of runes, is the same word as the sense of marks a blade can inscribe.[68] So swords were a particularly useful object to talk about writing with, since they were linked etymologically to it.

In addition, here the sword stands in for memory through time—not only because swords can be imagined as writing, or carrying written messages on hilt or blade, but also because the object itself has endured through time. Several scholars have pointed out that a sword hilt, even more than the blade itself, could typically survive over many generations; in fact, we have recovered examples of sword hilts with runic inscriptions. The poet, in short, was imagining the kind of hilt that would have been known in his day but which would have carried the sense of pastness.

In other words, if swords and spears and neck rings and other wealth are good things to think with throughout the poem, if they are linchpins in human relationships in the society depicted, if they drive the story forward as actors, then none of them, this example tells us, works better for those purposes than a sword. And they are one of the most important devices by which the poet imagines the past. From his Christian present, he laments the inescapable, cyclical violence of Beowulf's world. But he also creates a mythic past for that society, even more fantastical and monster-ridden than Beowulf's present.[69] The sense of a created past is in part the result of the archaic language in the poem—but especially in the story of the sword hilt, which literally carries that past into the present of Beowulf's time.

To translate the work that swords are doing in the tale into evidence about how things *were* in the actual lifeworld of the audience around the year 1000, we must stress this sense of distance the poem creates. This is an orally derived text, a work "that emerges from oral tradition along pathways we cannot now retrace," which the poet deliberately stresses by hiding the fact that he had to have been working from written texts in some measure himself to produce the rendering we have.[70] There are several narrators whom the poet allows to tell the tale, and he includes scops, thereby both evoking a world of oral performance and obscuring his own reliance on writing. In fact, he defers to the authority of his supposed witnesses and tale-tellers when he is in fact at his most inventive as a poet.[71] The digressions or episodes added to the audience's sense of remoteness by mimicking a gathering of oral tales.[72] The distance from this created "historical" past is reinforced by the fact that the character Beowulf dies without heirs. Even though Wiglaf's sword has killed the dragon, the great warrior king who has kept the peace throughout his long life is gone and his lineage ends. After him, his kingdom is beset with strife. We, in the audience, lament the dead hero, but we do not regret the violent world in which he lived. Rather, we pity Beowulf because fame and worldly goods were all that succeeded him.

In the present of the twenty-first century, we cannot know whether the precise descriptions of swords rang true for tenth-century contemporaries, whether they seemed understandably archiac or even faintly ridiculous.[73] In fact, we are deaf to much of what the poem accomplishes, because the poetics are alien to us—and not just because few of us control Anglo-Saxon, the language of the original. The poem is a text composed with writing that preserves much oral residue that predates its rendering in writing. The "text" that we have relies on phrase units (often thought of as "formulaic units") whose variations and, hence, whose nuances we can barely appreciate. We are, in short, deaf to much of *Beowulf*'s language because it is ripped from the context that endows it with much of its meaning. It would seem, for example, that the scene where our attention is focused on the extraordinary rune-inscribed hilt could have been an experience of "presence effect" for the contemporary audience—but we can only guess.[74]

We can be more certain that members of the audience were attuned to prestige objects as focuses of attention, longing, and pathos. Things in their world rewarded, displayed, and mobilized loyalty, bravery, and identity. Great swords were familiar characters, their presence expected in such a tale. But perhaps, by the year 1000, things no longer literally drove action, if they ever had. This hyperattention to things, expecting things to be willful actors in the world, some with mysterious power, may have been nostalgia, already even fantasy. As I have suggested for *Maldon*, nostalgia could accomplish reconciliation. *Beowulf* harks back to a day and age where stuff alone could start feuds or make peace, where gifts and booty were justly gained and freely distributed, lost and won again. Warriors in the tenth century could indulge their longing for a world of loyal retainers and bountiful rewards, unrestrained by rules and regulations, by written wills and calculated heriots, and claim it as their ancestral world, all from a safe distance from the harsh reality of Beowulf's sixth century.[75]

Swords are the connective tissue that do the work of linking the two worlds. We have seen that they link the two pasts together, the poet's past (of Beowulf's time) and the character Beowulf's own past, the before-time when giants made swords and monsters were born. They can do that work within the poem because they also link Beowulf's day to the poet's present day. Swords are indispensable as a narrative device; they are present at almost every turn of the action, they are invoked at every moment of mourning for a fallen king. Swords are also the primary instrument, as in *Maldon*, that expresses the pathos of heroes in this flawed world: their powers are limited, they will die, peace will not come, in their world at least. The grief that the poet evokes in his audience by means of swords happens in his present. A lament for what men and swords could not do in a remote past, when magical powers were already waning, made sense in a society where swords are both the most valued weapon and an essential symbol of lordship yet never sufficient for either adornment or even reliably for self-defense and, like the most potent exemplars from the past, still offer no guarantees.

CHAPTER 2

Swords and Chivalric Culture in the High Middle Ages

In 1191, in route to the Holy Land, the English king, Richard "the Lionheart" (d. 1199), made a gift of arguably the most prestigious object he owned. He presented the sword Excalibur to King Tancred of Sicily. In return, Tancred gave Richard some nineteen ships for his army's passage across the Mediterranean. This exchange of gifts preceded a formal settlement of disputes between the two rulers. After seizing the throne of Sicily from the legitimate heiress, his aunt Constance (the wife of the Holy Roman emperor), Tancred had dispossessed and imprisoned Richard's sister Joan, the late king's wife, who had supported Constance's claim. Richard seized Sicilian territory in retaliation for Tancred's move against his sister but formally agreed some months later to recognize Tancred's rule in return for the monies owed to Joan. No doubt, the presence of Richard's crusading partner and rival, Philip II of France, had spurred the negotiations. Whatever Richard had gained, he had expended King Arthur's sword, with all its symbolic might, to guarantee this one relationship and its strategic possibilities.

What are we to make of this object? What *was* this Excalibur? And what kind of exchange did this gift represent? In gross material terms, the transaction clearly favored Richard: one sword in return for his sister's safety and fortune and for guaranteed passage of his entire army and all its equipment. While the weapon's prestige would have bolstered Tancred's fragile legitimacy, it might have been superfluous to Richard's stature in any case. He already enjoyed a reputation as a daring and canny warrior but he was skilled above all in logistics, and what he needed at this moment was cash, supplies, and transportation.[1] Whatever we may know about the circumstances of the exchange, however, we still need to explain the object, the sword. For Excalibur to "work," it had to have a potency both parties would recognize. How was this actual sword brought into being and endowed with the significance it had? And what was the nature of that significance, that potency? How did it take and give meaning from swords and their lore, from other objects and stories? In order to understand this transaction, in other words, we want to know about the gift economy at play, about the life of swords amid other objects at the time, and about this sword itself.

The centuries from about 1000 to 1300 were not a period of especial artistic or technical innovation in the case of swords. But though the properties of swords did not change much in this period, much changed around them. Western Europe in the central Middle Ages was a world of dramatic economic growth and social and political change. The material signs were everywhere, even as early as the mid-eleventh century. Lords had the resources to project their power also over long distances, such as the Norman invasion of England and, most notably, the First Crusade (1096). Both presupposed adequate manpower, hence growing population, and extensive resources in craft labor and materiel. Increased wealth enabled a handful of lords to build their residences and strongholds in stone for the first time; more and more stone castles appeared in the decades after 1100. New goods were imported for the first time or in greater numbers; gemstones, for example, brought back from western Asia, created novel possibilities for personal adornment when set in finger rings, as they were by Richard's lifetime.[2] Excalibur thus came to life amid an expanding array of other positional objects, and even this sword was more a prop than an actor on the stage.

The fact that Richard claimed to have not merely a potent sword but the Excalibur itself situates the gift in a further context: the history of the creation, reworking, and circulation of the Arthurian legends. There is much that was new also about the world of texts in the twelfth century. The earliest vernacular romances, that is, stories of chivalric adventures, came from the orbit of Richard's parents, Henry II of England and Eleanor of Aquitaine, and by Richard's adult life they had found one of their greatest crafters in the verse romances of Chrétien de Troyes (d. ca. 1190), who may have spent part of his writing life at the court of Richard's half sister Marie, Countess of Champagne. Preceding those romances was the *History of the Kings of Britain* (ca. 1136) by a Welsh cleric known as Geoffrey of Monmouth, the origin point for the many later French- and English-language romances of Arthur. Geoffrey's text claimed to be a history; it traced the British realm back to one Brutus, the great-grandson of the Trojan hero Aeneas, and went on to position Arthur as a defender of post-Roman Britain against Saxon invaders. Many reworkings of Geoffrey's *History* followed in the twelfth and thirteenth centuries, as did numerous other histories grounding the claims of elite families in an ancient past. Aristocratic and royal families sponsored and consumed genealogies and histories. Not only did they have the money to commission the work but increasingly they themselves were literate consumers of romance and history. As the expanding economy gave lords and rulers more resources, self-definition and self-advertisement in histories represented vital political work. Excalibur itself constituted a specific historical and genealogical claim.

To call Excalibur a prop therefore does not imply cynicism about the meaning attached to this sword or the work it could accomplish in its day. Rather, the term refers to the process of its deliberate creation. One particular sword "became" Excalibur as a result of an interplay between circulating stories, present need, and a suitable object. The actual sword was likely a ceremonial sword with added value already attached to it, in circulation before Geoffrey's *History* was written. (Legends about Arthur had been circulating orally, we know, before Arthur's reign was cast into a historical narrative by Geoffrey of Monmouth.)[3] It may in fact have been the sword that was presented to Richard's grandfather, Geoffrey Plantagenet, Count of Anjou, at his knighting in 1128 by King Henry I, shortly before Geoffrey's marriage to Henry's daughter Matilda. This sword, a chronicle tells us, was from Henry's treasury; it bore an "ancient inscription" and the mythic sword smith Wayland had "sweated many hours" to make it—clearly, a recognizably antique sword, an heirloom in its day.[4] Thus an existing sword could be made into a new entity as another known identity was grafted onto it.

An almost identical process had resulted, also in the twelfth century, in an embellished reliquary being reimagined as a donation by the Emperor Charlemagne, centuries earlier, to the French monastery that held it, a sign of his having favored that house above all others. In this case also, historical texts compiled at approximately the same time as well as legends circulating orally constituted the raw material, together with the actual object, that created in effect, a new object—an object with new significance because it was "remembered" to have always represented what it was now taken to signify.[5] Nor was Excalibur the only sword or piece of warrior paraphernalia from story or legend to make an appearance at the time. Richard's brother John (r. 1199–1216) counted, among his treasure, the legendary Tristan's sword. And, a few decades earlier, their older brother, Henry (d. 1183), had taken posses-sion of the hero Roland's sword when he plundered a monastery in southern France. Meanwhile, Roland's battle standard had been "discovered" and put to use as the French king's sacred banner.[6]

In the case of swords and banners and reliquaries alike we are witness-ing the workings of what one historian has termed "imaginative memory." The circumstances in all these cases were similar in that the identity of each object, and the work it was doing in its day, was anchored both in legend as well as in contemporary written texts. In addition, each was the product of some immediate need—institutional or political rivalry, dynastic legitimacy, and so on. But each was endowed with new life at a time when the num-ber and range of objects available to warriors and rulers (and monks) was expanding dramatically, thus it was distinguished from a vast field of like objects more insistently precisely because of the company it kept in among them, circulating in its world, from which it drew and reflected meanings.[7]

The potency of Richard's Excalibur lay in its comparative heft vis-à-vis other swords and thus in the evolving symbolic life of all swords during his lifetime. In what follows, I will sketch the material, social, and political con-texts that prevailed in France and Britain in these centuries, with particular attention to the way swords became a new means of staging lordship and demarking status. Even as they became more numerous, thus more ordi-nary in warrior society, swords became instruments of social exclusion and a favored, if not ubiquitous, symbol of both lordship generally and royalty specifically. I will also sample the representation of swords, particularly of Excalibur, in the growing corpus of histories and romances sponsored by elite consumers. These texts, particularly the romances, provided contem-poraries the opportunity to wrestle with contradictory requirements now at the heart of elite life, such as the expectation that warrior men be bellicose and fierce but also mannered and courtly.

They also provide, for us, a means of glimpsing the range of symbolic resonances swords now enjoyed in elite imagination. These texts were also important because, though reflecting orally circulating stories, they increas-ingly had a physical existence in writing, in books owned by warrior families. Dependence on writing and on literacy mattered for how signs other than words—such as swords—could also matter. Imaginative literature explored and celebrated identity even as the need grew to represent oneself in written documentation in order to manage property and safeguard political claims. This chapter brings together the implications of literacy with the symbolic meaning of material objects to build an understanding of the cultural shap-ing of warrior identity.

At the same time, as the economy expanded, new material means were available to represent a man and advertise his status in public ways. In other words, more swords came into a world where signs of identity were needed that could represent a man in his absence, and where documents but also other objects—seals, coats of arms—proliferated. The question is: what role did swords have; how were swords unique among such signs?

The tenth and eleventh centuries may have seen the creation of literature celebrating memorable swords, but, not coincidentally, the days when such swords were created were already waning. These were the centuries when Viking raids dwindled and the economies of western Europe took off. Objects such as stirrups and brooches and even swords were manufactured in towns, already by the eleventh century, by artisans who sold their work for cash. Only a handful of swords for those of highest status survive after about 900 that have rich trappings such as gold pommels or gold-wrapped grips, or designs carefully crafted in silver, such as the symbols of the evangelists on the pommel of the well-known Abingdon sword. More swords were now being produced, and they were, in the main, less masterworks and more simply workaday weapons. Moreover, the high-quality steel from Asia used in some early medieval swords was no longer available. Examination of the microstructure of swords manufactured between about 1000 and 1300 reveals, unsurprisingly, the composite structure made necessary by limited amounts of good steel available: steel edges welded onto an iron core or various small bits of steel of differing quality worked together to form a blade. Swords would certainly have been more plentiful than in earlier centuries, as manufacturing capacity grew, but were not more distinguished in any aesthetic sense from those of earlier ages.[8]

The changing political landscape that accompanied economic expansion led to changing practices in warfare which, in turn, caused swords to lose some of their practical importance, particularly as booty, and some of their symbolic importance as a prestige possession. Historians now posit that the mid-eleventh century represented a watershed of sorts in the conduct of warfare in France and, soon thereafter, in England; war among landed magnates and would-be aristocrats appears to have become less savage than it may once have been. Scholars note, for example, the growing practice of ransoming one's captured enemies, rather than slaying them outright—and appropriating their signature belongings. The roots of this development, they suggest, lie in economic growth. Why kill an opponent, when his lands, especially the bustling towns within them, generate income you could tap as a ransom, or castles that could change hands in exchange for his freedom? How fighting actually proceeded when it occurred, indeed whether it occurred at all, also reflected greater wealth in warriors' hands. Better-equipped opponents, above all, better-armored men, were quite simply harder to kill: yet another reason to seek ransom rather than press on to the death during battle. By the 1130s, the English monk Orderic Vitalis could criticize the savage treatment of prisoners after the battle of Bourgtheroulde (part of a Norman rebellion against Henry I of England) by saying "it was not our custom."[9]

By the early twelfth century, being an elite warrior in France or in Anglo-Norman lands meant being an armored (that is, mailed) and mounted warrior, adept at using both sword *and* lance. It was an expensive business, and fighting was increasingly about protecting resources: productive land and the prerogatives of lordship over it. It made more sense to besiege a castle, and perhaps win it and its dependencies for your own use, or to hold it for concessions, than to seek to destroy a rival and his kin and claim all their accoutrements—and risk future revenge. Moreover, recognition of a fellow adept, a fellow member of this increasingly privileged elite, likely fed the disinclination to dispatch him in a cold-blooded way. The more extreme fighting that prevailed in England until after the Norman Conquest is the exception that proves the rule: Anglo-Saxon lords like the unfortunate Byrhtnoth at Maldon were fighting Norse invaders. After the conquest of 1066, and the initial savaging of Anglo-Saxon resistance, Anglo-Norman warriors continued to treat fallen enemies ruthlessly when—an important caveat—those foes were in the economically marginal Celtic borderlands and, notably, did not have the resources to be similarly protected by armor.[10]

It is easy to exaggerate this change in the character of warfare, of course. Economic and demographic expansion also produced increasing numbers of warrior youth eager to establish reputations and amass property. Localized violence and feuding continued and outright slaughter persisted even within England and France, especially of garrisons and other low-ranking fighters as the hierarchical distinctions powered by economic expansion led dependent warriors to lose status relative to knights.[11] Nevertheless, even the treatment of garrisons was coming to be loosely governed by conventions.[12] And sieges, in any case, were much rarer than we have imagined. Castles were used as sites of administration, social cohesion, and display—thus of lordship—far more than as defensive sites or launch points for attacks on others. Indeed, even in the early days of stone castles, all sites were vulnerable to concerted attack and their defensive elements worked in part because they were decorative in a strategic way; they were built to deter the very presumption of challenge, politically as well as militarily.[13] Moreover, coincident with the relative restraint in practices of warfare came the rise of tournaments to occupy martial energies. In fact, the practice of ransoming opponents may have evolved first in tournaments.[14] Above all, it is not just a question of how war was fought, but whether and when it *was* fought at home.[15] Social hierarchy was expressed militarily, and aristocratic society was martial in its identity and self-expression. But it was not militarized, nor was warfare endemic.

The same forces that led to new limitations on warfare drove the explosion of new material accoutrements of knighthood and lordship to share the stage with swords: banners, heraldic devices on shields, clothing, and even buildings. Like the building boom that produced elaborate manor houses, stone keeps, and private oratories, this was partly a simple ripple effect of economic growth. Once fighters could afford the protection of a coat of mail, it became harder to tell men apart from one another in a fight, and heraldic symbols multiplied. Tournaments, in fact, may have been where the need for signs of identity was first felt. Almost as soon as tournaments are attested in the sources, so are the first heraldic devices: images on surcoats worn over mail or on banners affixed to lances. These symbols began as very simple designs and became more elaborate as time went on, though the requirement that they be recognizable in the fray limited the kinds of images that would serve. The surcoat itself probably appeared first among knights on crusade, in imitation of local garments that protected their wearers from the sun. One of the first textual references to a knight wearing a surcoat was a Syrian chronicler writing after the First Crusade (1096–99), who notes that the European man wore "his colors."[16] Heraldic devices also appeared, early on, on the small banners affixed to warrior's lances. When lances had been thrown, like javelins, banners or flags of any kind would have impeded their flight, but when wielded exclusively by an armored, mounted man, the "couched" lance, designed to be delivered by the full force of a moving horse, could carry a small banner or pennant as it went. The wealth and training necessary to produce such fighters in number thus produced new opportunities to advertise their identities to each other: in addition to their lances, pendants appeared on horse harnesses; over time, innovation in shield construction made it easier to execute a heraldic design on its surface as well. The first coats of arms on shields appear in the 1160s.[17]

Expanding wealth made it possible, as well as imperative, to claim and broadcast status ever more emphatically and precisely by material means, beyond the use of heraldic signs. Now swords became important, both in symbol and practice, in a new way: they were to have a special role in this scramble for distinction. Before the late twelfth century, all aristocrats were knights—that is, all were warriors, but not all knights were part of the warrior elite. There were many fighting men in elite retinues who were common men. In the late twelfth century, the ceremony of formal dubbing, creating a knight through ritual, became widespread and created a distinct status in custom and, in some cases, in law for the men who went through it. No longer would members of a fortress garrison, for example, describe themselves as "knights." The formalizing of the status of knight helped fuel the cascading effect of status-envy by all those below the very greatest magnates, which was being driven, in any case, by the ambitions wealth created.

Some lords began to claim the greater distinction of being "banneret" knight, for example, with the right to have a stylized banner precede them in their entrances, at tournaments as well as in battle. The practice of using banners to organize forces on the march or in battle derived from Roman legionary ensigns, and in medieval practice drew on the mystique of Roman precedent. Banners were composed of a symbol, usually executed on cloth, and the pole, lance, or staff on which it was fixed. Like swords, banners had more than a military function. Examples are attested in histories and chronicles of the ninth through the eleventh centuries of banners in the hands of kings, dukes, and earls, given as gifts to other princes or favored allies, which were often associated with the sacred power of a saint. We can imagine a process of memory akin to that which created Excalibur operating for objects such as the banner of St. Maurice (a third-century Roman legionary, martyred for refusing to kill Christians) given to a tenth-century English king by Hugh the Great, father of the first Capetian king of France.

By the twelfth century, some dukes—above all the Plantagenet dukes of Aquitaine and Normandy—were invested in their titles in formal (religious) ceremonies with banner as well as with sword and represented themselves on seals with both sword and, on the reverse, with banner. Using a banner, with or without sacred associations, became widespread among magnate families— counts, earls, dukes—in the twelfth century. By the end of the century, banners had become firmly associated with aristocratic identity and the power of command over others. By the 1180s, a man just below magnates in the hierarchy— perhaps untitled but nonetheless in command of a group of knights—began to be called a knight *portant bannière*. By the thirteenth century, the term "banneret" designated a social distinction above the common knight.[18] Above the bannerets, the counts, earls, and dukes set themselves apart by adding other distinctive insignia; some dared to affect a coronet or diadem, some wielded rod or scepter, at least on their seals. Even the lowly knight, though he did not enjoy such special insignia, could claim a heraldic device. He could also anchor the family's status with other kinds of displays: he could affix the family arms on the gate of a priory it supported, create a memorial site of family tombs in a local church, or commission tapestries to memorialize ancestors' deeds.

FIGURE 2.1. A personal seal displays sword and banner. This thirteenth-century wax seal depicts, on one side, the Count of Flanders wielding his sword and, on the other, bearing a lance with a personal banner. © RMN-Grand Palais / Art Resource, NY.

New titles and dignities went to whoever could claim and make them stick in the twelfth century, but the greater the social mobility and the greater the political prize—especially standing vis-à-vis royal or princely power—the greater the felt need for barriers and gradations of status. Being dubbed a knight became, by around 1200, a nonnegotiable rite of passage into a politically and, to some degree, legally privileged aristocracy.[19] In this sense, then, the sword became a centerpiece of warrior identity more firmly than ever before. A warrior could not be a knight without it, and the significance of the sword was now formally staged.

It shared that stage with two other objects. In the dubbing ceremony, the knight was ritually clothed with his sword belt and his sword as well as with spurs. The sword belt, we have noted, carried the symbolic weight of the weapon itself such that it was often deployed, as in early medieval graves, when swords themselves were absent. Spurs were a more recent piece of knightly paraphernalia. Though spurs had existed since pre-Roman times, it was only with the widespread expectation and practice of mounted fighting that the spur became a definitive marker of elite status. Then it quickly became a prestige object available for embellishment. The earliest gilded spurs are recorded in 1128, for Geoffrey Plantagenet's knighting by Henry. Sometime thereafter, gilded spurs became a commonplace symbolic attribute of the knight, alongside his sword; squires, where that was a recognized niche in the elaborating hierarchy, wore silver spurs.[20] Swords were now more numerous on the ground, but they, together with sword belts and other paraphernalia, had become a means of exclusion.

Now required for knighthood, swords were both more and less than a weapon, but in ways rather different from swords in earlier centuries, when they could be humanlike agents whose potency and grievances caused action. The sword, belt, and spurs were not ritually deployed to create just a fighter, a warrior, but a culturally distinct being, the knight, whose political privilege flowed from his claim to this identity. It is the *political* valence of swords that dominated their use in ceremony and image in the eleventh through thirteenth centuries. The cascading status-envy had as its motor the growing power of kings and regional princes. Thus, knights' swords existed on a continuum with swords imagined as symbols of rule.

On gravestones and memorial brasses, on seals, in tapestries, it was the dukes and counts, those just below the royal dignity, who had to rely on the sword above all. As we have seen, by the twelfth century they were often formally invested with swords when assuming their titles. They claimed banners and other devices such as coronets when they could, but the staged use

PLATE 2. The sword as scepter. In the first frame of the Bayeux Tapestry (top), the aging King Edward the Confessor holds his royal scepter as he sends Harold to France, to promise the throne to Duke William of Normandy. When Harold is taken prisoner by a rival French lord, William negotiates his release with the lord's envoy in a later scene (bottom). William is depicted in a posture echoing Edward's: seated, gesturing with his right hand while his sword rests on his left hip and shoulder, like Edward's scepter. Erich Lessing / Art Resource, NY.

of the sword is omnipresent. The swords are often depicted distinctively as swords of command, and not primarily as weapons—the less exalted symbol mimicking more traditional emblems of lordship and authority such as a scepter. A duke or count might be depicted, as was William of Normandy in the Bayeux Tapestry, seated and in civilian clothes but bearing a sword upright, as a scepter would be held. His ceremonial seat, of course, also mimicked royal stature.[21]

So, as dukes' or counts' symbolic work with swords echoed the uses of imperial regalia, it also reflected swords' own increasing resonances. Where previously they had rarely used swords for this purpose, now kings and emperors adapted the sword as a symbolic instrument to their own purposes. Swords began to be used to represent the royal power of command, supplementing and partially eclipsing earlier iconography derived from Roman practice. Early images depict Holy Roman emperors in the tenth century, for example, holding staffs that reflect the Roman practice of bearing a standard (such as an eagle) to signal the commander of a legion. Royal staffs or lances as well as scepters all derived from this earlier Roman imagery and remained in constant use—borne, for example, by the French king in the ritual inauguration of the Basilica of St. Denis. As early as the eleventh century, however, they were often supplemented by swords in paintings and manuscript illustrations. Swords could represent Roman inheritance too, of course, such as in the example of the sword of the legendary legionnaire St. Maurice, whose sword (as well as banner) appeared among royal regalia in later centuries.[22]

The deliberate, almost choreographed uses of swords in certain surviving sources reveal the political work such a symbol could now accomplish; it could embody the power of command, but also acknowledge the relative authority or stature of other lords, something the Roman-derived regalia could not. Later scenes in the Bayeux Tapestry's narrative show deliberate use of swords to signal Duke William's precise relationship to his rival Harold at different points in the story. When Harold greets William the first time, acting as emissary of Edward the Confessor, William's sword honors Harold by being presented point downward. Later, the relationship shifts. William has knighted Harold and now watches as Harold, in effect his vassal, touches a reliquary as he takes the famous oath to honor William's claim to the English throne. Here, William bears his sword like a scepter, with the point raised. In both cases, he is seated, and the sword's disposition distinguishes the degree of William's authority. Several times, the tapestry depicts William surrounded by men bearing swords. Surviving images of the Emperors Otto III and Henry the Lion are more explicit—an honored courtier bears the ruler's sword ceremonially, while the emperor himself holds staff or scepter and other standard regalia.[23] As knighthood became an exclusive rank, swords become a requirement even of kings; the knightly attributes of the ruler simultaneously became an indispensable part of royal identity and image.

Of course, swords were not always chosen to represent royal identity or convey its mystique. The Capetian kings of France never portrayed themselves on funerary monuments or on their seals girded with or bearing a

FIGURE 2.2. Symbols of rule, ca. 1000. This image from an illuminated gospel book depicts the coronation of Holy Roman Emperor Otto III. He holds a staff with an eagle, echoing Roman precedent, as well as an orb. Note, however, the courtier bearing his sword standing to his left. HIP / Art Resource, NY.

sword. This choice, one historian argues, reflected the fact that the English kings, as dukes of Normandy and Aquitaine, had appropriated the sword at their investitures as a symbol, thus their Capetian overlords chose to distinguish themselves from such symbolism. In addition, whether a sword was present or absent in an image or in a ritual also reflected the weight of precedent in a particular medium. For example, effigies on tombs, with or without swords, were rare before the twelfth century, because what mattered was how close a powerful man could be buried to the shrine of a chosen saint, not whether the man's tomb was itself eye-catching or artful in its use of symbols. Over time, the tendency of memorial objects to constitute an artistic program constrained the use of any particular image: once a mode of representing a dynasty was established—say, the Capetians' use of the fleur-de-lis in contradistinction to their Angevin rivals—there would be little reason to change, to start using a sword on a seal or on a tomb in place of other symbols.

In some cases, the absence of a sword may simply reflect lost evidence, such as in the case of some burials. Royal remains that survived into the modern age, long enough to be examined and documented, occasionally included swords buried with the great man, in reprise of pre-Christian weapons burials. The Emperor Frederick II (d. 1250), for example, was entombed at Palermo in all his regalia, including a sword girded over his ceremonial garments. John of England (d. 1216), buried at Worcester Cathedral, was also reportedly entombed with royal crown and mantle as well as with a sword in its scabbard.[24]

The fact the stone effigy on John's grave also depicted him holding a sword probably reflected, at least in some measure, the family program of effigies reflecting the deceased's funeral tableau. John's remains have disappeared, but we know how his father, Henry II (d. 1189), was arrayed for burial and can compare it with the effigy on his tomb. A chronicler reported that Henry was "dressed in rich array," which included gloves, a gold ring, boots made of golden cloth, with crown and scepter, but also spurs and a sword, which both appear, as do the scepter and crown, on his tomb in the Abbey of Fontevrault. The sword lies in its scabbard, not girded on, as the chronicler reports, but placed by his side. Richard Lionheart rests near his father, similarly arrayed in stone.[25]

In John's case at Worcester, interestingly, the sword is depicted as a naked blade, drawn from the scabbard: a unique presentation within the family and virtually unparalleled in all funerary architecture of the period. John is crafted with jeweled eyes, so he would have appeared awake, rather than asleep as were his father and brother. His stone crown, his clothing, and the hilt of his sword all bear carved niches where further semiprecious stones would have been placed. Perhaps we are looking at the funeral array also of this king, yet why is he awake, in an active stance, hand on drawn sword? The fact that an unsheathed sword is being represented in an ecclesiastical space is another discordant piece of information. And the power of the sword is tested, perhaps diminished, by a little carved lion busily gnawing on its point. A bold and complex message may be embedded here: about John's reconciliation with the pope (represented by the two bishops, standing in for the more common angels, holding John's crown); about his authorization by the Church to bear arms in its protection; about the sword itself—which may be Tristan's sword Curtana, whose blade had a portion missing, in legend.[26] All these messages—or others—are accomplished emphatically by a drawn blade.

Swords did, by the twelfth century, become regular props in coronations, on both sides of the Channel. Precisely by what process or by what date is hard to establish, since we lack records about specific coronations. We have liturgies—prescriptive manuals for officiating clergy—written for such occasions and some lists of and references to regalia, and must assemble a notion of what actually occurred from these hints.[27] Lists of regalia are also problematic as sources because, although swords eventually became a

FIGURE 2.3.   The naked blade on King John's tomb. In this side view of his tomb in Worcester Cathedral, we can see the unsheathed blade John holds beside him. His feet rest, typically, on a lion, which, in this case, gnaws the tip of his sword. Erich Lessing / Art Resource, NY.

regular prop, they were not always considered regalia proper, which consisted, first and foremost, of the clerically inspired ceremonial vestments and a crown, and sometimes the instruments related to the anointing of the king. Acclamation by the "people" and unction, anointing with holy oil, were the bedrock of coronations; the unction made the king unique, priestlike, and was especially important before primogeniture (ca. mid-thirteenth century) sealed claimants' right to rule. The scepter appears as coronation regalia, and as part of the monarch's image on coins in the ninth century, both in the case of Charlemagne and his heirs and that of Anglo-Saxon kings. The rod or staff, bearing Roman precedent, appears at about this time.[28]

Like all rituals, coronations were malleable performances; they varied over time, and supposed precedent and claims of interested parties influenced components of the ceremony. For example, it was part of the effort of the Abbey at Westminster to gain unchallenged control over English royal coronations that led to privileging the personal regalia of Edward the Confessor (d. 1066) in the ceremony, supposedly bequeathed to the abbey by him for that purpose.[29] Swords' role in the coronation appears to have evolved slowly too. Early medieval kings likely wore their own personal swords during the ceremony, which were then blessed or presented by the officiating clergy, as a way for them to attach sacred meaning and their own authority to this secular object; but the process was not considered, in the early liturgies, to be part of the coronation per se. The earliest coronation order in England, from the ninth century, does not mention a sword at all, only scepter, staff, and crown.[30]

By the twelfth century, the role of the sword is firm enough that mention of it is sometimes made in lists of regalia. In most surviving liturgies, from France, England, and Germany, the king is arrayed with garments and then with ring, sword, scepter, and orb or rod. Sometimes the liturgy specifies a special prayer to be said at the presenting of the sword or adds another accoutrement, such as a mantle (a Roman official garment). Spurs, that other attribute of knighthood, were first formally included in the ceremony in England in 1189, at Richard's coronation. With the addition of spurs, the coronation could appear to be an amalgam of knightly practice: the king as preeminent knight, the bearer of the sword as symbol of rule, a blade recognized, blessed, and bestowed by clerics.

In fact, dubbing of knights developed in tandem with these coronations in which the sword had become essential, both by about the year 1200. In both cases, the boundaries between secular and religious control and symbolism were not fixed. No one doubted the religious gloss or underpinnings of knighthood, but the ritual handling of the knight's sword was not in clerical hands. Generally, the would-be knight passed his vigil beforehand in sacred space, such as a chapel, even with his sword resting on the altar, but only very rarely would a knight actually be girded with his sword by a cleric. In royal ceremony, however, clerics generally maintained control over the sword; no lay aristocrat could present it or gird it onto the king's body after it was handled and blessed (sometimes multiple times) by the clergy, even though, in some ceremonies, lay participants could dress the king in his spurs and sword belt. The royal sword had become a site of contestation of authority and meaning. (Theologians at the time were clear on the matter: the two swords, spiritual and temporal, were both in the hands of the Church; the Church merely delegated use of the temporal sword to rulers.)[31]

A sword with sacred origins and duties was a formidable thing. Though clerics dominated the coronation ritual, the king's sword was ultimately a material object with knightly connotations, and not wholly in clerical control. After the king was crowned, his sword, as a marker of rule, symbolically overshadowed the symbols of clerical power such as vestments and crosiers. Once a king was solemnly invested with a sword, his sword could later stand in for him and could be ritually displayed on formal occasions. And, bearing the sword at the opening procession of, say, a later coronation or at other solemn moments became a coveted honor for a chosen courtier-companion, not a cleric.[32]

Faced simultaneously with knightly competition and clerical appropriation, it is not surprising that both Richard and his brother John now found "special" swords to attach to themselves. Dependent now partly on knightly imagery, the king was moved to distinguish his own weapon as special, unique, exalted: hence Excalibur, which first appears in 1191, and John's sword Curtana. It is also about this time—the twelfth century—that French coronations begin to use "Charlemagne's sword."[33] These swords were all, so far as we can tell, distinguished by certain attributes, especially the design of the pommel, that marked them as venerable in their day.[34] But the sword remained an ambivalent symbol; always necessary but never sufficient, it was appropriated for royal rule but by being grafted onto another, preexisting set of symbolic objects that were considered more wholly regal. And the swords used in coronations, however emphatic the clergy's role, were not automatically considered regalia; for example, the vestments and staff of Edward the Confessor remained in the guard of Westminster Abbey, but the "sword of state" was not stored with them, not preserved as regalia as such until the end of the Middle Ages.

Later, other specially hallowed items joined the king's sword. In England, John's son Henry III (d. 1272) began to use St. Edward the Confessor's crown,

FIGURE 2.4. "Charlemagne's" sword. Used in French coronations, perhaps as early as the twelfth century, this sword is a composite artifact, as most swords were. Its pommel dates from the tenth or eleventh century, the guard, with its distinctive animal faces, from the twelfth, and the grip and the jeweled top of the scabbard from the thirteenth, with modifications as late as the nineteenth century. Thus, it is "Charlemagne's" sword only by means of imaginative memory. © RMN-Grand Palais / Art Resource, NY.

in addition to the sainted Edward's vestments. Henry encouraged the cult of the Confessor (and rebuilt both Westminster Abbey and the saint's shrine within it). The saint's crown, so far as we know, remained in use until all the regalia were melted down during the revolution in 1649. Like Excalibur, it collected more resonances as it went. As we have seen, Excalibur likely began as a suitably old sword used to dub Geoffrey Plantagenet and to confer the then king's favor; St. Edward's crown, one century after Henry III, began to carry an association, in contemporaries' minds, with an august and even more remote ancestor: Alfred the Great.[35]

In France, a sacred banner, the Oriflamme, became attached to the crown in the twelfth century, even as Charlemagne's sword also appeared. It was a version of the Roman battle standard, a banner or ensign atop a wooden pole. First attested in 1124, the Oriflamme was most likely a creation of Louis VI (d. 1137) and his adviser Abbot Suger. At this point, the French king faced aggression not only from the dukes of Normandy and his other great vassals, but also from the Holy Roman emperor on France's northern and eastern borders. And the emperor had, since the tenth century, had a holy lance—in fact, he claimed, *the* Holy Lance, once wielded by the emperor Constantine. More than one such lance had actually been discovered, including one unearthed in Antioch by a monk on the First Crusade. The French lance was an amalgam of this artifact and a literary allusion. The lance itself was crafted to look like one of the lances known to be circulating in the empire, but it also drew its inspiration from the epic story of Roland, where a flaming ensign helps the army defeat the Muslim enemy (whose own banner falls, presaging their defeat).[36] The Oriflamme guaranteed the victory of the French king, so the story went. In addition to the Oriflamme, the French kings shortly afterward also advertised their sacral associations with a heraldic device rich with Christian symbolism, the fleur-de-lis. Royalty searched for sacred props of outsize power, beyond iconic swords, and the French kings had a symbolic advantage, for a time, over their English rivals—who turned to Arthurian legend for symbolic material.[37]

What of swords in warriors' own hands? It is still too early, before 1300, to find many documentary traces of ordinary knights' swords in household records; we do not know how many swords a lesser or greater aristocrat owned, and have few indications of how he used, valued, or bequeathed them. Swords are occasionally mentioned in some records of arms and they survive, after a fashion, in material remains such as statues, graves, tapestries, and illuminations—but above all they exist for us today in literature. By the time the dubbing ceremony became commonplace, in the decades after

1200, a body of historical and imaginative literature was in place, and growing, with which warriors at all levels could understand themselves and their position in a hierarchy, not one purely of force, in their imagining, but also of moral value. Swords are as obligatory in these histories and romances as they had become in life. But, as in life, they take and give meaning in a crowded field of objects and texts. They are less subjects in these texts, capable of moving men to action as in *Beowulf*, than they are symbols and props. Signs, perhaps, of character, of conflict, of command, but not quasi-human actors.

Historians and scholars of literature distinguish several kinds of oral and written texts produced by and for elite families in this period, including histories, genealogies, and imaginative tales. They subdivide imaginative literature into the genres of epics or chansons de geste (stories of heroes and their great deeds) and courtly or chivalric romances, which are also stories of knights and adventures, but with the additional tensions of court life, romantic love, or religious quest. The term "romance" usually refers to verse or prose "chivalric" stories, but it is also a technical term referring to narratives written in the vernacular, French—the common language of elites in both Britain and France at this point.

The first such tales to appear, in the mid-twelfth century, were not imaginary exploits, but histories, loose translations and elaborations of Latin epics. These included a reworking of the tale of Aeneas, for example, and a vernacular version of Geoffrey of Monmouth's *History of the Kings of Britain*. After about 1160, verse stories more fully fictional (though there were of course fictional elements in the "histories") began to be composed for consumption at court by a Frenchman we know as "Chrétien de Troyes."[38] All these stories and histories celebrated and parsed the conflicting requirements of warrior life. In the twelfth and thirteenth centuries, this meant accommodating the growth of regional princely courts and, soon, royal ones; it meant integrating the growing pull of an invigorated Church and of crusading outlets and the alternative form of celibate masculinity they offered; it meant investigating courtly as well as violent masculinity, and celebrating lordship and its responsibilities as that terrain was increasingly contested.[39]

Family histories commissioned by aristocrats reveal an acute need to recast the past in terms required to make sense of their present, one in which royal power had dramatically increased and encroached on their own. Many of these historical or genealogical texts enabled great families to better assert their claim to privilege by imagining its antecedents in an august lineage. For example, in the early thirteenth century, magnates in northeastern France sponsored the writing of histories that claimed their families' descents from Charlemagne, in direct challenge to the Capetian king's preeminence. Some of these histories took the same ancient texts that rulers used to justify their power and reworked them to create criticism, unflattering comparisons, or counterexamples. They might reuse ancient texts about Roman history in order to make Caesar the exemplar of a just ruler and thus undermine present kings' claims that their aggressive rule followed ancient precedents (or, conversely, to argue that Caesar was an unworthy ruler, the epitome of a tyrant who did not respect his regional underlings).[40] In this way, magnates accomplished the same thing that kings were doing when they integrated swords into coronation rituals and into representations of themselves: appropriating stories and symbols in order to contest the ground of lordship. Just as both warriors and kings had a stake in swords as a symbol of lordship, so did they all in how the past was represented in narrative, composed in writing that survives to us.

In fiction, too, more palatable rulers could be imagined—for example, in retellings of the story of Roland. The best-known version of the poem, which we think of as the *Chanson de Roland* (Song of Roland), dates from about 1100, though versions of it circulated as early as the middle of the eleventh century.[41] In the text version we have, Charlemagne is an aged ruler who takes advice from his barons but remains above the fray: an emperor, not a knight. By the early thirteenth century, the Charlemagne in prose renderings of the tale is no longer a remote, imperial presence but a knight himself, who can hew an enemy in two with his sword; he is also a warrior in God's army of crusaders. Rather like the version of Arthur in many courtly romances, he does not threaten the warriors under him by actually ruling.

The concerns of the knightly characters in romance tales also changed and became more complex over time. Protagonists evolve from prideful epic heroes who, much like Beowulf, face impossible odds (and usually die trying) to more nuanced characters with tangled emotional lives who face the thorny challenges of being a *courtly* warrior. Beginning in the twelfth century, romances advocate and explore both ferocity and decorum, prowess and elegance, and celebrate both loyalty to companions and fellow aristocrats and love of a powerful lady. Many later prose romances of the thirteenth century, meanwhile, tend to emphasize certain themes from twelfth-century tales at the expense of others. The tension between ferocity and decorum continues, but is sometimes resolved by an emphasis on the goal of religious quest. An ideal knight, versions of the Grail stories relate, is fierce and single-minded but also pure of heart. In these later texts, it is hard to find the balance of Chrétien de Troyes's earlier stories, such as his tale of Yvain, likely from the 1170s. The knight Yvain can be both rash and moderate, torn by doubt but nonetheless a worthy champion of the downtrodden; he can love a high-born woman and work to win her approval, even though he abandons her for a long personal quest. In the end, he is successful in both quest and love—though, in the latter case, largely on the lady's terms.

In many later stories, it is the snares, rather than the opportunities, of court life, of love, and even of adventure that are emphasized. Passion should be reserved for religious quest, some tales argue. The hero Roland, for example, in some thirteenth-century versions, has lost the tragic flaw of pride that doomed him in the original (as we consider it) but he is not troubled by the bonds of family or fellows-in-arms. He is an exemplary warrior in the mold of monastic and crusading orders now on the ground in the early thirteenth century: a self-abnegating militant Christian knight.[42] In such tales, ideal knights seem to be impossible heroes, the tales more extravagant and pessimistic.

In histories as well as in imaginative literature, swords are omnipresent, and fulfill a dazzling variety of symbolic purposes and narrative roles, though rarely as the quasi-human actors the *Beowulf* poet imagined they had been. In Geoffrey of Monmouth's *History of Britain*, Arthur figures as one of the historic rulers of the island and his sword, Excalibur, represents just rule, not simply force, however charmed the sword may be. Thus, it helps Geoffrey account for the very mixed history of rule in the island—Britons, Romans, Anglo-Saxons, now Normans—without the tale becoming one of chaos or woe, and without slighting any ancestor of the present peoples in the era of his writing.[43]

As Geoffrey's history was translated and adapted by other writers in subsequent decades, Excalibur changed attributes and function according to the circumstances of each retelling. One of the ways English and Anglo-Norman authors reconciled the complex ethnicity of Arthur and his subject peoples was to make him emphatically Christian and an instrument of divine will and chastisement. In some versions, he is the means by which Saxons become Christian. The sword in many of these cases is a tool, a vessel for divine force and nothing more. The real potency is God's will; Arthur and his weapon merely channel and direct it. In a history by the Norman cleric Wace (ca. 1155), Caliburn (Excalibur) is an instrument not of divine purpose, but one that justifies de facto power when it is successful. By Wace's time, early in Henry II's reign, the Anglo-Norman rulers needed to legitimize rule of their far-flung territories, including England, Normandy, and the Angevin lands in central France. The only possible logic for this accretion of lands, for Wace, was feudal tenure. The great sword represents the right of a family to rule when they can make a legitimate and successful claim to land. It is an instrument of force, but just force in the interests of legitimate heirs. Caliburn, in fact, is almost personified in the battle sequences, which contributes to the sense of another family taking over, another presence.[44] The sword, here, is above all an emblem of lordship.

A great variety of additional symbolic and practical uses of swords appear in imaginative literature, particularly in works written after dubbing became a formalized entry into knighthood. Not surprisingly, dubbing ceremonies are common scenes in these stories. But it is the detail, the variations in these stories, that are interesting. In an anonymous version of the Lancelot story, the description of the ritual of dubbing is described in detail only to lead to a surprise ending. After the night vigil, the young men enter the church in full armor, which symbolizes, by their right to be armed there, their role as defenders of the Church. Yet they are not truly knights until they leave and are girded with their swords by the king. This moment captures tensions between secular and sacred authority, and the aristocrat's collaboration with both powers-that-be in order to claim knighthood. But, in this version, the young Lancelot hares off on an adventure before receiving his sword. He wants to accept his sword from the queen, Guinevere. The transgression of their love relationship is dramatically highlighted by this violation of ritual. The sword's power to confer knighthood and the king's presumed contribution to effect the ritual is what makes this violation, this transgressive stretching of the possible, telling and dramatic.[45]

It was the centrality of the sword to the identity of knighthood, the very security of that identification, that allowed the wide variation in its thematic treatment and its symbolic properties in literature. Individual swords could signal one particular character, be a clue to a hidden identity, or could symbolize something else entirely, such as a perilous journey or an ordeal. The physical properties of the object are put to use in some of these cases. For example, a sword in another tale about Lancelot and Guinevere serves, literally, as a bridge Lancelot must cross to reach the castle where the queen is held captive. The edges of the sword wound him as he crawls along, so the sword is not his helpmeet, but his challenger; it represents a test. (The blood from his wounds later betrays his presence in the queen's chamber to the knights pursuing him.) The two blade edges of a sword are also imagined, in other texts, conveniently to symbolize force and justice, and the point of the sword, obedience. A sword can represent a kingdom because its edge symbolizes boundary, and the capacity to divide one entity from another, even as they are part of the whole of a single blade, a particularly convenient symbol for Britain, especially under the Plantagenets.[46] Another kind of symbolic possibility appears in one text from the Grail cycle, where a sword in a floating stone (echoing stories about Excalibur itself) washes up at Arthur's court. The characters in the tale recognize the object to be a symbol of the worthy Galahad, who will undertake the quest.[47] In this case, a sword symbolizes identity, and echoes the ability to extract a sword from a stone as the recognition of special power—kingly or quasi-saintly.

In addition to its physical properties, it is the taken-for-granted presence of the sword that allows for this riot of symbolic uses, yet the sword's symbolic heft is muted, in some respects, by this constant, almost mandated presence. The battle sword is rarely a marker of special status, such as was the case of Byrhtnoth's abandoned weapon in the *Battle of Maldon*, an imagined sight that asks us to pause and invites us to consider loss by its means. In addition, the lifeworld of increased consumption of all kinds is also reflected in these romances, in tandem with complex narratives of longing, questing, and suffering, and swords are not the only knightly accoutrements to receive concentrated attention, or that assist in great feats, in either history or fiction. Now essential in life, a knight's armor is vividly, even lovingly, described in many texts.[48] Wace, for example, is careful to provide Arthur with an array of armor, and mentions his shield by name as well as his sword.

There are many other objects with magical properties in twelfth- and thirteenth-century tales. In these verse and prose romances, the main character usually has emotional depth; he has choices and he must change over time, which means his actions are not definitively scripted by feud or fate. The cause and effect sequences in the stories are sometimes fantastical yet permit a complex working-through of aristocratic experience. Feuds foretold and endlessly reenacted are replaced by random, inexplicable motors for action, all in the service of driving a hero's adventures or love or religious quest. All kinds of marvelous things can impel the hero on his journey, such as the magic fountain that Chrétien's Yvain journeys to attack, for no other reason than the boasts and challenges he has heard at Arthur's court. Yvain is proud and impulsive and this mysterious fountain, we understand, is an opportunity to prove himself—for that purpose, the more unlikely the object, the better.

The consequences of Yvain's rash act, and his continued quest for prowess, provide the narrative arc of the tale, but they also lead him to a personal epiphany, after which he grows in loyalty and honor as well as in prowess. He kills the splendid, fierce knight who naturally appears to defend his fountain, then is so moved by the grief of the widow (which Yvain can witness close at hand because he is magically invisible) that he falls in love with her. The lady is no cipher; she eventually comes to return his love and accept him as the defender of her territories, but she sets conditions when Yvain proposes to set out on new adventures, as knights "must" do: he shall return to her within one year. But he loses track of time as he pursues quests and does not meet her deadline. Cast out by her in a dramatic scene at the court, Yvain wastes away in his grief in a forest. Here begins his transformation into a worthier man and knight with the help of a remarkable lion, who behaves like a truer and more loyal knight than Yvain has yet been himself. Yvain is also healed, initially, by means of a wondrous ointment supplied by a gentlewoman who happens to encounter him in the forest in an almost bestial state.

Magical objects, in other words, become more not less important as motors of action in worlds such as Yvain and his real-life counterparts inhabited: a world with an increasing surfeit of prestige goods, many of which are newly crafted and carry no relationships or loyalties with them. Though they are plot devices, they remain largely external to the central narrative point about the quandaries of the human subjects and how they navigate the challenges of warrior life. As objects multiply, as character-centered narratives grow in response to the more complex settings where knights live, the power of the objects really to *participate* in human life contracts. Hence, the many symbolic valences of the sword.

We should not characterize warriors' swords as diminished because of all this symbolic versatility. First of all, we should be on guard against exaggerating the process of change. The textual world in which warriors were immersed cannot be clearly demarcated as old versus new, heroic tales with larger-than-life swords versus newer tales where swords are symbolic material only. (Nor should we think "only" symbolic work insignificant.) Though we can sketch a historical progression of this literature from epics to courtly romance, that trajectory is an approximation after the fact of what was a much messier world of literary production and consumption. Compared as genres, the contrast seems clear: the chansons de geste focus typically on war and violence, on the workings of a closed system of personal-political relationships sustained through gifts, where things maintain relationships with and between people and have some power to impel action; the world of romances, on the other hand, contains many objects that are just that— artful and valuable objects, perhaps, but which operate as symbols of warrior skill or status or as magical agents, outside influences in the ordinary human world of cause and effect.

In elite life, though, epics and romances were present together, produced not only in sequence but overlapping significantly in time. Men and women alive in the thirteenth century could read or listen to a wide sample of this literature: early epics, early verse romance, later prose versions as well as new stories. In fact, all the copies we have now of twelfth-century verse romances are thirteenth- and early fourteenth-century copies. Warrior families were discriminating consumers: in surviving manuscripts, tales are grouped together purposefully, not in abstract schemes, such as by author, but thematically, such as a grouping of tales of Arthur's knights, or various versions of a single tale, or a tale by an early author like Chrétien paired with a continuation of the tale by a later author.[49]

Whether the tales were verse or prose, early or late, delivered orally or read by a book owner or both, all of them circulated orally as well as in written form, and were amended, continued, recombined, and retold in many media over the succeeding centuries. They constituted what historian Brian Stock calls a textual community.[50] The telling, retelling, and illustration of tales reflect the fact that there was "two-way traffic" between this literature and everyday life. We know that knights were familiar with and actively engaged with this literature, because, in addition to sponsoring editions of it, they referred to it in other contexts.[51] We also know that these tales were not only read and heard, but also seen, in the very spaces where the tales were performed and read. Their themes were represented in tapestries and wall paintings and on chests, stone capitals, chess pieces, and even on mirrors and hair combs.

The various tales were a means for warrior elites to explore the tensions inherent in their lives in this period: the tension around the desirability of passion, one in which both warriors and clerics had a direct interest; the tensions between belligerent warrior behavior—prowess, honor, derring-do—and courtly standards such as elegance, appropriate speech, and self-control. Such conflicting standards were not wholly new; the muscular hero Beowulf also speaks well in the mead hall, indeed tells stories with great skill. But the presence of women and their roles of inspiring honorable behavior or of instantiating lordship through their own powers of command is new in twelfth-century tales, as is the possibility of imagining masculinity that is almost entirely courtly or celibate.[52] In fact, given the rising importance of clerics in the life of the aristocracy, masculinity across a wide spectrum, as well as femininity, was actively negotiated in these tales.

These tales were not mere venting mechanisms, then, but textual worlds that represented and reinforced the *cultural* identity of this aristocracy. The tales both constituted and reflected that grab bag of ideals and practices we know as chivalry, together with warriors' conduct in the courts, tournaments, churches, and battles. Chivalric literature was part of a cultural shift that required justification of violence toward others at the same time as it delimited violence among themselves and, above all, reinforced their privileged identity by maintaining the allure of martial behavior. The elaboration of conflicting, even impossible standards contributed to a felt sense of exclusivity; chief among them were the simultaneous requirements of prowess, thus violence, and courtliness.[53] Tensions were not resolved in this literature, but rather investigated, even indulged. The most skillful among these texts are subtle and multilayered, even playful in the way they moved their audiences with the full array of possible elite predicaments.[54]

Hence the value of swords in these tales. A sword could represent almost any aspect of knightly experience within them because almost anything might be required: a symbol of rule or resistance, of prowess or purity, of an oath honored or broken, an instrument of God or a magical cause of violence or harmony—or a stand-in, a symbol for the knight and all his various attributes, the sword as emblem of challenge, courage, or for the very fact of lordly stature. As elites enjoyed the multivalent texts that we, with different emotional expectations and political circumstances, can find confusing, so too they would have delighted in the plays of meaning on this signature possession, since the fact of the play was itself an enactment of privilege. Certainly, they were accustomed to the intellectual habit of thinking in binary terms, and embraced all the paradoxes that engendered: a sword could be both an instrument of war and of peace; an extension of a powerful body and simultaneously, like a relic, a celestial instrument.[55]

Imagining the sword as a multifaceted sign in warrior life, as these texts do, in its many contradictory possibilities, in fact not only composed a new range of symbolic powers invested in swords, but reflected the wider importance of representation, of symbols themselves, in the changing material circumstances of the era. In this era of economic growth and political consolidation, representing one's identity and authority at a distance was increasingly necessary. The practice of affixing a wax seal to a document, to guarantee the authenticity of the contents in the absence of the principals, was perhaps the most important innovation of this kind, around 1000 CE. It enabled the uncontested transfer of property that both generated a permanent record more precise than an object (a knife, say) could do, as it was exchanged as a token of conveyance; the transfer also could be accomplished without the presence of the individuals involved. Clerics executed and controlled most of these documents until later in the Middle Ages, but their existence meant that aristocratic benefactors got used to having a constructed "double"— their seals, with images of themselves or their property—representing themselves in the world.[56]

Like seals, the coats of arms that began to develop at this time became another means of representing a warrior at a distance from his person, thus making him present in his absence. Royalty were particularly effective at deploying coats of arms in this way, to symbolically be present over a wide territory (in addition to their attention to the precise images on arms themselves).[57] Seals and coats of arms enabled the felt presence of the king's or a lord's identity and authority at a distance. So did swords, though they did so in slightly different, complementary ways. A sword was an adjunct to the physical person, to the body. It could represent a lord in his absence because it was a bodily appendage that both represented his power to kill and ensured the status to do so; an individual sword also had recognized attachment to his person or his family. Otherwise why would signature gifts work, or swords be taken as trophies? In their attachment to the body, the sword gained its power to represent that body though, unlike seals and coats of arms, they were not designed to work at a remove from the warrior—though they might do so in ritual.

Within stories, however, they freely circulated in the awareness and imagination. In the world of the chivalric imaginary, a sword could symbolize almost any aspect of a warrior's person or his conduct or his circumstances or his authority over land or people, or his relationship with God. Dubbing ceremonies, ducal investitures, and royal coronations made swords particularly potent stand-ins for a warrior or lord, even as coats of arms and other means proliferated. Their very materiality guaranteed they embodied a spiritual power: swords were cruciform by design. A sword fixed into the ground or in a stone—a common trope in many tales—mimicked the cross on an altar, or even the cross on Calvary. One thirteenth-century writer argued that the cruciform design of the sword symbolized the authority of the knight to wield it on behalf of the Church, echoing the Church's justification for its own notion of the "two swords" it controlled.[58]

Swords were present by being on every warrior body and ubiquitous in the imaginary and symbolic world. They could never be out of mind. It also matters that the imaginary world, like swords, seals, and coats of arms, had a physical existence. The earlier tales that do not now exist in original manuscripts refer to stories heard and repeated, or even read and then passed on orally before being written down again. In one of Chrétien de Troyes's tales, for example, the prologue states that he heard the story from his patron, Marie de Champagne. Many scholars now argue that these references to oral origins (and the imagined narrators, in the tales, who rely on them) are artful inventions of the authors rather than direct renderings of oral narrative.[59] These scholars point, too, to growing literacy in elite families, evident by the early thirteenth century.[60] Of course, even later stories, created as reading became more common and manuscripts subdivided and illustrated to be more reader-friendly, could be performed for audiences; thus, both reading and oral/aural reception of these tales coexisted until the end of the Middle Ages. Nevertheless, the existence of this increasingly literal *body* of literature also shaped the roles swords played within it. Together with the histories that aristocrats also sponsored and consumed, and other literature it responded to, chivalric literature represented a dependence on, even deferral to, the authority of texts that were, increasingly, texts with a physical existence, whatever the oral origins of the material. The text itself had become a thing, an object, alongside the other goods and accoutrements an elite family now enjoyed. Texts were still often consumed orally, but now were, in one historian's words, "everywhere interposed between experience and reality." This fact, this awareness of texts available to be consulted, underwrote the creation of family histories that some aristocrats sponsored, and helped make character rather than role a driving force in legends and stories. A character such as Yvain can think, reflect, and make choices, rather than follow either fate or his immutable "nature."[61] It follows that swords, as signs, could be nimble and multifaceted yet still be iconic symbols by which a warrior is identified. Different material entities, they nonetheless were like other ubiquitous signs, like coats of arms, in that their presence and their attributes could be decoded.

And yet it was certainly possible, amid this rich nexus of old and new, orally derived and written stories, where swords played many symbolic roles, for an "old-fashioned" sword to make an appearance. One example might be the case of the John de Warenne, Earl of Surrey, who famously confronted an agent of Edward I (d. 1307) carrying out the king's quo warranto investigations in the 1280s. When it was demanded "by what warrant" he claimed his rights and jurisdictions, the earl supposedly brandished an old, rusted sword that an ancestor had wielded at the Norman Conquest and declared "this is my warrant." This incident may be apocryphal, but either the earl himself or one of his contemporaries thought in these terms or assumed his audience could.[62] Here, the sword does not merely represent but *embodies* the authority of lordship. In this scene, we are invited to think that this actual sword, grasped in the earl's hand, won these rights for his forebears and for him, thus reflecting the residue of an oral culture where the past and the present blend, and an invocation of a past when belongings instantiated affiliation, honor, or privilege.[63]

The authenticity of the claim lies partly in the ancientness of the sword. Witnesses, or those hearing of this encounter, are invited to think, "Could this be the very sword that won these rights? Is this an heirloom from days gone by, when swords were more potent than now?" Warenne's pugnacious gesture worked, at least on the contemporary imagination, because of the pull of this nostalgic vision. The old stories, where weapons live on to move men to action, and where they carry the memories and power of their past deeds, are themselves still alive despite the more complex themes of chivalric tales and the flexible symbolic roles swords have in them, representing men and their various powers but not standing in for them as beings too.

We should note, also, that the appearance of such a sword as Warenne's meant that keeping unused, aged weapons among one's gear was something that happened, and not just in the earl's household. If many households had such a venerable sword to hand, or hoped to have such a relic, it would have contributed to the plausibility of Warenne's performance for his contemporaries. Like saintly relics, a potent object like this had to be reused, restaged, or somehow made visible, its meanings invoked anew.

What, then, did a sword like Excalibur signify, in the circumstances? Swords are still named individuals, at times, in the twelfth and thirteenth centuries, but rarely do they, by themselves, arouse desires in those who wield them. The emotional economy depends on swords and other accoutrements largely as symbols, not as actors. They are now part of a gift economy different from that of the *Beowulf* poet's imagined world, where rulers were "ring-givers," and much wealth was movable booty. This later world is fairly awash in *stuff* by comparison, but control of land and its resources is what matters most. Much of this stuff forms a language justifying power over land and people—attributes at once of identity and lordship. Indeed, the importance of the dubbing ceremony, the *clothing* of a man with his sword, should not be underestimated. It meant that the sword was now an identity tag, its many legendary potentials concentrated and domesticated in the interests of creating an exclusive status.

Excalibur came and went in the twelfth century, before the dubbing ritual was ubiquitous, but with Arthurian legend already circulating in numerous versions. It was a gift that encapsulated many tensions: originally imagined in order to make a dynastic claim, as swords became attributes of royal identity too; a signature sword, authenticated by texts, with great value, nonetheless exchanged for mere military hardware; a material symbol memorializing a political alliance, that is, Richard's success in coming to terms with Tancred, which his rival Philip Augustus would envy.[64] The presentation of Excalibur might also be understood as an instance of "keeping while giving," where much of the prestige or power of the gifted object remains with the giver. Among the many positional goods an aristocrat enjoyed were some that one scholar terms inalienable possessions, belongings that could not be given away to others willy-nilly, even in a society where competitive gift and countergift was a norm, because they helped constitute the identity of the person who controlled them.[65] Successfully creating such an outsize object would also mark the owner as especially powerful, which is another vantage point on the Earl de Warenne's sword-rattling moment.[66] The need to make such magnetic objects had grown in the century separating the earl from Richard, and the possibilities for doing so fewer. Excalibur had been the product of decades of careful "imaginative memory," necessary to create so potent a symbolic object.

The power of such an object could be increased when it was given away. Richard gave Tancred the sword of Arthur, which was connected inextricably to his own lineage. That connection to his lineage would only be advertised by the gift; no one would imagine that Tancred could by himself claim the connection. In fact, it would only "work" in Tancred's hands if he had received it, ostentatiously, from Richard's. We should keep in mind, too, that the gift took place under Phillip Augustus's nose. Richard was bolstering his stature in that crucial encounter, before the rival rulers both went off on crusade.

Richard also bolstered Excalibur itself by using it in the exchange. Treating an object differently than it was intended to be used (if the use is successful, of course) adds to its aura, and the aura of the owner. When a fictional version of William of Orange, a companion of Charlemagne celebrated in a twelfth-century text, went to pay for food and drink during a visit to one of the monasteries he patronized, he did not merely dispense the required funds, in fact, he was not merely generous; he *threw* money out by the handful. This was not simple liberality, which was well known, but treating the money as a different kind of object.[67] When Richard presented Excalibur in return for ships, he was daring to use something as money that is not money. The daring itself, giving the greater gift, marked Richard as the superior in the relationship.

Excalibur's potency was constructed over decades, but it was also ephemeral; its greatest power was embedded in, and spent in, this single moment of competitive gift-giving. Once it passed out of Richard's hands, it disappeared, at least so far as extant records can tell us. Curtana, on the other hand, had a longer life. The sword was simply called "Tristan's" in a list of items of royal regalia in 1207, during John's reign. It was identified with Tristan because its point was broken, as, according to the story, the hero's sword had been broken in his fight with a dragon. After John's death, a sword labeled "Curtana" appears in a list of items used at the coronation of his son's (Henry III's) queen. There is a catch, however: Tristan's sword in John's effects had been among the vast royal treasure lost with the king's baggage train in a river crossing shortly before his death. Yet Curtana appears not only in the following reign but, again, a century after that, in a list of royal regalia from the reign of Edward III (d. 1377) and, again, in the following century, enjoying a prominent role in Richard III's coronation in 1483.[68]

These glimpses of Curtana's continuing life emerge from inventories that document the work of the succession of royal treasurers, including receipts verifying the movement of the coronation regalia back and forth from the treasury. We can glean, in those inventories, that coronation clothing and other props were sometimes newly made and sometimes reused, with great antiquity claimed at times. Items worn by the king on the day, such as spurs, were sometimes given away to honored companions afterward. Sometimes the wrong items, such as some humble swords covered only with leather, were sent by the treasury for use and had to be sent back. Curtana could have been "rediscovered" for John's heirs and made part of this malleable set of regalia. Documentary traces of its existence (the same ones we now use and more that have not survived to us) would have allowed it to be "rediscovered" if the previous namesake had been lost and if its presence were felt necessary. For Richard III, in 1483, we have a record of payment and so can attest that his Curtana was made for the occasion. It was *a* Curtana, but could not claim to be *the* Curtana.

Perhaps Richard the Lionheart's Excalibur had a long life that has left no trace. But its potency would have diminished in subsequent generations, once the connection to him had been severed, or if the blade's aura had not been renewed in some way via ritual, thus further symbolic enhancement. The memories attached to special objects faded after two or three generations, the cycle of living memory, when a man could say "I remember my grandfather telling me of the day when he saw . . ."[69]

The power of the legend behind this Excalibur was also ironically dispersed and muted by the increasing elaboration and circulation of the myth, particularly in written form. The existence of the texts themselves, of increased literacy and elite engagement with a proliferating world of imaginative literature helped transform swords from truly potent actors who could move men to action into weighty, complex symbols—capable of carrying multiple, even contradictory meanings because they were no longer actually subjects, actors in their own right. Swords were symbolically flexible artifacts in an expanding world of objects, objects that increasingly mediated face-to-face encounters and subtly differentiated status. They were capable of individuation, of standing out from like objects, and of marking and conveying a charismatic identity, but they were not immune to the same fading from use and memory that affected all symbolic objects.

In the case of Curtana, there were additional processes at work. Curtana faded into a stage prop for the king as a result of the same pressure that led swords to become a compulsory piece of aristocratic costume; once it became required, its unique power was lost. That loss was accelerated and sealed by the very documents that now enable us to chart Curtana's several lives. The list that names Curtana becomes one of the ways of beholding it; it is a form of ownership and of consumption. In the fourteenth and fifteenth centuries, as Curtana's life continued, royal and other elite paraphernalia would become even more elaborate but would also be displayed and consumed increasingly by means of writing—in fact, by lists.

✎ CHAPTER 3

Swords, Clothing, and Armor in the Late Middle Ages

In January of 1458, his *Chambre des comptes*, the officials who managed his property and revenue, wrote to René, Duke of Anjou, Count of Provence, titular king of Naples and Jerusalem, to report that his tapestry keeper, Nicolas, had found armoires in which to store the king's extraordinary (and, today, famous) six-piece apocalypse tapestry set, which had been commissioned by his grandfather. The hangings have been duly delivered to Nicolas, René's officers record. Later that year, we learn, King René tried to track down other opulent hangings that had been ordered by his father more than forty years before: white satin bed hangings with designs of falcons and other birds in flight, together with a coverlet for the bed in white wool. The record from his father's lifetime verifies that a payment in full of 4,000 *livres tournois* had been made to a go-between, an Italian financier, and notes where so large a sum had been found at the time. This Italian also had been given another 1,600 *livres* for a set of red silk hangings, also by the orders of René's father.

The long letter to René from his officers makes it clear that the king wants to know what has become of the bird hangings. An agent in Paris is at work on the problem. "Sire," the letter reports, "we have asked [the agent] Monsieur de Précigny and have shown him [the written record] and he says the bird hangings were indeed finished and were given to the late queen your mother and then to the Count du Maine [René's younger brother]. And," the letter continues, "as for the red silk hangings, Monsieur de Précigny cannot remember them ever being delivered . . . so the heirs of [the Italian] owe back the money paid for them." Four years later, in 1462, another workman is paid for repairing four large pieces of tapestry and ten tapestry cushions. The tapestries had been in the actual room where the *Chambre des comptes* met, in Angers, but René "had ordered them taken out of the said chamber to put on his boats to travel to Saumur [another of his fortresses, near Angers on the Loire river] and elsewhere on different days . . . and as a result of which the tapestries were damaged and ripped in several places." The next year, his men sent René four large pieces of tapestry bearing his coat of arms, together with a few other chosen items, all dispatched on horseback from Angers to the duchy of Bar, another of his fiefs, in the Holy Roman Empire on France's eastern border, where René was lodged at the moment.[1]

"Good King René" of Anjou (1409–80) was hardly an average warrior, or even an average aristocrat, of the late Middle Ages; he enjoyed extraordinary wealth and successfully claimed royal status, even if he never actually reigned in either of his kingdoms. He had the resources to defend and administer his scattered domains and to commission, manage, and trace movable property over the years, like many of his royal and ducal peers.[2] We can note, for example, the forensic accounting revealed in the inquiry about the missing hangings: René's officers are even able to document where the monies for the lost set had come from forty years before. Only the most elite households had such resources.

However, René was typical of the wider cohort of elite warriors in the ways he cared about and attended carefully to the representations of his identity and status located in objects. Indeed, though René owned vastly more accoutrements than most, he was typical in the fact of his personal investment of time and attention in them. The officers trying to trace the missing tapestries in 1458 report directly to him and the phrasing of their report suggests that René has inquired specifically about these items. Most telling is René's attention to the details of display when he chooses which tapestries should accompany him on the river journeys four years later and which set needs to travel beyond the borders of the kingdom in 1463.

This chapter treats warrior families and their material surroundings in the late Middle Ages, the late thirteenth through the fifteenth centuries, set in the contexts of the politics and warfare of the age as well as in that of the changing conditions of material life and the documentation that recorded it. In recent years, historians have revised their view of these later medieval centuries from one that characterized the period as distinguished almost exclusively by chaos and decline, an interruption in the development of culture and institutions, to a more balanced view that emphasizes continuity with what came before and what followed.[3] Not surprisingly, some investigations of material culture now treat the centuries after ca. 1100 seamlessly, emphasizing, for example, further elaboration and new uses of accoutrements that had long been in place, such as wider deployment of coats of arms to represent the person of the warrior, particularly in his absence.

Continuities in material culture across these centuries can be masked by the fact that record keeping increased over time also, which can exaggerate, for us, the magnitude of change: put simply, more stuff becomes visible to us. It is also true, however, that although these centuries were no more "chaotic" than the turmoil of, say, the sixteenth century, there were nonetheless new opportunities and new challenges associated with political life. We cannot ignore the unique circumstances of the Hundred Years' War for the warrior elites of France and England. Neither the stakes for self-representation and the maintenance of honor nor the possible rewards of political alliance and military participation had ever been higher. A sword, a sword belt, spurs, even banners or a coat of arms were no longer enough, either to perform a warrior's privileged identity or to mark his political affiliation. In addition, despite certain continuities, the material world elites inhabited did change, some would argue dramatically, after 1300. Technological innovations enhanced the symbolic possibilities of clothing and, to a lesser degree, of armor. Technological change and endemic warfare together also permitted more swords than ever before to be manufactured, deployed in battle, and circulated among fighters.

What symbolic resonance could one warrior's distinctive sword have in this crowded and newly inflected material world? Here, I will first consider changes in clothing and its ripple effects in the creation and use of other belongings and then treat the changes in metallurgy that permitted new varieties of armor as well as the production of swords in much greater number. The significance of swords must be weighed against the importance of and attention to these other goods that warrior bodies also carried and displayed. Often overlooked, I argue, is the importance of tournament life for the way warriors invested in, and how they valued, armor. Finally, I will return to the phenomenon of written records, which make all these accoutrements visible to us, to argue that they barely capture the continued importance of a warrior's signature swords. Amid more belongings, and more swords, elites demonstrated their capacity to make a commonplace accoutrement, as swords increasingly were, into a signature belonging emblematic of their special status, by means of special decoration, deliberate collecting, or calculated display.

The decades around 1300 constituted a watershed in some features of the material environment surrounding warrior families. New kinds of goods appeared, made possible by continued commercial expansion and by technological innovations. Perhaps the most dramatic change in a warrior's belongings occurred in his clothing, which in turn became a backdrop for other goods to take on new aesthetic and symbolic roles. In the calculated gift economy among elites, in the staging of identity and in its transference through time, clothing had a leading role.

High-quality fabric had of course long been a staple of distinctiveness and display. Representations of kings with their emblems of rule and clothed effigies on tombs, before about 1300, show off status by means of detail, such as jeweled and embroidered borders on the robe, but particularly by the generous, weighty draping of the fabric alone. These luxury textiles were the most important commodity in European trade in the twelfth and thirteenth centuries, and demand for them sparked innovation over time. By the fourteenth century, silk manufacture had begun in Italy and furs used to embellish garments were traded over long distances. Woolen cloth manufactured in northern Europe improved with new weaving techniques. These more densely woven woolens in turn allowed new tailoring methods. For the first time, a close-fitting garment could be fashioned: for men, the iconic combination of doublet and hose appeared.[4]

More important than any one fashion was the possibility of fashion itself. Before the early fourteenth century garments for men and women alike were essentially big rectangles of fabric passed over the head, cinched with a belt or tightened with laces, with squared-off sleeves all of a piece with the robe. Now, close-fitted garments were possible for the first time, and it was also possible to execute decorative details such as scalloped or pointed edges; true sleeves attached to tailored armholes could now be deliberately fashioned in a variety of shapes. In short, *style* was now possible, and with style came mutability.

Men's clothing began to emphasize the torso and shoulders, while women's gowns developed weighty trains and low, off-the-shoulder necklines.[5] For men, the doublet had a brief life as a solitary garment in the first third of the fourteenth century, covered, sometimes, by an equally close-fitting and similarly constructed jacket. By the third quarter of the fourteenth century, however, the doublet was usually covered by a houppelande, a heavy overshirt of sorts that had a fitted bodice but, often, exaggerated shoulders and sleeves and, below a belt, a pleated or gathered skirt.[6] The effect of such an array was to take up space, but not with the mere amplitude of floor-length drapery, even though some houppelandes were full-length. This created torso was a larger, broadened silhouette, with more defined edges. Copious, flowing costumes now were reserved, in the images of the time, for saints and deities. The movement of fabric, showcasing its high quality, was retained in the new men's garments in the pleats of the houppelande, in sleeves elongated, sometimes exaggeratedly, at the elbow, and by means of playful tricks with layering, such as slashing the overgarment to reveal contrasting doublet or chemise beneath. Illuminated manuscripts from the

FIGURE 3.1.   New fashion for men. This padded doublet, made of imported silk, is an outstanding example of the kind of close-fitting garment that new fabrics and tailoring methods could produce in the fourteenth century. Note the set-in sleeves and the buttons rising up the lower arms; buttons like these could be left open for draping shirt sleeves to peek out. The garment probably survived intact because its owner, Charles of Blois, Duke of Brittany (d. 1364), was venerated as a holy man, and his belongings treated like relics. © Lyon, Musée des Tissus—Pierre Verrier.

heyday of such works in late fourteenth century capture the striking possibilities in dress—in the words of one scholar, images that were "veritable
odes to novel ways of dressing."[7]

Of course, not every knight or nobleman could vie to be as fashionable as
elites at court. But even without the pressure of *fashionableness* warrior men
now performed their gender more explicitly than before if only because,
by donning short garments, they differentiated themselves not only from
women, but also from clerical masculinity. In addition, for a decade or two
in the first half of the century, male fashion was briefly militarized. The doublet was essentially a redesigned gambeson, the padded tunic usually worn
under chain mail. Doublets could be so close-fitting as to be constrictive of
movement, but many were fitted out with padding in the chest nonetheless
to mimic the increasing armature warriors now sought.

The new styles also provided novel aesthetic opportunities for other prestige goods to make their mark. For example, hats with plumage and hoods
with long trailing peaks could create the illusion of movement at the same
time that they artfully balanced the bulky torso beneath them. Daggers also
became a fashion accessory. Everyone, men and women of virtually every
social level, wore a knife routinely for practical reasons such as cutting food
at table. Some of these knives were quite large and could easily function as
a weapon. Indeed, the term "dagger" probably meant a knife thought of as
primarily a weapon. According to a contemporary, when Henry IV of England (d. 1413) confronted the Earl of Northumberland and accused him of
treason, the king "drue to hym his dagger," which must thus have been on
his person.[8]

If knives and daggers were common, wearing a dagger as part of an artful
ensemble was new, in the fourteenth century; the squared male torso could
also be visually balanced by suspending a dagger from the belt. Now, stylized
hilts increasingly distinguished these weapons; in records of belongings we
note rondel daggers, named for the metal disc that formed part of the hilt,
and ballock daggers, with ball-shaped extensions on the hilt that mimicked
male genitalia. Daggers begin to appear, together with swords, on many effigies and memorial brasses of fourteenth- and fifteenth-century knights.[9]

Inventories that document the transfer of goods in and out of a guardian's control, or in and out of a treasury, capture the elegance and decorative
heft of some of these weapons in the most elite hands. In 1408, for example, an inventory written shortly after the death of the French prince Louis
d'Orléans and his wife Valentina Visconti documents, for their heirs, the
return of goods that she had taken back to Italy with her shortly before her
own death. More than forty of the items had belonged to Louis, including

many jewels, chains, and collars, and bejeweled and enameled tableaux, as well as one "small dagger," decorated with pearls. Another inventory of Louis's possessions mentions "other jewels," including cups, fancy buckles, collars, and a "little dagger of gold" also garnished with pearls and a balas ruby.[10] Such jewel-like weapons were not necessarily worn but could constitute gifts from greater to lesser aristocrats. An account from Charles VII of France from 1458, for example, lists two elaborately decorated daggers—one with an embossed gold pommel—and a third dagger, also with a gold pommel, specifically made for the king to carry for the feast of the Epiphany. One folio later, the cost of four identical daggers with gilded pommels is recorded: a cache of prestige goods is thus created.[11]

Gifts from one aristocrat to another included a wide variety of other jewels and plate, and the wealthiest men and women by now had literal hoards of such goods—a kind of savings account that could be tapped to ensure favor and reward loyalty. The accounts of one French duke, for example, on campaign after the loss at the battle of Crécy (1346), reveals his household staff noting the dispersal of object after object to accomplish political work: falcons, chalices, rings are given to a monastery as recompense for their damaged land, to a knight whose horse was lost in his service, to another knight whose wages are in arrears. At the same time, his staff are busy buying or commissioning new items to have on hand.[12]

Clothing also circulated as gifts; these gifts included partial components of outfits, since hoods, sleeves, and other features of the new styles were detachable and could be handled separately. The distribution of pieces of clothing is most obvious in royal accounts: kings gave away many garments and accessories to their sons, relatives, and favorites—including gowns, belts, and the newly important hats.[13] But it also appears as a common practice in most surviving accounts and inventories. In the aftermath of one great nobleman's death in 1420, we can see his debts being paid and his retainers rewarded. One of the many items listed is a gift of fur that had been removed from a certain garment and is now given to a particular knight to compensate him for another robe that the duke had previously taken back from him, to give to someone else.[14]

What is different about these collections of items and the gifts of clothing and jewels, compared to centuries before, is, first, the scale of the collecting and dispersal, but also the way it is increasingly dependent on commercial relationships. The circulation of goods reflected political ties sustained by giving, but also reflected and depended on a widening and far-flung community of craftsmen and purveyors. Accounts reveal goods commissioned, goods transferred, squires or serving women reimbursed for travel to and from a particular workshop, to and from a jeweler to retrieve an item repaired. Noble men and women even *bought* items from each other's collections when estates were settled at death. The greater availability of records for these centuries may emphasize an impression of a greater scale of accumulation and exchange, so we should underline that clothing and other accoutrements were not merely created and exchanged in (apparently) greater number but with a new deliberation about their effects. Partly, this was a consequence of the imperatives of fashion; one must now be not only richly arrayed, but also fashionably so. Yet clothing, in particular, in addition to fashionableness, carried more meaning because it was ritually deployed, and because it carried encoded information about identity and affiliation in the form of badges and personalized designs. Here, the increasing presence of writing and written texts in elite life makes its mark.

An elaborately illustrated book of advice, prepared for Charles VI of France by a secretary, meticulously depicts the king, in one illumination, sporting not only his signature colors but also a personal motto and devices on clothing and bedding alike. The best-known motto from this period is that of Edward III's Order of the Garter, "Honi soit qui mal y pense," but Charles's, in this image, is pithier: "Jamais," never. This single word reprised, for those in the know, the longer epigraph "Jamais desormais nul autre ne le verra": never again will anyone see this. It refers to a passage from one Grail epic, in which a winged white hart flies away and disappears—a representation of the transcendent that Charles appropriated to stand for royal power.

In the illustration, the word *jamais* marches across Charles's houppelande as well as the bed canopy above where he reclines in majesty. Meanwhile, Charles's other signature devices also envelop him: representations of the broom plant, for example, also bedeck his garment and bed hangings. And one device is not enough: other plants and animals long associated with Charles are included on the fabric. Charles's nemesis, John the Fearless, Duke of Burgundy, stands near the bed, recognizable because his own plant device—hops—climbs up his robe. John is overmatched by Charles, who is completely framed, within the image, by rich furniture and clothing with their abundant signature devices and colors.[15]

A further power of devices like these wearable signs came from the fact that they changed over time. One could not perform one's privileged relationship to Charles, for example, by wearing the same badge over many years. "Jamais" was an abbreviation of the earlier, longer motto, and any reader of the image needed that intertextual reference to decode this one. Earlier in his reign, Charles had also used altogether different animals than appear in this illumination. Indeed, these personal devices mutated organically over time,

Figure 3.2. King Charles and his personal signs. Charles's clothing and the bed where he reclines in this manuscript illustration display several of his personal motifs, including selected plants, animals, and the word "Jamais," repeated on his black gown and on the red canopy. The fringe on the canopy alternates his signature colors: red, green, black, and white. Charles's nemesis John, Duke of Burgundy (standing, right), is identified by his own signature plant, hops, which embellishes the elaborate sleeve of his houppelande. © Bibliothèque nationale de France. Ms. Fr 23279 f. 19, Pierre Salmon, Les demandes faites par le roi Charles VI.

just as Charles's short "jamais" derived from the longer motto. The collar of the Order of the Golden Fleece, Philip of Burgundy's chivalric order, for example, included, as a pendant, a stylized version of the eponymous fleece but it also included, as links of the chain supporting the pendant, a rendering of a steel for striking flint. This sharp steel was itself a further development of Philip's father's device of a woodworker's plane. That device of John the Fearless, who also represented himself with hops, as we have seen, had arisen in response to one belonging to his rival and mortal enemy, Louis d'Orléans. That prince's device was a wooden club, represented with the stubby remains of branches still visible—which his nemesis John the Fearless's plane could shave away.

Devices changed over time in deliberate conversation with and in response to others, and, though royalty set standards in this domain, rarely was an aristocrat or even a more lowly knight represented throughout his life by only one sign or only one motto.[16] Their complex, ever-changing emblems and mottoes appeared on every kind of object imaginable: textiles themselves and badges on garments, but also furniture, dishes, tapestries, armor, horse trappings as well as bespoke objects such as manuscript illustrations or jewels, like one version of John the Fearless's plane, executed in precious metals and gems, intended as a gift. Some personal devices were deliberately transient, such as a badge made for a special occasion and distributed to a chosen few. A mutable vocabulary of badges and other devices constituted a sophisticated means of performing both identity and affinity in which both the originator's and the wearer's aristocratic identity were enigmatic, always in motion.[17]

Clothing itself was changeable not merely because of the demands of fashion but also because courtiers and more lowly retainers regularly received, not merely occasional gifts of clothing, but outfits created anew for special occasions. Worthy garments were a popular gift from the king or high-ranking nobleman to a typical young warrior upon his knighting.[18] In 1458 alone, Charles VII of France gave celebratory outfits or special accessories to selected courtiers in honor of Candlemas, Mardi Gras, Lent, Easter, Pentecost, the feast of St. John the Baptist, and the birth of the Virgin—not to mention the Epiphany daggers he also commissioned and distributed.[19] That Charles's Mardi Gras gift was of hats intended "for Morris dances" is evidence both of the imperatives of fashion but also of the power of performance to enable aristocrats to engage in elaborate but safe play about identity. By participating in ritualized play, such as Mardi Gras dances and Maying processions, knights and aristocrats performed their inclusion in privileged circles. Yet symbolically potent clothing, decoration, and accessories were not just donned for staged amusements or solemn occasions, wholly distinct from daily life. Staged and spontaneous performances bled into each other;

the honor of a warrior always depended on performance in some register. Gifts, countergifts, pieces of fur and fabric, daggers, jewels, and hats were deployed in life in ways that represented both identity and affiliation and transferred them across time, from one body to another. It did no good to own a merely serviceable gown or belt or sword; to be a privileged warrior, one's belongings had to be made distinctive, not merely one iteration of many like objects but personalized and emblematic of one's identity. Not merely a thing, but a performance by means of a thing.[20]

Belts are a useful example. Belts are everywhere in accounts; they were an essential item in a man's wardrobe and were symbolically and practically connected to swords. We know that Henry III of England (d. 1272) kept a large cache of sword belts that included trophies taken from defeated rebel aristocrats, and that he made gifts of belts to his familiars and allies. He also commissioned a jewel-encrusted belt that most likely celebrated the occasion of a formal meeting with the French king; it memorialized the companionship of the English lords who accompanied him to the meeting by including careful renderings of their family crests. Even so small an object as a belt could be carefully crafted to further the program of Henry's rule, which, after the loss of French territory by his father, King John, included ambitious monuments such as the rebuilding of Westminster Abbey. The belt, on a smaller scale, was designed to celebrate the Englishness of his dynasty through identification with English saints and lineages. Most importantly, it was not merely created to mark the occasion in some abstract way but was deliberately gifted to a French ally of the moment, Thibaut of Champagne. It wound up being gifted again to one of Thibaut's relations, the heir to the Castilian throne, with whose remains it was eventually buried. Memorable and deliberately grand as this specimen was, it claimed attention partly because it was a familiar object, one of many belts in Henry's collections, which were talismans of identity to bequeath or to hold as a form of triumph over an adversary.[21]

Another memorable belt created about fifty years later appears in a will from the end of the fourteenth century. Blanche of Navarre, dowager queen of France since 1350, lived into the 1390s and left behind a will in which she scrupulously described the provenance of the worthy objects she bequeathed to her many relations. Blanche had briefly been the much-younger second wife of the first Valois king, Philip VI (d. 1350). Now, in 1392, Philip long gone, her only child already dead, Blanche bestows gifts on the current king, Philip's great-grandson Charles VI, as well as on his wife, on her own nephew, the King of Navarre, as well as many other relations, in order to stage her royal identity and connections one last time. The first bequest named is the sumptuous jeweled belt. It had belonged to her late husband, thus Charles's royal ancestor, Blanche points out. The belt bears Philip's arms, but it is also decorated with pearl-encrusted lozenges that open to reveal relics. This potent object, Blanche relates, had been given to her husband by his first wife *pour porter sur lei quant il alloit en guerre*: to wear on his person when going to war. She now passes it on to Charles. Blanche also gives Charles a signet ring with an even deeper ancestral connection, since it had belonged to Charles IV, her husband Philip's predecessor and the last Capetian king before his collateral Valois line took the throne (an ascent that had given Edward III of England a chance to mount a counterclaim to the throne). Blanche notes that both she and Philip had both worn the ring, which thus guaranteed the provenance of the object by means of transmission literally on their bodies.[22]

Personal attachment is what these objects convey. They are not just beautifully crafted adornments; rather, they carry the identity of the original owner, as Blanche makes clear in her descriptions. Both ring and belt carry layers of meaning: the association with the original owner and a personal seal, on the signet ring, or relics, in the belt. In addition, we can see that both items were *worn*; the belt is particularly interesting because it was a necessary part of every man's apparel, every day, yet could be a powerful object—one with talismanic power or trophy-like associations, owing to its association with the sword. The one Blanche bequeaths was potent enough to be worn "to war." We have a suggestion of the *choices* of raiment that have become possible, perhaps required, of elite warriors, even regarding appearance in war, and the powerful associations that were transferred from body to body.

Like clothing and its accessories, body armor could convey an intimate connection when gifted or bequeathed. Like clothing, it evolved and changed form, if not quite as abruptly, in the late Middle Ages. By the early fourteenth century, chain mail began to be regularly supplemented, then slowly replaced, with breastplates fashioned from larger pieces of metal and, eventually, from single pieces of iron or steel. The earliest surviving single-piece breastplate dates from the late fourteenth century, but experimentation that led to the one-piece full plate began about one hundred years before. Good mail could withstand a blow from a sword, even when delivered with force by a trained swordsman, but it did not protect against arrows or, especially, against crossbow bolts, particularly at close range. Crossbows came into use over the thirteenth century, and experimentation with better armor was well under way before 1300.[23] Small steel plates could be fixed onto a padded shirt or jacket, or added between the cloth layers of the gambeson, and when worn under mail gave somewhat better protection for the wearer than mail alone.

Larger metal plates required more steel, in a single piece, than could be produced by smelting methods until the late thirteenth century—though, as with textiles, innovation did not happen overnight; we have evidence of iron processing on a larger scale as early as the twelfth century in Sweden. By the early fourteenth century, larger "bloomeries," furnaces for processing iron ore into iron (cast and wrought) and steel, existed in several locations in Europe, spurred in turn by demand for iron for cannon. In the fourteenth century, then, it was possible for the first time to craft an all-steel sword blade from a single piece of steel. By the mid-fifteenth century, entire suits of plate armor could be made, with each piece formed from a single bloom of steel.

The transition to full suits of armor was nonetheless very gradual. Men wore chain mail routinely under plate armor through the fifteenth century, and coats of mail are named in wills for a long time after this transition begins. The first innovation, when more steel became available, was the "pair of plates," which were overlapping pieces of metal affixed to a fabric or leather covering. Across the fourteenth century and into the fifteenth, even modest knights assembled and bequeathed hodgepodges of this plate armor and coats of mail.[24] One London vintner who rose to become a knight and rural land-holder in the late fourteenth century had a collection of armor including a pair of plates covered in red velvet, but also helm, aventail (mailed neck protection), and hauberk—in other words, a coat of mail—all described as "used." His arm coverings are "feeble."[25] Many mail garments, we know, were composed partly of links salvaged from damaged ones, hence the garments' longevity, and variable quality; this vintner's armor was secondhand and likely second rate.

Like sword belts, coats of mail had the potential to be highly charged belongings, uniquely capable of conveying the intimacy of connection to the body—in addition to the continued utility of the garment. In 1399, for example, we find Eleanor de Bohun, widow of Thomas of Woodstock (youngest son of Edward III) bequeathing to their son a hauberk that had belonged to his father. She had retired to a monastery, two years before, and now, her health declining, she sought to formally bestow this coat of mail of his murdered father to their son. Naming the mail coat in her will suggests that Eleanor had kept the garment and was concerned it might be gifted or even sold by the monastery at her death. In 1420, agents for the late Philippe d'Orléans very deliberately bought back a coat of mail from a knight to whom it had been given in order to present it to another.[26]

In his 1325 will, Fulk of Pennebrugge (modern Pembridge, Herefordshire) is careful, above all, to make sure that his sons are well provided with armor. To the eldest son, also named Fulk, he leaves more than twenty separately named pieces of armor. First, the essential quilted gambeson and a coat of mail, then "a pair of the best plates." Next, a "bassinet [a style of helmet, new in the fourteenth century] for tourneys." Then follows a list of other individual pieces, including older pieces such as a hardened leather cuirass (chest protector) and an aventail, the mail neck guard, but also plate coverings for shoulders, thighs, shins, arms, and hands and feet—indeed multiple pairs of some of these items. With the addition of the pair of underarm protectors also listed, and "a helm for tourney and a helm for war," young Fulk would have been as well shielded in tournament or battle as anyone in his day. Then come a few accoutrements for young Fulk's horse. The bequests to the three remaining sons follow this pattern: whole body armor—gambesons and coats of mail—named first, then bassinets, aventails, and smaller pieces of plate. The youngest son receives only two coats of mail.[27]

There seem to be several impulses at work here. The most obvious is that Fulk wanted each of his sons to have the most essential and expensive bit of armor—a coat of mail—provided for him. All five coats of mail cannot have carried an intimate association from their father, however, and they represent a deliberate distribution of Fulk's accoutrements that must have been thought out in advance. The other obvious commitment here is that the eldest son and heir has not only Fulk's name but also the gear he will need to immediately assume his father's place as the head of the family.

Armor conveyed identity in ways that spoke to others, beyond the immediate family. Like surcoats worn over mail, the new pairs of plates could carry a man's insignia, signature devices, or colors on the attached cloth. Surviving accounts and inventories contain many notations of payment for plates together with fabric jupons, or of plated garments—pairs of plates—covered in an array of velvets and silks. Full garments are presented as gifts to chosen relations, and further gifts of lengths of cloth are made specifically for the purpose of covering armor, of some kind, for the torso.[28] In an inventory of some of the belongings of Humphrey de Bohun, Earl of Hereford, dead in battle in 1322, we can see that his "pair of plates," worn with his hauberk, were covered in green velvet, reprising the color of his personal device of a swan on a green field. The inventory lists more mundane jupons (which could be worn over mail or later over plate armor), a couple of coats of arms (whether banners or something else is not clear), then four pairs of ailettes. This is turn of the century armor in transition: ailettes were a kind of flat shoulder covering, both functional and decorative, that would be soon superseded by curved pieces that would better protect the shoulder joint. These ailettes, we are told, sport Humphrey's coat of arms. So, Humphrey had a good-quality coat of mail, supplemented with added plates and ailettes that were not merely serviceable items, but also functioned to advertise his identity.[29]

All these garments, accessories, and distinctive pieces of armor, all closely associated with the body, were further additions to an existing menu of signifiers that deployed family and personal identity beyond that individual, and asserted the presence of the individual and the lineage in space. Families' arms, which had existed since 1100 or so, now adorned all manner of surfaces: battle standards and shields had carried coats of arms since the twelfth century; now, so did castle gates and decorative elements, like fireplace surrounds, inside castles; so might the wall of a nearby family-sponsored priory or the altar in a parish church they patronized. So did tapestries, such as the ones René d'Anjou required to accompany him to one fief, or on his barge for river journeys. The depiction of Charles VI of France we noted above, so well adorned with signature emblems and mottoes, frames him within a chamber where, with the aid of hangings and furniture, he dominates the space and isolates his enemy. Crests and coats of arms and family mottoes also appeared on platters, chalices, even spoons by the dozen.[30] Tableware of this kind was often gifted, carrying affiliation with it. Together with a family's emblems affixed on or attached to buildings, they served to create a diffuse presence of the elite man (or woman) in frequented locales, and in the daily experience of their dependents, allies, or rivals, that complemented his well-arrayed actual presence in person.[31]

Where are swords, whether old or new, in this crowded world of embellished clothing, decorative daggers, and personalized armor—especially vis-à-vis armor, which garners so much attention in the documents we have? And in view of the wider effort to stage identity in space, with fixed emblems on buildings and portable emblems such as shields and banners? Again, we will pause to further consider context first: the manufacture of swords and their circulation among the many ranks of fighters during the Hundred Years' War. Then we will dig further into records designed to track ownership, maintenance, and gifting for more insight into how swords were handled and valued.

In one sense, swords were a more commonplace object than before, particularly when compared to armor, since the increase in production of iron that enabled the development of plate armor led to production of many more swords than were previously available. The best swords could now be made entirely of one piece of steel, though this did not guarantee their superiority over older weapons, since finishing a blade by tempering the metal was still an art that produced variable results. In fact, increased production of iron meant that, by the end of the fifteenth century, it became possible to manufacture larger quantities of decidedly inferior swords. Though many were inferior weapons, it is nonetheless important to imagine the difference from, say, the early thirteenth century, when a knight's one or two or even four swords distinguished him from all others below him in rank. By about

1400, a member of the growing ranks of infantrymen such as an English archer could be found carrying a sword of some kind along with his bow.

Bladed weapons grew in variety as well as in number, in part because the form of swords adapted to the emergence of plate armor. Increasingly,

FIGURE 3.3. Varieties of late medieval blades. A typical late medieval sword (above), had cutting edges as well as a sharpened tip to penetrate joints in armor. Metropolitan Museum of Art, Open Access. This fourteenth-century falchion (p. 107), could be used to slash with its single edge and pierce with its tip. Like many swords, it was embellished with a decorative pommel. © RMN-Grand Palais / Art Resource, NY. The long, slim estoc (p. 108), could be suspended from the saddle and used for stabbing when wielded on horseback as well as for hand-to-hand fighting on foot. This example was recently discovered at the site of one the last battles of the Hundred Years' War. © RMN-Grand Palais / Art Resource, NY.

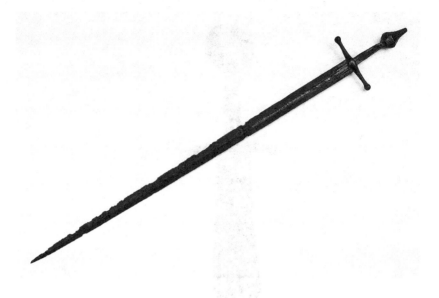

they were tapered to a sharp point that could pierce joints in armor. One form of sword, the estoc, was a long—sometimes two-handed—sword that had no sharpened edges at all and was used only for thrusting. We also find baselards among knightly belongings: a short sword that retained the form of a dagger and was used also for stabbing. In addition, increasing numbers of warriors would also own a falchion, a long curved-bladed weapon akin to the scimitar. The falchion had a single edge, but also a point that could stab—and demanded its own specialized techniques to be wielded success-fully. This diversity of weaponry was part of the lore of arms in the day. The French poet (also a squire to the Dauphin and a fortress governor) Eustache Deschamps (d. 1406) celebrated such an assortment of offensive and defensive arms in his ballads that it has proved difficult for modern interpreters to know what objects he intended in each case.[32]

But a sword of any sort, we also know, was not always a warrior's first choice in combat in the fourteenth and fifteenth centuries. On horseback, knights often wielded a lance first. Whether mounted or on foot, many fighters used a mace or hammer to pound an opponent's armor, or an ax to cleave it.[33] In 1314, the Scottish king Robert the Bruce used an ax to kill his English opponent in single combat—while on horseback. A century later, in 1424, the English commander and regent for Henry VI, John, Duke of Bedford, wielded a two-handed poleax in battle and with it split the armor of many French knights.[34] A sword or the ubiquitous dagger or knife could dispatch a fallen or concussed opponent through the visor or a joint in armor.

Traditional swords could be used for their concussive force, too, but they could not penetrate good plate armor.

Meanwhile, after the opening salvos of the Hundred Years' War in the late 1330s, an elite warrior could encounter good-quality armor and weapons in his opponents of all ranks, given how continuously troops operated in France and how mixed the cohorts of fighters were. Groups of fighters under captains (as they were officially designated by the English at least) included familiars of the leader, such as members of his household, but also humbler men signing on for pay and the opportunity for plunder or because they were felons seeking pardon. Under pressure of need, as fighting wore on, troops were raised by both the French and the English however they could be with whatever monies, or promises of money, were at hand. More than 150 self-styled "captains" operated as independent agents in the decade of supposed peace after the Treaty of Brétigny in 1360 (drawn up in England's favor after the French loss at Poitiers in 1356.) These were not mere bands of rabble, but effectively led companies of experienced soldiers, now without official employment, who could best even royal troops sent against them, such as at Brignais in 1362. Their quality was also attested by the fact that they were recruited by the principals contesting thrones in Spain and in Sicily, as well as in various local quarrels and even in crusading ventures, before being reabsorbed—that is, rerecruited—by English and French armies when the dynastic fighting reopened in France in the 1370s. In many respects, these free companies, though lacking aristocratic leadership, and the display and perks of status that implied, would otherwise have been indistinguishable from the "royal" forces on either side all along.[35]

We must imagine, whether among "royal" or independent cohorts throughout the wars, contingents of men in diverse bits and pieces of armor, armed with equally mixed weaponry. Humbler men did not remain humbly armed; they could be found wearing pieces of good-quality armor looted from manors or taken from prisoners or pulled from the dead. Indeed, it is likely that better body armor or a steel helmet would have been the first items any fighting man would have appropriated when the opportunity arose. Skeletal remains of infantry killed in one fifteenth-century battle, whose remains were excavated in the 1990s, reveal the high proportion of head wounds—both fatal on the day but also received in action earlier in life—versus wounds to limbs, except for the fighting arm. Very few rib injuries were noticeable, suggesting that padded chest and back protection had been effective enough for these fighters, but that good helmets were rarer, and of potentially great value.[36] Particularly significant is that the bodies found in the mass grave had been stripped before burial of virtually all their arms and armor, by other fighters or by local civilians scavenging, who knew their worth.[37]

So, fighting men of all sorts might wield weapons given to them by a freelance recruiter or stolen from a baggage train or salvaged on the battle-field or bought locally or brought with them from home. The chronicler Froissart reports that some French men-at-arms, included in a would-be inva-sion fleet in 1386, had to sell their equipment locally at a huge loss to feed themselves; supplies had run so low—one reason the plans for the fleet had been abandoned—and local fighters or arms dealers were the beneficiaries.[38] The circulation of arms by means of gift-giving or lending was common enough to attract the attention of Christine de Pisan. She devoted a section of her 1405 work, *The Book of Deeds of Arms and Chivalry*, to the case of what should happen when a man who fights with borrowed equipment loses it in battle; does the original owner deserve compensation?[39] The slightly later anonymous narrative of Henry V's reign *Gesta Henrici Quinti* relates that, at Agincourt, English archers "seized axes, stakes and swords . . . that were lying about [and] they struck down the enemy."[40]

We also have records from town governments, particularly in areas where fighting raged, insisting that all heads of households have weapons to hand, and trying to survey and inventory exactly what was available among their citizens. Whoever knew how to use a crossbow was urged to have one, not surprising given their usefulness in urban defense, as a bowman could be protected by walls when reloading. These inventories also reveal the wide-spread presence of other armaments, including defensive armor and a range of weapons: lances, axes, even swords. One fourteenth-century inventory from the small southern French town of Vence reveals that in 97 households are 35 crossbows, 97 lances or other poled weapons and 24 swords.[41] Swords are common enough in such households that sometimes they include rusty ones languishing in a cellar. By the mid-fifteenth century, particularly, when swords were manufactured in a greater number, there would have been blades aplenty in many bands of armed men—whatever "side" they fought with and whatever their station—whether purchased, borrowed, or appro-priated. Of the 201 names on a rare surviving English muster roll at the time of the battle of Towton in 1461, 69 infantrymen were equipped with a sword in addition to a bow or a long-staffed weapon like a bill or poleax.[42]

Swords, in short, appeared in many fighters' hands. Not only were more swords available, this was a world of swords in motion, in a kind of cha-otic circulation. The sheer numbers of recruited men active in France until about 1450 meant a circulation of both armor and swords down the economic and status scale. French and English knights and great lords alike could lose swords and armor or face high-quality armor or weapons randomly, in almost any adversary. High-quality weapons were desirable in and of themselves and, for an ambitious soldier of modest origin, they could display the increased status to which he aspired. In other words, prestigious equipment that moved down the social scale enabled the men who displayed and used it to move up.

The rise in wealth and status by many initially humble fighters was noticed by contemporaries. Already in the 1350s, one English knight, writing while a prisoner of war, commented that many fighters who had been "unknown youths, from different regions of England . . . [started as] archers, then [became] knights, and some of them captains."[43] Even a man of very humble origin could wind up captaining a troop of sought-after fighters; many men, commanders or otherwise, compiled significant wealth from plunder, ransoms, and extorting protection money, as well as from a magnate's or royal favor if their military skill warranted it. Not merely goods and wealth but also social standing accrued to such men; their raised status was their best protection against arbitrary execution when fighting went against them, as it well might.[44]

One Englishman named David Holgrave, for example, briefly an independent captain, rose through the ranks in princely service, eventually to gain estates through marriage to the heiress of a knight in his native Northumberland. He was described, while a captain in France, as carrying two swords, one on his belt and another fixed to the pommel of his horse. What is interesting here is not merely the vignette itself, but the fact that it is reported by the French chronicler, who narrates the death of this "proud captain" at the hands of the Duke of Bourbon's men. The two swords on display were this "grant David Olegrève's" signature accoutrement; he is known by them.[45] We do not know the precise attributes of these two swords, though many contemporary images show mounted men wielding long, tapered swords that would have enabled a man on horseback to reach opponents either mounted or on foot (so-called hand and a half swords, since a longer hilt was required to balance and maneuver the blade). But knights also wielded the shorter swords that be most useful on foot, and could be worn as a matter of course. These shorter swords were most likely to be found in the hands of ordinary men on the battlefield. Holgrave signaled his rise in status, perhaps, by the fact that he had acquired both varieties. His signature weapons reflect the continued importance of iconic swords to the persona of a leader of men.

Catching glimpses of the swords owned by already established elites, by means of inventories and accounts their households left behind, one is struck by the fact that as swords became more common, swords designed as pure ornament did also. Like daggers, swords could be fashioned to be more a jewel than a weapon and could be found gathered with other treasures in the care of subordinates. For example, an inventory from 1417, made as control of the treasure in one French chateau changed hands on the death of the guardian, reveals a tiny sword stashed with other precious goods in a large armoire. The armoire's two upper shelves are filled with books, but on the lowest shelf is a leather coffer containing a mass of cups, gilded and enameled tableaux, jeweled pins, crosses, and collars, rosaries holding relics, small boxes with more relics, rings, bracelets—more than fifty items in all and, among them, a "little sword" with a ruby in the pommel, a scabbard decorated with gold, and even a diamond on the chape (the protective fitting at the bottom of the scabbard).[46] The little sword was likely a gift, though this inventory does not record its provenance. Another little sword appears earlier in the accounts of the *argenterie* (the treasury of precious metalware) of King John of France (d. 1364) when it is repaired by a silversmith; it had belonged to Philip III, his great-grandfather, and had been a gift to the monastery of St. Germain des Prés to mark the occasion of a tournament. It had since found its way back into the royal collection, where the record carefully inscribes its journeys as a memento.[47]

At the end of the century, less than two months after he seized the throne of England, Henry IV had precious goods sent to him from the treasury "for his use." Amid a quantity of tableware, chalices and a pyx for the Mass, candlesticks, salvers, mirrors, rings, buckles, loose jewels, clothing, rich fabric, and belts are two swords: one is for display only—it is decorated with jasper and comes with its own pearl-studded pedestal, so we can imagine it to be small, a jewel rather than a working weapon—not unlike other ornaments on the list, such a "stag lying under a tree, the horns and the branches decorated with twenty-six pearls."[48] These miniature jeweled weapons echo the unusable blades, bows, and axes deposited in graves some eight hundred years before. They are jewels, to be sure; they could be regifted, melted down or refashioned as many such items were, but they are also swords, and constitute one somewhat playful instance of the expanding variety of swords elite men now assembled.

The second sword in the cache delivered to Henry, meanwhile, was a full-size weapon with a sword belt decorated with gold, pearls, sapphire, and balas ruby and a scabbard that also sported gemstones. The sword itself had pearls, sapphires, and rubies on both sides of the pommel, as well as on the guard and the grip. In short, a jewel-like sword—not the same as the coronation swords discussed in the previous chapter, but worthy of occasions of state, a prop for this new king of questionable legitimacy.[49] Ten years later, a jeweled sword belonging to Louis d'Orléans, brother of the king of France, was recorded along with his jeweled dagger, as his goods were disbursed after the death of his widow; like his dagger, Louis's sword had a balas ruby in the hilt and a sheath decorated with pearls. We know that Louis's Italian wife took this sword with her back to Italy after his assassination in 1407, along with the dagger previously described above, out of all the precious objects she might have chosen. In other words, the sword was costly jewel and weapon and memento all together.[50] It is still in her hands at her death in 1408, returned to their children by a lady-in-waiting.

That kings and princes owned expensive showpiece weapons is not surprising, nor a departure from past practice, except that some of these weapons advertised no connection with an illustrious forebear. The records of swords in the possession of other aristocrats, and on down to aspiring gentry, reflect a similar need to secure a signature weapon of appropriate grandeur as well as an impulse to collect additional noteworthy swords—including a richly bejeweled or embellished weapon, or perhaps one carrying a relic or the sign of a warrior saint or some other kind of trophy or souvenir weapon. Examples are the four swords left behind by Humphrey de Bohun, the Earl of Hereford, at the time of his death in 1322, in rebellion against Edward II. Included are one with the arms of the earl (presumably on the pommel); one "of St. George" (again likely referring to decoration on the hilt), "the third, Saracen," and finally, "the fourth, for war."

These details come from the inventory that recorded the earl's belongings. Like most inventories, this document is a checklist of sorts, a control on and protection for a temporary guardian of goods—in this case, the man charged with receiving this rebel's goods in the name of the crown. Also like many other lists, it includes multiple inventories initially achieved separately—three in this example—and then copied into a single composite document. The first collection is a reservoir of treasure: a huge deposit of jewels and plate deposited at an abbey founded by the earl's ancestors in the south of England, including more than two hundred diadems, plates, cups, clasps, buckles, loose jewels, enameled images, spoons, girdles, belts, and rings. The third lot comes from a chapel, probably a foundation in Scotland that had once been under the earl's control; it contains liturgical books, reliquaries, and a sack of charters.

It is the second section of the combined inventory where the earl's swords appear, and where our attention to the precise composition of the list bears fruit. The list reveals a mixed cache of luxurious textiles, armor, and arms. Here is Hereford's hauberk, his green-velvet-covered plates and the distinctive ailettes we have already noted, as well as his four swords. The order of objects on the list appears to reflect the way they had been packed together.

First, come seven rugs or hangings in the earl's signature green sprinkled with white swans, then the hauberk of good quality, identified by its place of origin, then the pair of plates, followed by the jupons, the coats of arms, and the ailettes. Next come two lengths of elegant cloth: "one cloth of gold for a bed," and "one small cover, in saye [a particular kind of woolen cloth] for an infant's cradle." Then the document announces the "four swords," and cursorily describes them.

We can envision the swords cushioned between layers of cloth as the list continues with three quilts: one made of white silk, another of red velvet striped with peacock feather, and a third with the earl's arms quartered with those of England. The list then concludes with one book, two helmets, further bed furnishings and rugs, one pair of hose, one covering for a horse "with the arms of Hereford," and, finally, a packhorse itself.[51]

When the earl was killed in battle in Yorkshire on March 16, he and his allies had been moving quickly north to avoid entrapment by royal troops after a skirmish earlier in the month. These items must have been in Hereford's train, the packhorse his own, the elegant armor kept somewhere within reach of him on campaign, if not on his body at death. He would not have left behind a sword with his arms on it, or a quilt depicting his arms quartered with those of England—a bold way of reconfiguring heraldry that was new in the early fourteenth century, which reflected, in this case, the fact that Humphrey had married a daughter of Edward I. At this moment, the quilt would be vital visual propaganda, for himself and his retinue, as he rebelled against Edward II. We can also speculate about the sentimental weight of the cradle blanket—perhaps a memory peg, recalling a son who had died in infancy?[52]

From their presence together, intermingled with other valuable effects, we surmise that Hereford kept these swords close; they bear his arms, they carry the charisma of a saint, and—in the case of the "Saracen" blade—represent a trophy, perhaps inherited from his great-grandfather, the second earl, who had gone to the Holy Land on pilgrimage. From the way they are labeled by the inventory makers, we can further assume that swords that could be heirlooms, trophies, or otherwise especially potent were, on the one hand, essential, but were not necessarily used in battle. In other words, a sword could be a potent weapon valued for its symbolic resonances, a signature prop, but not deployed in actual fighting. The fact that all four traveled with him suggests that they were precious to the earl as a collection, as well as individually. We must also consider the possibility that the fourth sword, "for war," was special not in appearance, to an outsider, but by reason of long use or association that only Humphrey or his intimates knew, and recognizable as "for war" by the quality of the blade or signs of use.

It is also likely, given what other wills and inventories tell us, that these four swords represented all the swords that Humphrey owned, beyond a possible fifth blade he may have carried to his death and which disappeared in the ambush that killed him. His contemporary, Fulk of Pembridge, for example, bequeathed a total of only three swords in the meticulous allotments to his four sons. One hundred and twenty-five years later, the staggeringly wealthy would-be king René d'Anjou had about six, whose attributes resemble those belonging to the Earl of Hereford. At various junctures, René's accounts list a richly embellished one made for his son, as well as "a simple sword," "another sword," a "ceremonial sword" a "Moorish" sword, and his own sword—described simply as "the lord's [René's] sword."[53] Like Humphrey, then, he had at least one workaday blade beyond "his" sword, by which he is known; he also owns an elegant ceremonial sword (and perhaps has another made for his son) and a blade of presumably Muslim manufacture.

We thus can be confident that the increasing numbers of swords and numbers of fighters who wielded them meant that individual, high-value swords had not lost their cachet. Rather, the reverse. The more common swords became the greater the need to make those in elite hands special and distinctive. These caches I have examined were deliberate assemblages of unique blades; wardrobes, of sorts, of swords valued for different purposes or to represent different attributes. Fashioning a "ceremonial" sword mirrored royal practice and thus was an understandable presence among René's belongings. Precisely how other swords—a trophy blade or an iconic family heirloom—were thought about or deployed in life is harder to establish. One insight comes from a later appearance by one of the Earl of Hereford's swords. In 1345, more than twenty years after he died in battle, the earl's sword bearing the family arms, captured in 1322, is still in the hands of the king.[54] The family estates had been returned after the fall of Edward II's hated favorites in 1326, and two of Humphrey's sons had since established their reputations commanding in Edward III's forces early in the Hundred Years' War. The elder had resumed Humphrey's title and would hold it until his death in 1361. Precisely *why* their family heirloom was still in the king's hands we cannot say; what is significant is that, whatever happened to the other swords taken in 1322, this one, above all others, had landed and remained in the royal treasure. Whether it was ever used in battle, a distinctive sword like this one, bearing the family's arms and known to others as such, represented, and in effect, captured, that lineage. The fact that Humphrey had carried it with him on campaign anticipated royal appropriation and likely served to prompt it.

We do not know whether this blade was actually an heirloom—a well-used sword, perhaps refurbished over time, with memory, not just identity, attached to it. The point was the role it played, not its etiology. In use, it is akin to John de Warenne's sword, brandished to threaten agents of the crown some four decades before. Instead of being old and battle-worthy, Hereford's sword bears his coat of arms, and it might even be new. If recently made, the sword was a grand gesture, a performance in a newly inflected vernacular of heraldic devices and luxurious goods; regardless, it instantiated a claim to a political identity, which is why the king kept it.

In fact, when records reveal nothing else, they reveal the presence of such distinctly decorated swords. In mid-fourteenth century Marseille, the chevalier Bérenger de Boulbon's property includes three swords, of which one is embellished with silver and has a belt made of silk.[55] A century later, the great soldier-opportunist Sir John Fastolfe left large caches of plate and armor and elegant clothing behind in his main residence at his death—and one sword, which the inventory makers distinguish by decorative features of the scabbard: in this case, the sheath has a gilded chape.[56] In 1483, the Duke of Norfolk's staff pays an armorer to have "my lord's sword" polished and sharpened, as well as a goldsmith for a new belt and gilded chape "for my lord's sword."[57] These improvements postdate the coronation of Richard III earlier that year, though they were surely related to needs of courtly display, since refurbishing Norfolk's Garter pendant was part of the improvements done at the time. But, however it was used, this was "my lord's sword"; it was a weapon, though perhaps not used as such, as well as an elegant talisman of identity.

We can also occasionally see up-and-coming men securing just such a distinctive weapon as they rise in status. The hundred-year war, and the leveraging of French resources, meant that many English fighters, particularly, who would otherwise have remained on the margins of elite status could move up, but the rise of families into the gentry and petty nobility was ongoing over the fourteenth and fifteenth centuries, regardless of the special opportunities represented by war. Consider, for example, the case of one Paul de Sade from the region around Avignon whose *livre de raison* from the 1390s survives to document his business enterprises and his efforts to climb the social ladder.[58] A son of a bourgeois of Avignon, Paul traded in salt, shipped up the Rhone from the coast; he also traded in textiles, acted as a small-time banker of sorts and was a property owner enjoying rental income from dwellings in and around the town. Not surprisingly, Paul had connections at the papal court clinging on at Avignon (several cardinals were among his tenants). He counted among his acquaintance the chamberlain of the Duke of Orléans, the connection close enough that Paul lent money to one of the crossbowmen in the chamberlain's employ. Among Paul's outlays is the full outfitting of one man-at-arms—with armor, sword, lance, and mount—to serve the city of Avignon in his place. The right to provide a man-at-arms was a privilege, and sinecure: Paul records in the book the existence of an accord whereby the fortunate man serving in his name shares his wages with him, his benefactor.

Paul worked doggedly to display the status he sought to claim. He staged his betrothal to a woman from the local petty nobility by arriving at her family estate with a retinue of ten horses, bearing gifts of cloth, fur, and jewels, with his own notary in tow to draw up the marriage contract. After the union, his rise in status is marked by being named an honorary guard (*huissier majeur*) at the papal palace. Among his outlays after that are funds to create a family coat of arms and display them on the walls of his townhouse. Paul procures weapons and armor for himself too—a full set of armor, plus extra helmets, leg and arm fittings—and, at some point before the beginning of these accounts, a sword. His sword appears, here, as it is sent out to be garnished with decorative enamel, by means of the same process by which one of King Charles VI's swords was embellished.[59] Paul de Sade does not want just *a* sword; he wants a sword in the latest fashion, worthy of his new stature. In a different way than David Holgrave, though perhaps with the same motivation, Paul seeks to make his sword a signature prop. Great nobles such as the Earl of Hereford could afford more than one ceremonial or ornate sword, as well as a trophy or two and one or two others specifically "for war." In fact, we can imagine a man like Bérenger de Boulbon or the Earl of Hereford on horseback, like David Holgrave deploying two swords at once: both signature swords, of different styles or dimensions. In any case, it was essential to the likes of Paul de Sade to at least have one distinctive, embellished weapon.

We learn about Paul de Sade's sword and his other belongings via what amounts to a personal account book, where we can track some of their comings and goings, rather than merely catch sight of them in his household at one point in time. We can see in its pages that Paul lends armor to a friend, and notes when it is returned. In particular, we can remark that Paul has, in addition, the use of a full set of jousting armor (which he may have borrowed to start with). In these pages, he lends the ensemble out and records its return. We also know, from another source, that some seven years later he fought in a duel, "on horseback and armed as is incumbent upon a nobleman."[60] Both the fact and the tenor of this observation are important: a nobleman of more secure lineage would not have elicited such a comment. Recently minted noble or not, Paul wanted to be in the club of elite men who had access to the world of tournaments.

If swords were not unique to knights any longer, what was still unique to elite warriors, and particularly to aristocrats, beyond their deliberate collection of embellished, special blades, was the ability and the expectation to fight in battle mounted on horseback, protected by high-quality armor and wielding a lance in a cavalry charge and, above all, the costly enterprise of practice in the staged encounter of a joust. Participation in tournaments remained an essential pastime for warrior elites well into the sixteenth century. Tournaments were not just a sideline, a diversion, from the "real" business of being a warrior. Keeping them in view enables us to appreciate the context of other signature belongings a warrior would have invested in, particularly the overriding importance of improved armor and the variety and symbolic heft of weapons he might now own.

Early tournaments, staged as early as the eleventh century, had consisted of massed charges between two teams of spear- or lance-bearing horsemen followed by a melee where fighters mostly wielded their swords to stun or unhorse their opponents and win ransoms, sometimes multiple ransoms in a single tournament.[61] Thus a knight of modest stature could win both renown and riches and, perhaps, an elite patron's notice. William Marshal (d. 1219), later the right-hand man to four kings, literally made his fortune and his reputation in tournaments as a young man. The relationship of tournaments to other aristocratic pursuits was not one of mere diversion, for this reason as well as others. Indeed, tourneys got their start, we believe, in the Low Countries, where counts and other magnates ruling over small but wealthy territories resorted to these not-quite-mock battles to shame, to intimidate, to bloody their rivals within the protection—for the fighters, for the land and its resources—of a staged, thus delimited, encounter.

Group encounters waned by the early fourteenth century in France and England owing partly to royal disapproval, especially during crusading ventures or other campaigns abroad, or during periods of baronial rebellion—though individual warriors continued to participate in tournaments and invest in appropriate gear regardless.[62] Over time, jousting became the more exclusive focus of tournament combat and with these more choreographed contests came the elaboration of pageantry associated with it, including an initial parade of contenders, culminating in a ceremony of choosing a rival by striking his shield, which represented the warrior in his absence. Above all, these formal occasions were opportunities to display a meticulously calibrated persona, composed of armor, certainly, by the identifying cloth worn on or over it, the signs carried on banners and pennons (and on one's tent), a tournament helm with a distinctive crest, a shield painted with one's heraldic device, all atop a horse that was clothed in similarly rich signage: a virtual carapace enclosing the living bodies of man and horse, creating a unique hybrid being. Performance not just of prowess but also of identity and thus status mattered, and jousts continued to be effective means of formally displaying and bolstering an individual's claims to both. The performance was powerful precisely because it mimicked—and sometimes virtually repeated—the array a man would wear into battle.[63]

Tournaments thus had political valence, but they were also an important ingredient in success in actual battle. Prior experience in tournaments helped to mold the cohesion of forces demonstrated by the armies of Edward III in the great victories of Crécy and Poitiers, for example. Edward III came to the throne as a young man, having always known he would be king (unlike his French counterpart, Philip VI); he perceived the need to build a coterie

PLATE 3. A knight's symbolic array. In this image from the Psalter he commissioned late in life, Sir Geoffrey Luttrell is literally encased in symbols of his status and lineage. His wife ceremoniously hands him a great crested helm, while his daughter-in-law holds his shield at the ready. Their gowns replicate the signs on Geoffrey's horse and his own surcoat and ailettes. While this rendering of himself was a nostalgic gesture, in Geoffrey's old age, the importance of the symbolic trappings of identity would have been legible to younger contemporaries. Only the fact that his lance is not blunted at the tip reveals that this is an imagined departure for battle and not for a tournament. © The British Library Board, 9/12/2019, Add. 42130, f.202v.

of loyal knights about him as he wrested control from his father, then from his mother and her over-mighty ally Roger Mortimer. Edward proceeded to bolster the loyalty of these companions by being careful not to favor one at the expense of the group (a mistake his father had made), by awarding them commands and preferment judiciously, as well as by means of a veritable program of tournaments. The timing—celebrating early victories against the Scots, for example—and the sheer magnificence of these occasions accomplished the political work of creating Edward's authority by means of performing and celebrating it, but they also worked to fashion the group ethos of the privileged cohort surrounding him. These men often received luxurious outfits and armor to match the king's (indeed he often thus celebrated himself as "one among equals" which reflected the fact that they were indeed his companions); they performed worthy deeds of arms before audiences of courtiers and purveyors, and simultaneously honed their skill and their mutual regard. It was this group of men who led English troops on the battlefields of Crécy and Poitiers. Fighting cohesion in these battles was possible because the English commanders knew and trusted each other and had long experience of winning renown and admiration as part of a group, as well as individual fighters; the French commanders, more independent politically, with far less experience of collective rituals and entertainments, had no such common experience.[64]

Tournaments were also important because lance-wielding cavalry remained a vital military arm through the first quarter of the sixteenth century. It is true that in Scotland, in 1297 and 1314, and in Flanders, in 1302, respectively, the English and French cavalry had been humiliated by opposing forces that relied on disciplined infantry. After that, the French, so the story goes, did not learn their lesson, as the English did. In their victories at Crécy (1346), Poitiers (1356) and Agincourt (1415), the English deployed their elite men-at-arms largely on foot, in coordination with massed archers. Recent study of these battles, however, argues that they were more complex affairs than that of complete dominance by more "modern" cohesive forces, willing to forego individual glory in the interests of effectiveness.[65] At Crécy, the French cavalry enjoyed some tactical success during the battle, though ultimately were hampered by unfavorable ground as well as by the countercharge of English horsemen. Poitiers was a resounding English victory because the king of France was captured, but it was a very near-run battle that could well have gone the other way. Agincourt was decided by terrain and poor coordination as much as by the failure of cavalry per se. And beyond these clashes, the record of lance-wielding cavalry was by no means uniformly negative. The French had particular reason not to abandon the tactic, as they had witnessed its success on several occasions, including in an engagement not long after their shameful defeat by Flemish infantry in 1302. In 1362, French royal forces were themselves defeated at Brignais because mounted fighters in the free companies they faced made a surprise attack on their flank using hastily cut lances. In their turn, in 1370, French cavalry bested a group of poorly armed men of the companies. Led by the constable Du Guesclin, the French dismounted and faced the men of the companies on foot, but they were only able to prevail when reinforced by a late-arriving contingent of mounted lances.[66]

Contemporaries, by and large, did not condemn the cavalry charge either. Rather, for them, the pressing issue was how to control and manage such fighters, and, above all, how to combine them effectively with infantry, especially versus opposing infantry. In short, it was the question of discipline, which Edward's tight-knit commanders exemplified, early in his reign. Writing in the early fifteenth century, Christine de Pisan envisioned a role for cavalry as a component of mixed forces and urged the French to—somehow—adopt the discipline their enemy's successes reflected.[67] Other writers echoed her, including one French nobleman who wrote, after the end of the Hundred Years' War, that lances were still the most "dangerous arms in the world" because nothing could stop the force of a cavalry charge.[68] He was a veteran of Verneuil, one of the bloodiest battles of the war in which foreign cavalry fighting for the French had had some success against English archers—though the French eventually lost largely because they did not properly manage their disparate forces.[69]

As it turned out, this veteran of Verneuil, Jean de Beuil, was right to have faith in the cavalry charge. For another seventy-five years or so, heavy cavalry would succeed in battle when it was properly deployed.[70] In Paul de Sade's lifetime (which more or less coincided with that of Christine de Pisan), jousts thus remained good practice for what was still—and for what would remain for another century and more—a vital combat tactic. Thus, participating in a tournament continued to be part of the real business of the elite warrior, as it had been so pointedly in Edward III's reign. But the joust was something more: participating in jousts could differentiate him from the burgeoning ranks of not-quite-honorable fighters, men such as the freelance captain Holgrave, whose swagger consisted of displaying two swords. Paul de Sade was eager to separate himself from those below him by these means.

Of course, all participants knew well, especially by the fifteenth century, that actual combat away from the tournament field might have to occur on foot. Their appearance, then, in tournaments was a claim to an exclusive status that, in this domain too, included an element of nostalgia: an evocation of an imagined past where a warrior was literally known by his elaborately coded exterior and who could defend his renown visibly on horseback. Tournament combat also now began to include the variety of weapons and the fighting skills that dismounted knights also needed to master. Two men, or pairs of men, might face each other first by jousting, then on foot with pole-axes, then with swords, and finally with daggers.[71] That foot combat was part of elaborate ritual, a ritual that included traditional jousting, meant that aristocrats (and wannabes like Paul de Sade) were claiming a kind of exclusivity even when fighting on foot, which ordinary foot soldiers could not hope to mimic. Thus, it was another version of the same impulse that led elites to gather distinctive blades, not merely effective weapons.

The desire and expectation to participate in tournaments is reflected in the material record. In 1349, we note that the young Duke of Normandy—who would reign later as Charles V of France—pays the staggering sum of 297 livres for a complete "harness for the joust."[72] But we mostly do not often find "jousting armor" listed as a tidy package, as in this account or in Paul de Sade's record of loaned equipment. As plate armor improved and became more expensive, tournament wear included purpose-made helms, shoulder protection, and attachable braces for the lance, but chest and limb protection could be the same as battlefield wear. Thus, we often find mention only of a piece or two that suggests equipment worthy of both battlefield and tournament, not whole purpose-made "suits."[73] This high-quality armor, including items designed solely for tourneying, were a steady focus of investment and individual pieces were accumulated and replaced over time. Already in the eighteenth year of his reign, thus just before Crécy, Edward III had, in one cache of belongings, a great helm, clearly worn at a prior tournament (it has a damaged crest). There were also three other helms "of various sizes," plus two other helms "for the tourney, of little value." Judging by their position on the list, these last two helmets were gathered with other bits of outmoded armor, including leg pieces made of leather.[74] Running expenditures in the household of Edmund Mortimer, Earl of March (d. 1425), as he kept company with King Henry V in 1413–14, include predictable expenses on falconry, on alms, on games and clothing, but also payment for rerebraces (armor for the upper arms) decorated—at significant cost—with gold.[75]

A lengthy inventory of goods sold after one aged knight's death in the early sixteenth century suggests also the piecemeal nature of the acquisition of horse armor and decorative trappings for tournaments. From the array of goods offered for sale, one fellow knight buys an old coat of mail, which still, at this point, sports an impressive velvet surcoat.[76] He also buys two "old tourney saddlecloths," also of velvet (along with bedding, napery, plate, and Turkish carpets). Another fellow knight buys a splendid saddle decorated with gold embroidery and green velvet, together with the matching bard for a horse. The bard, the decorative horse covering, is crimson satin, and the bridle crimson velvet with gilt and copper fittings. The dead knight's collection also includes at least four more saddles and sets of trapping, including white and black velvet harnesses, bards of white and black taffeta, and one of sarcenet, a particular weave of silk. There are gilt bosses for the bridles, and several sets of gilt and steel spurs. There is no high-quality armor in the long list of sale items, certainly none worthy of the joust, so whatever this knight owned in that domain had been dispersed to his sons, or was located in a residence other than the ones surveyed for this inventory. Regardless, the quantity of the black and white saddles and decorative fitting for mounts is arresting. There are enough to have clothed several horses at one time, for the same event. So, here we get another vantage point on the steady investment that this kind of display mandated; all these accoutrements for horses were in excess of whatever got passed down to heirs, and another knight gladly purchased the lot.

The material record regarding tournaments includes abundant evidence of investment in written texts about it: participating in the life of tourneys meant collecting and savoring accounts of actual and mythical encounters. Some were illustrated manuscripts celebrating individuals, such as the so-called Beauchamp Pageant, chronicling the achievements of the Earl of Warwick (d. 1439), commissioned by his daughter late in the century.[77] Others depicted imaginary or idealized tournaments, such as a highly detailed instruction book written by none other than René d'Anjou.[78] Still others were compilations of texts that might include celebratory narrations of well-known contests or accounts of the challenges or proclamations that initiated famous tournaments. One outstanding example was the "Grete Book" assembled by Sir John Paston in the mid-fifteenth century. It includes records of famous encounters, the formal challenges preceding others as well as instructions for would-be contestants, such as precise directions for appropriate clothing and armament, and what other equipment to bring to a tourney: for example, the need for a kerchief to hold up the visor of one's helmet when necessary. Paston's text was lent out and returned by friends and relations who wanted their own copies made and, in itself, represented a gathering of material procured from others, and thus reflects the availability of individual and other collected texts in circulation.[79]

Insofar as they read about their own actual or ideal behavior, one scholar has suggested, these men were reconstructing scenes of action. Reading was a form of performance recall, or performance imagined.[80] Thus, reading

Figure 3.4. Fighting on foot in a tournament. This illustration from a late fifteenth-century manuscript, written to celebrate the career of Richard Beauchamp, Earl of Warwick, shows, in a single frame, three stages of individual combat. On the ground lie broken lances from an earlier phase when the men clashed on horseback; now the earl and his opponent fight on foot with axes, while attendants hold their swords ready for the next stage. The earl has just wounded his opponent in the shoulder, however, and the sponsor of the tournament, the Duke of Mantua, is ready to throw down his staff to end the contest. Note his ceremonial sword-bearer to the duke's right. © The British Library Board, 9/12/2019, Cotton Julius E. IV, art. 6, f.7v.

these texts, like actually witnessing or participating in a tournament itself, was an experience of virtuosity. Tournaments constituted practice in and celebrated exclusive forms of fighting, on horse and foot, with a variety of weapons; but they also served, in the event and in the remembrance of it in texts, to aestheticize violence. One historian has concluded that the textual world around tournaments constituted as dense an imaginative world, a textual community as rich and significant to its participants, as the world of epics and romances two centuries before, and that it was directed largely toward similar ends of glorifying both prowess and decorum.[81]

Once we appreciate the role of the tournament in life and in imagination, it proves difficult to come away from records of elites' material goods without having our impression reinforced that good armor was as important to them as any sword. Paul de Sade, though on the lower rung of the hierarchy, reflected this preoccupation with armor: having access to the right pieces, lending it out, making sure it was returned, having the proper accessories to use in the tournament field, and so on. In Fulk of Pembridge's will, from 1325, the swords are listed in the detailed shares each son receives—that is, they appear separately from each other, and at the end of the portions each of the two oldest boys are given.[82] Each provision of armor to a son consists of a list, loosely organized from the largest and most valuable pieces on down. Fulk Jr.'s begins with acketon (gambeson), then the "hauberk of steel," then "a pair of his [the father's] best plates," then a bassinet for the tourney, an aventail and so on down through the "gloves of plates" and several pairs of cuisses to protect the upper leg. The lists of belongings destined for the younger sons are organized in the same way. At the end of each list, when there is one, lies the sword; at the end of Fulk Jr.'s share is "a sword for war," *and* "a sword for tourney," and a set of spurs. Closing Robert's (the next eldest) list is "a pair of shoes and a sword." The will thus suggests that Fulk was intent, above all, on carefully dividing his collection of armor among his heirs.

Here, to conclude, we will weigh the characteristics of the written records themselves in order to nuance our understanding of the relative value of armor and swords in contemporaries' eyes. In fact, the kind of precise, rank-order list deployed in Fulk's will is quite rare. Inventories tended to be very literal: room by room, item by item as they are pulled from trunks, like the Earl of Hereford's belongings. There had to have been a prior moment of reflection on Fulk's collection of armor. Alternatively, the lists in the will could have been assembled from prior inventories of the items, in order to accomplish the choices required in disposing of his armor. The swords—barely described at all—appear almost as codicil to each bequest. It is not that swords are meaningless or insignificant; they are a backstop. They guarantee the status of the elder boys. Notably, the heir, Fulk Jr., must have one for war and one for tourney. Neither is identified as his father's "best" blade, or in any other specific terms. The attention to detail in this document is expended, apparently, on the armor.

Yet the growth of record keeping in this era should not lead us to believe that all that was important was written down; rather, documentary traces reflected and were dependent on personal memory and relationships, and this is key to perceiving the value of swords. When, in his 1319 will, Humphrey de Bohun declares that his eldest son should inherit "all my armor," he is calling on the memory of his servants and retainers, and perhaps the knowledge of his young heir, about twelve at the time, for that bequest to be fulfilled. The importance of memory and personal knowledge of the fate of objects is ironically revealed by Blanche of Navarre's long written description of the items she bequeaths in 1399. She tells us about rings she wore, about who had given her husband the belt she now bequeaths, and from whose hands she herself had gotten it. Knowledge of the life of an important object did not depend on a written record, though writing was useful for commissioning and paying for things, for recording guardianship of them, or in conveying them to others—such as in the long-lived Blanche's case, when the memory of recipients might not be adequate.

Thus, the relatively brisk references to swords we have remarked may reflect the importance of personal knowledge that superseded or undergirded the written record. In 1345, did the then-earl Humphrey, son of the man who died a rebel in 1322, need to know of, much less consult, a royal inventory, or any other document, to know that his father's sword, embellished with family arms, was in the king's hands? In 1399, his granddaughter bequeathed to her own son a velvet quilt with peacock feathers that had been named in the inventory of goods seized by the king from her great-grandfather some seventy years before. The connection to ancestors was surely known to her, just as her contemporary Blanche knew well the objects she bequeathed.[83] Why else would they have been deliberately passed onward?

There may have been less of a need to catalogue and describe swords than other belongings because creating and keeping documents, necessary for the staging and management of belongings, was necessary for goods that had lives to lead away from the person of the warrior in question. Swords were a requirement of elite status, but also required, in the fourteenth and fifteenth centuries, was investment in the wider array of ever-changing, fashionable clothing, rich textiles emblazoned with coats of arms, accessories sporting devices and signs, increasingly sophisticated pieces of armor, some of it specifically for the tourney, plus all the jewels, plate, relics, and exotic wares that a warrior could afford to amass. These goods, in turn, required managing—the commissioning, buying, repairing, protecting, transporting, bequeathing, and the management they required *in use*. All the tapestries in the world did no good if they were not strategically deployed, as Humphrey's green hangings scattered with swans must have been, or René's hangings chosen for his boat rides or dispatched to find him at a distant chateau.

René d'Anjou's relentless pursuit of lost pieces of tapestry in writing was in itself a form of protecting his honor by insisting on the attention and good service of go-betweens and craftsmen, and by defending his identity as it was represented in those objects. The paper and parchment trail he created was another form, another means, of staging his power symbolically and of reinforcing his connections with retainers and dependents carrying out his instructions. It also made visible to René himself the pursuit of the object as a goal, and it created another object—the letter itself, which bore his signature and seal. In short, documents we now mine for information were themselves valuable things, embedded in the world of goods they appear to document, and they were a further means of identifying with and relishing those goods, of extending their reach outward from the individual and impressing themselves, and their owner, on memory.[84] For someone like René, creating—which usually entailed dictating, thus literally a kind of performance—and handling documents were ways of staging his own status and experiencing the presence of an object.

Relative to other objects, swords in this world of stuff in motion appear thin on the ground to our eye, partly, I surmise, because they were kept close to hand by their owners. They are not yet numerous enough to be treated regularly as yet another commodity to track and manage. Yet where we can glimpse them, we can detect the forces of fashion at work, such as Paul de Sade's sword that is embellished by the latest method. We also note that an impulse toward collection building is extending to swords. In the most elite hands, in any case, it seems to have been important to have swords that could stand in different roles, representing different attributes of identity and power: lineage, divine protection, trophies from vanquished foes (and all the better when they were infidels), or pure luxurious excess, such as the sword-like ornaments intended for display only. Swords, even in these incipient collections, are surrounded by other belongings, other equipment essential to a warrior's status and to his functions—to the point of seeming to be eclipsed by them in the written record. Nor were swords always the killing weapon of choice in actual combat. But they were felt to be absolutely central, in their various incarnations, to a warrior's identity, to representing and safeguarding his power by both military and symbolic means such that the most marginal of the warrior elite—a mercenary captain or a parvenue from the world of commerce—sought out, even advertised, the distinction they embodied.

Chapter 4

Swords and Documents in the Sixteenth Century

Early in 1533, the twenty-eight-year-old French nobleman Jean de Dinteville found himself at the court of Henry VIII in London as an ambassador for his sovereign, Francis I. It was the second of what would become five stints as the French king's envoy to England, and it came at a crucial moment: Henry was in the process of claiming authority over the English church so that he could annul his marriage to Catherine of Aragon and marry his lover Anne Boleyn, whose crowning as queen Dinteville would soon witness. The international repercussions of Henry's moves were of great concern to Francis; he had only recently negotiated a treaty with Henry and was anxious to keep relations stable while he focused on his more powerful rival, the Holy Roman emperor Charles V. Meanwhile, Dinteville took advantage of his time at Henry's court to commission Hans Holbein ("the younger"), who had been working in England for six or seven years at the time, to execute a dual portrait of his fellow envoy, the Bishop Georges de Selve, and himself. This is the painting now housed in the National Gallery of Art in London known as *The Ambassadors*.

The Ambassadors was well known and admired in its own day and has fascinated modern scholars; it is one of the finest surviving examples of Renaissance portraiture, as well as the largest and arguably the most sophisticated of Holbein's extant work. It is almost mesmerizing in its artistry and complexity. Virtually all of the critical attention in recent years has focused on explaining the significance of the many objects depicted between the standing figures of Dinteville and Selve, on the two shelves of a wooden buffet. On the lower shelf, a book lies open to two pieces of music that were well-known Catholic anthems that had been translated into German for a Lutheran hymn book published in 1524—though these two selections did not actually appear on facing pages in the 1524 edition. The mathematics book on the lower shelf is propped open to a page depicting long division: the word "division" is easily visible. Is there an explicit message here about the dangers of discord, religious division? The lute perhaps contributes its "discord": one of its strings curls up, broken.

The subjects, Dinteville and Selve, each lean an arm on the upper shelf. Crowded there, between their elbows, lie six scientific instruments. Do these

PLATE 4. Hans Holbein's *The Ambassadors*. French nobleman Jean de Dinteville, left, and the young bishop, Georges de Selve, stand beside a buffet displaying books, a lute, and various calculating instruments. Note the crucifix almost obscured by the green drapes in the upper left corner. © National Gallery, London / Art Resource, NY.

objects contribute to some message of disharmony or, alternatively, since most of the instruments could function as timekeepers and seem not to be working properly, offer some hint about the passage of time or the times being out of joint? Or, as one recent scholar has argued, are all these instruments calibrated to depict one specific date and time: Christ's death on the cross on Good Friday?[1] And what might the most baffling element of all, the distorted skull at the men's feet, contribute to whatever message is intended: perhaps some invocation of the brevity of life? The only thing we can be absolutely sure of is that these two shelves full of instruments, books, and globes are not merely a display of riches; even if they were that, no one at the time would have missed the opportunity to make layers of comments with symbols of various kinds embedded in the selection of objects, which would repay their contemporaries' (and historians') attention. Speculating about the importance of the individual items is especially invited because Dinteville and his friend Selve stand on either side of the buffet, framing the marvelous objects between them.

Comparatively little attention, in contrast, has been given to the figures of the two men. Selve, we note, wears appropriately muted yet still luxurious robes in velvet damask. Dinteville, however, is the model of a fashionable courtier. He wears a skirted black velvet doublet over a rose satin shirt that has been artfully slashed to reveal the white silk shirt beneath. Holbein's artistry in depicting the textiles helps the viewer appreciate their splendor: the weight of the velvet skirt, the soft folds of the pink satin that respond to Dinteville's body beneath. Note, for example, the way the chain around his neck creates a ridge in the fabric and the pleats of silk on his forearm, poised on the shelf. Over the ensemble is a coat trimmed in lynx fur (note also that the fur peeks out of further deliberate vents, held closed by golden fasteners). His fashionable soft hat sports gold accents as well.[2]

The viewer's eye is drawn to the badge of the royal Order of St. Michel that hangs from his neck by a heavy gold chain and even more emphatically to the sheathed dagger Dinteville holds in his right hand. The dagger and its decorative tassel, like the pendant, were executed first in earth tones then finished with a process known as mordant gilding, which Holbein used in other works, and, finally, with gold powder applied meticulously with the finest of brushes.[3] We can note the elaborate design etched into the gold sheath and pommel and we can feel the weight of the blue and gold knotted tassel. The dagger is not fixed to his belt, where it would normally rest, but hangs loosely, almost insouciantly, in his hand, where we cannot fail to note the sexual reference.

Amid all of this suggestive sartorial display, Dinteville's sword is barely visible at all. We can just glimpse part of the pommel and guard set against the lynx fur on his left side and, behind his leg, the tip of the scabbard. Otherwise, the sword is completely hidden. The tip points to an object that lies askew on the floor underneath the buffet behind him: the case for the lute displayed on the bottom shelf of the buffet. The sword, in short, appears as an essential prop, but one that does not need to, does not even try to, call attention to itself. Dinteville's stance—left foot forward, arm raised—easily and naturally accommodates its weight. We note the sword's existence but require nothing else of it here. Unless it is an anomaly, somehow out of sync with its surroundings, a commonplace object cannot call attention to itself.[4] In this respect the sword contrasts sharply with the crucifix just visible in the upper left-hand corner of the panel, behind the edge of the green curtain. What is that most familiar of symbols doing *there*, almost offstage? Its anomalous position invites our curiosity.

But not so with Dinteville's sword. The sword is just present, less an object requiring explanation than simply part of the tableau, a necessary backdrop. In this way, it mimics how many swords are represented in contemporary documentation: there, but nonetheless hard to glimpse. In surveying inventories generated by elite households, as in viewing *The Ambassadors*, swords appear to be inconspicuous in comparison to many other material effects, in part because their presence is taken for granted. However, a closer look at when and how swords *are* mentioned in surviving documentation enables us to say more: they were taken for granted because of their significance, not because they were overlooked or marginal to elite life. They were, in fact, known to contemporaries in ways efforts at documentation did not easily capture. Their relative invisibility in some records is in fact evidence of swords' particular importance. Therefore, when they become the deliberate focus of documentation—as they do in the royal list of venerable weapons created in 1499—our attention must focus on what that written record, in its precise features, was designed to accomplish. This chapter closes with a reconsideration of that captivating source: what significance do those legendary objects, and the precise record of them, have now, in Jean de Dinteville's world?

In the opening chapter, I also posed questions about two other documentary vignettes of the life of swords in the sixteenth century. The first, from early 1525, was an inventory at the death of a French nobleman who had been fighting with the forces of Francis I in Italy. That document details the contents of an entire chateau in central France but captures the belongings that this Sire de Mézières had taken to Italy, all still in their trunks from the journey home. The second inventory, from half a century later, lists garments and accessories left behind when their owner traveled to England on

FIGURE 4.1. Hans Holbein's *The Ambassadors*, detail. The hilt of Dinteville's sword is just visible above his left hip, set off against the white background of the lynx fur. The tip of the scabbard is visible behind his left leg, next to the upturned lute case. © National Gallery, London / Art Resource, NY.

his own embassy of sorts. These snapshots of belongings hinted at a transformation over that time from a lifeworld in which a nobleman fought with
a battle sword that had some personal association and would have been recognizable as such hundreds of years earlier, to one where that man would
wear a sword in a matched set with a dagger, more an ornament, a piece of
jewelry chosen for an outfit, than a memorable weapon. Those who could
afford them, like François de Bourbon, Duke of Montpensier, in 1576, would
own many such "sets," just as they would doublets, cloaks, and actual jewels.

We have already complicated that narrative by noting that many blades, in
prior centuries, were neither simple workaday weapons or pure ornament,
but both, like the embellished sword that meant so much to Paul de Sade.
We have also noticed that individual aristocrats saved "foreign," or old or
outmoded weapons, some clearly as trophies; the Sire de Mézières carried
a gilt-embellished braquemart "of antique design" to Italy with him; eighty
years before, René d'Anjou had his "Moorish" blade, and, another century
before that, the Earl of Hereford his "Saracen" one. In this final chapter,
I return to the inventories I introduced at the outset and reconsider them
within the contexts of political conditions as well as of elites' material surroundings in the sixteenth century.

My sampling of inventories, accounts, and correspondence from French
and English aristocrats and gentry in the sixteenth century reveals that both
"kinds" of swords—working weapons and jewel-like accessories—coexisted
for a long time and were never wholly distinct in contemporary sensibilities. In fact, they were both part of an increasingly crowded landscape of
swords that included, now, crude weapons manufactured in large numbers
solely for ritual or sport. The sword did not somehow change character
over a few decades and leave its wearers denuded of their iconic belonging.
And the men who bought, wore, wielded, and bequeathed these swords
did not feel the need to "reconcile" one kind of sword with another. It was
and is the business of warrior culture to claim and stage continuity with the
past. Swords over time might take on new attributes, indeed provide new
symbolic opportunities, but old roles would not be jettisoned. Therein lay
a major component of its symbolic power: a sword could be unadorned
or elegant, memorable or alien—and always, simultaneously, be a weapon.
Because one dimension of its materiality was undeniable—its lethal cutting edge, or its point—the rest was a malleable form with many potential
resonances. Swords came into the sixteenth century capable of assisting a
man like Dinteville with his claim to the privilege of violence and with the
many roles that might be required of him as a member of the elite: warrior,
courtier, ambassador.

The strategic and material circumstances in which warrior elites were enmeshed by the early sixteenth century had changed, in certain important respects, in comparison with the century before. A Tudor monarch more secure on his throne than his Plantagenet forebears of the fifteenth century vied and sometimes cooperated with the French king, Francis I, across the Channel. For both of them, the rise of the Hapsburg emperor and king of united Spain, Charles V, was the major strategic challenge; fighting, including several large-scale battles between the French and imperial forces, lasted until 1558. Religious dissent led to uprisings, outright revolt, and civil war that plagued all these rulers and their successors, and forced stark choices about personal defense and political loyalty onto elites. Both religious rebels and political rivals made good use of the printing press to circulate information, self-advertisement, and images of political horrors and achievements alike.

Also new were certain weapons, particularly gunpowder weapons, and new uses of old ones. Artillery was now more mobile and thus more effective in battle itself, as well as in sieges; and, in battle between Francis's and Charles's armies in 1525, handheld firearms were first used in open battle to decisive tactical effect. By midcentury, most elite fighters would have owned a set of pistols, in addition to their swords. Pistols were not particularly deadly firearms to begin with, and they often malfunctioned. Precisely because they had to be used at close range, and were both finicky and expensive to repair, they were an elite man's weapon, too.[5] Armor and swords, meanwhile, benefited from further improvements in steelmaking, rendering strong breastplates that were proof against bullets and creating the possibility of increasingly supple blades. Not until the end of the century, however, did contemporaries use the term "rapier" and "sword" to distinguish two distinct styles of bladed weapon.[6] Throughout the century, swords existed in many varied types.

If we look more closely at warriors' belongings in the sixteenth century, we see that daggers continued to have a starring role. We have noted that, beginning in the fourteenth century, renderings of daggers embellish funerary monuments; ornate daggers are created to mark royal celebrations and are exchanged as gifts; certain daggers are so adorned with gold and precious stones that they are listed among the jewels in aristocrats' collections, when we find written trace of them. In the sixteenth century, daggers carry decorative power, captured in inventories, even when swords do not. Tassels specified for daggers appear often in lists of personal accoutrements. Jean de Dinteville's tassel-trimmed dagger in Holbein's portrait is a fine example of elaborate metalwork; a close examination reveals that his age (he is in his twenty-ninth year in 1533) is inscribed on the sheath. It is worth the effort the artist expended on rendering the golden thread and worked metal because a dagger could readily command attention. In another example, the inventory makers in 1525, taking note of the late Sire de Mézières's things, list two daggers with their velvet sheaths and two poignards; one is decorated with coral, the other with silver and, like Dinteville's, it sports a tassel.[7] Across the Channel, in 1526, the bastard son of Henry VIII, the duke of Richmond, owned, at the tender age of seven, an ornate dagger, "the scabbard and haft well-trimmed or garnished with silver and gilt," and a wood knife, "with a scabbard and girdle of green velvet, the buckle and pendants of the same gilt."[8]

We know from their own words that even modest warriors wore their swords accompanied with daggers as they went about their routines. In 1557, for example, one nobleman complained to his commander, the Duke of Guise, about one Sire de Beaumont who was always getting into violent scrapes with peers in the French camp, on campaign against the emperor's forces. The details of the confrontations reveal that all the men concerned carried swords and daggers on their persons.[9] While sword-and-dagger combinations were commonly worn by even modest warriors, the ability to collect and to wear luxurious versions of them set aristocrats apart, as they were intended to do.

Meanwhile, surviving records reveal the sheer number of weapons of all types now in private hands. Many grand chateaus and modest manor houses alike both in France and England were provisioned with cannon, handguns, crossbows, longbows, and pike weapons in number, sometimes virtual stockpiles of these weapons and of armor, reflecting a warrior's (or his relatives') service in war, and the needs of many fighters beyond himself. Sir Robert Wingfield, for example, in 1541, carefully dispersed his valuable armor and two swords to his nephews, and added to each bequest armor for foot soldiers (the elder nephew gets twelve sets) and halberds enough for them all. The armor in question is "rivets," meaning chest protection composed of joined small plates of steel. The first Earl of Southampton made a generous bequest to his young son, and also presents his son-in-law with a portion of plate and other goods, including *one hundred pairs of* rivets—body armor enough for a raft of retainers.[10] When the young Earl of Arundel was attainted in 1589, he left behind substantial supplies of armor and lances that probably dated from his grandfather's (the prior earl's) career, who had been an active soldier on the continent into the 1550s: not fewer than 436 pikes, and some 300 chest plates or other protective armor, plus tools for fabricating and maintaining most of them.[11]

Supplies of these weapons and armor circulated between these elite families too. In 1560, for example, one English knight buys some three hundred staff weapons, handguns, and pieces of armor from the estate of a fellow knight, for whom he served as executor.[12] In a later inventory, from 1586, we learn that collections of light horse armor and staff weapons sufficient for thirty men are now all in the hands of other knightly families.[13] Among the most frequently purchased or bequeathed items are horse armor and other trappings produced for war, for ceremonial occasions, and for jousting, just as in the fifteenth century.[14] Knights purchase elegant saddles and bards from other estates, and they are discriminating in their choices, in ways we cannot parse—choosing, for example, a well-used velvet saddle cloth over other, seemingly less worn, items.[15]

And there are guns. Cannon had been common in chateaus and manors since the fifteenth century, but now harquebuses, early versions of muskets, are present in many households, as are pistols. Robert Dudley, Earl of Leicester, owned at least two sets of pistols, and bequeathed them as memorial heirlooms to his friends. By midcentury, handguns had already earned a role in ritual. In 1568, for example, a magnificent procession from ducal chateau to the cathedral was staged for the baptism of the infant Catherine of Gonzaga, daughter of the Duke of Nevers. As always, luxurious textiles played their part—in this case, the entire journey from residence to church was covered in cloth and lined with tapestries. First to march in the actual parade to the cathedral, however, was a troop of harquebusiers "in good order, both in attire and in arms," says the witness, who estimated their number as "about three or four hundred."[16] And individual guns could be embellished and honored in ways we have previously noted swords might be. At the time of his death in 1557, François de La Tour d'Auvergne, Viscount of Turenne, was conveying, in his baggage, four wondrous items together: an ensign "with a number of persons painted on it," a chemise that "it is said" belonged to Notre Dame de Chartres, a spoon made "of unicorn horn bordered in silver," and an "harquebus *for war, gilded.*"[17]

When we turn to track gifts among elites, the picture of their lifeworld widens to include the great variety of their prestige goods beyond these growing collections of weapons. Foremost among gifts was expensive, ornamental plate—tableware mostly intended for display in domestic spaces or for ceremonial use. Pieces of plate were, aside from full suits of armor, the most expensive items that a warrior owned. In 1568, for example, when the king of France sends a raft of items to the noble governor of strategic northern towns, with instructions regarding how to disperse the goods to other commanders in the area, all the gifts are pieces of plate. The highest-ranking noble in need of a "reward" gets one basin and one vase, both gilded, two large covered chalices, two saltcellars, and a buffet on which to mount all of it: total value 749 *livres tournois*. Cups and chalices presented individually, to more junior commanders, are described in some detail so that they are distributed to the right recipients. One has a "little Bacchus" on it, but most of them sport a "man at arms" or, in one instance, a man-at-arms wielding a lance. These cups might bear a military theme but above all they were prestige items cementing and advertising a connection—and a source of ready cash for the recipient in case of need.[18]

Gifts among warriors routinely included such chalices and platters, as well as jewels, pendants, and collars. Elite men also exchanged hunting paraphernalia, including dogs and birds for the purpose. And they continued to exchange clothing, especially at times of important public events such as royal marriages or funerals.[19] Worthy gowns and cloaks are specified in wills, to be given to noble attendants for the funeral solemnities and for their personal use thereafter, or simply to the men and women in allied families to reward friendship and strengthen the alliance for heirs. The new owners of gifted clothing, through a will or in life, often passed it on to others of their acquaintance, or dispersed it to dependents.[20]

But gifts between gentry or aristocrats virtually never included swords, except in rare instances when bequeathed in a will, and only then when there was no obvious heir, for whom particular items need not be mentioned.[21] Typical of a will that does not identify many individual bequests because sons survive the testator is one from an English knight, in 1517. He specifies only that his wife get what belongs (already) to her, whatever that may be, plus some gilt spoons, a saltcellar, and his best bed (meaning all its rich covers and hangings); the eldest son gets the second-best bed and a gilt spoon, younger children spoons also, and to daughters, money for their dowries. He thus concentrates on the precious items he wants to share out fairly, and there are no arms or armor among them; the rest of the will is devoted to directing the executor to establish Masses and support the priests who say them after his death.[22]

In 1541, another knight, Sir Robert Wingfield, carefully enumerates valuable bedding left to his wife, bequeaths some clothing to his close friends and allies, and then divides his arms and armor among his nephews, echoing the careful dispersals of arms we have noted from the fourteenth and fifteenth centuries.[23] The luckiest (likely the eldest) nephew, John, gets luxurious horse trappings of crimson velvet embroidered with Robert's crest and a tent with all the accessories required, a small shield and Robert's light armor, a saddle for the joust and, finally, "mine arming sword." But his brother gets the armor "made in Augsburg"—which produced the finest armor at the time—"and my two-handed sword," a weapon usually often chosen for ritualized combat on foot. Sir Robert, one could conclude, was most interested in sharing out his showiest equipment, likely for the joust: horse trappings to one nephew, the best armor to the other. Though he is careful to share them out too, swords are not singled out here, above and beyond armor, as signature bequests.

Often, weapons are not mentioned at all, just armor and its accessories, with the catchall term "harness." For example, the Earl of Southampton wills to his minor son in 1550 "all my harnesse and furniture of my armore not hereafter bequeathed." (Later in the document, we learn that the executors are to choose which "harness" actually goes to him and which to the earl's son-in-law.) He is careful also to state that his son will enjoy the use of four hundred marks' worth of plate—gilded and partially gilded, he specifies—while young, which he will then own when of age.[24]

The will of Elizabeth I's favorite, Robert Dudley, Earl of Leicester (d. 1588), bequeaths one sword among gifts of horses, armor, plate, jewels, and guns, all very deliberately passed to chosen friends and relations, before the rest is settled on his illegitimate son.[25] This will is worth picking through in some detail for the glimpses it provides of the circulation of objects: what items had been gifted before the will was drawn up; the personal associations the items convey and the hints of the life of swords amid these other objects. First, after a long preamble of praise for her, is a bequest of jewels to the queen. Then, to each of his "dear friends," the lord chancellor, his brother the Earl of Warwick and Lord Howard, Leicester makes three detailed bequests in which richly ornamented plate circulates in a leading role, as signature gifts that ensure remembrance. His "old dear friend" the chancellor, Christopher Hatton, receives a gilt "great basin and ewer"; his brother, explicitly "for remembrance" gets a "cup of gold which my Lord of Pembroke [a courtier closely allied with Leicester] gave me"; third, to his "most noble friend" Howard, another gilt ewer and basin, decorated with one of Leicester's personal devices. Here we have an explicit mention of one characteristic that many of these bequests—including plate, jewels, as well as armor—would have shared: decoration with personal devices and other versions of heraldic signs.

After mentioning the plate presented to each friend, Leicester honors both Hatton and Warwick with his orders of the Garter—in other words, the medallions of the Order worn around the neck—heraldry of literally the highest order. Hatton gets "my best" one, "not doubting that he shall shortly be enjoying the wearing of it," while Warwick gets a medallion that is both the English Order and the French Order of Saint Michel "in one." Hatton also gets "one of his armors which he gave me." There are other testatees, including no less a person than William Cecil, Lord Burghley, Elizabeth's most trusted adviser. He and a few other peers and kin receive cups or basins and ewers too.

Weapons and armor are mentioned in only three of Leicester's bequests: his brother-in-law gets a ring, a horse "with its furnishings," and a case of pistols. His stepson, the Earl of Essex, receives Leicester's best armor, which, Leicester notes, Hatton had previously given to him, as well as two horses and another "George and Garter," again with hopes that he would be authorized to wear it shortly (Essex is pictured wearing the Garter medallion in a later portrait). Only Lord Howard, his "most noble friend," gets a sword: in fact, "my best sword," as well as his best horse, his best cannon, and, once again, a case of pistols.

Leicester's bequests remind us that precious ware like cups and basins circulated between friends and would-be allies, doing the simultaneously personal and political work of creating obligation, thus currying favor, in the recipient.[26] Armor circulates here too, as we have noted in records from prior centuries. All of them could have displayed personal devices that may not be recorded in the will, but were known to those involved. Displaying an embossed platter or wearing a recognizable collar or piece of armor publicized the recipient's connections, past and present.

Concerning swords, we have less information. Leicester owns more than one, as he writes the will, but we cannot tell how many he might have had or what their features were. He expects his contemporaries to know, however, and thus need no descriptions. In fact, he expects his executor and Lord Howard, at least, to recognize which sword is his "best sword," the one destined for this "most noble friend," just as he seems to expect that the identity of "his best Garter" will be obvious to all the principals involved. His will does not spell out what his closest friends and allies already know.

So, we face a problem of the relative silence of these sources on the subject of the swords; we want to know more about how this near silence should be interpreted. As we have seen, this relative silence concerning swords existed in fourteenth- and fifteenth-century sources too, but it persists in sixteenth-century records, when more and more family records survive. The fact of this silence for us of course always reflects lacunae: a document is missing, such as an inventory after death; some documents are created only for limited and immediate purpose, such as to keep track of Montpensier's belongings left behind in 1576.

Another reason for the information missing for us, now, was confusion about what category of goods swords constituted at the time. Many inventories cover the furnishings of houses and castles, while clothing, books, and, above all, precious tableware and jewels are often given inventories of their own. Thus, one type of inventory can survive from a family's goods, but other categories of belongings went unrecorded for posterity.[27] "Arms," however that was understood, can appear in multiple places. Armor for man and horse can be found in trunks within a chateau or, as the century wears on, in rooms labeled "armory," though the contents are not always detailed in an inventory of the residence. "Armory" was also a concept, a category, and could constitute a way of recording information that did not mean the items were all in one place, much less a dedicated location.[28] Arms in the sense of weapons are typically scattered throughout chateaus, too. Great halls sport pikes, lances, and halberds, gatehouses have canons—all of them likely captured in any inventory of the chateau's contents. Meanwhile, crossbows and harquebuses and more staff weapons are scattered, at the ready, in several chambers.

But in many inventories of both personal belongings and of castles, there are no swords, because the inventory considers only furnishings—and personal items are not treated as such—or, more rarely, because an inventory lists only clothing and what we would call accessories, such as jewels, caps, belts, and shoes, and the inventory maker chose not to include armor, daggers, or swords. One inventory from the late fifteenth century is an exception. The inventory after the death of a Hertfordshire gentry man, Robert Morton, records the contents of various chambers plus certain categories of belongings such as "nappery." One category, "gowns and other wearing stuff," includes nine furred gowns, twenty additional gowns, some lengths of expensive fabric, two doublets in damask and silk, and two brigandines, body armor fitted like a doublet made of small plates fastened to fabric. The only sword among Morton's belongings appears here, with other "wearing stuff." The inventory makers classified Morton's sword as they imagined it to be: something that he wore.[29]

Swords, in short, were a category unto themselves, consistently neither furnishings nor clothing nor arms nor ornaments; even their mere presence, much less any detail of their appearance or value, can elude written records. Running household accounts could be an exception: in them, we can see purchases and repairs, and thereby glimpse swords, which is how we often spied important weapons in prior centuries. In 1520, for example, the household accounts of Sir Thomas Lestrange, sheriff of Norfolk, note the cost of refurbishing *"your* sword." The sword does not need to be identified by appearance or decoration: there is only the one. Two years later, "master's arming sword," likely the same weapon, is cleaned and, three years after that, "trimmed," that is, given a new scabbard, by the same artisan who provided a stylish velvet bonnet purchased at the same time.[30]

Where inventories are concerned, we often find only brisk references to battle-worthy swords. While the daggers among the Sire de Mézières's things, as we noted, are depicted in some detail, his swords are not. They are listed simply as two "epées d'armes," arming swords, one of which has a gray velvet scabbard. His contemporary, the child duke of Richmond, had an ornate dagger and a knife, both described with their decorative features. His two swords, on the other hand, were just that: "two swords."[31]

The exceptions were the multiple sword-and-dagger sets in the hands of great aristocrats that now required managing as luxuries, often accumulated and left behind in a guardian's care, as the Duke of Montpensier's collection had been in 1576. Such collections appear earlier in the century as well. François de La Tour d'Auvergne, Viscount of Turenne, one of the French commanders killed in 1557 at the battle of St. Quentin, owned at least eleven sword-and-dagger sets at his death at the relatively young age of thirty-one. An inventory of his belongings held at two chateaus dutifully notes some of their distinctive features: "a sword and dagger, with gilded guards"; "another sword and dagger with rounded guards and sheaths covered in cloth"; among those at a second residence, "a sword and dagger with velvet scabbard, with a leaf design executed in gold, with a guard in the bastard style."[32]

Turenne's inventories are complete enough to see that a man of his status owned many sword-and-dagger "outfits" but also a variety of other blades, some potentially usable in battle, as well as trophy-like curiosities. Back at his ancestral residence in the Auvergne, the viscount had left more than twenty swords and other bladed weapons. Of them, five are listed with their matching daggers. The other blades are identified by particular features, typically of hilt or scabbard: for example, "a sword made with a twisted guard in the form of a snake," likely a recent hilt form, or "with a cross like the beak of a falcon." A few of the swords are described more cursorily as "large," one is specified as "two-handed," four are described as "bracquemards," thus single-bladed weapons, three are "espieus," a long-bladed staff weapon used for boar hunting. In the midst of all of this appears "a Turkish scimitar hanging from a fine chain, with a leather scabbard." The collection also includes a grab bag of other weapons: crossbows, longbows, "Turkish" bows (likely compound recurved bows), harquebuses for war and for hunting, then, randomly, dog collars, several well-used horse trappings, bits of bridles, some gilded spurs, and empty cases of various descriptions.

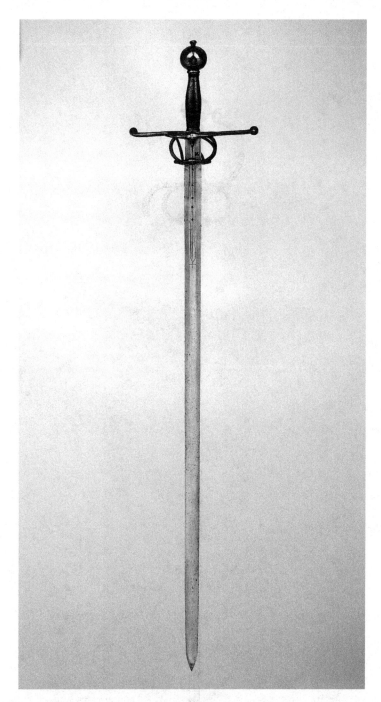

FIGURE 4.2. Two sixteenth-century swords (here and the following page). Both of these swords date from the middle of the sixteenth century, though they differ in style, and are distinct in dimensions and weight. The cruciform-hilted sword, left, is about two inches shorter than its contemporary, but at more than four pounds, weighs one and a half times as much. The elaborate gilded hilt on the second sword covers the widest portion of the blade, which tapers quickly to a much narrower point. We might call the second type a rapier, but that term was not used in contemporary documents, such as those recording the swords of François de Turenne. Credit: Wallace Collection, London, UK/Bridgeman Images.

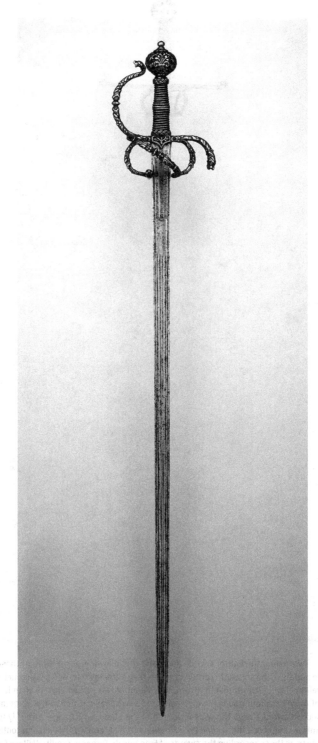

The belongings left behind at his northern estate, on the Ourcq River, on the other hand, reveal that Turenne had more recently been in residence there. He kept tableware and plate, including two chalices displaying the arms of the Order of St. Michel, which he had just been awarded earlier that year. And there are boots and hose, shirts, doublets, coats and capes, as well as a stash of surplus buttons and fasteners in gold and enamel, no doubt for further garments, as necessary. Among them, sandwiched on the list between pairs of boots and more dog collars, are six of Turenne's sword-and-dagger pairs. There are also books and surplus armor. At the end of this lengthy catalogue lurk the four one-of-a-kind items: the painted ensign, the chemise (a woman's undergarment) of Notre Dame de Chartres, the spoon of unicorn horn, and the gilded harquebus. These are precious items that he kept close by, like the fragment of the true cross that shows up in the Sire de Mézières's belongings returned from Italy. What Turenne does not leave behind here, close to where he died, are any other swords.

The partial and sometimes total silence on the subject of swords in many documents is thus telling: it suggests not the insignificance of swords but rather that personal association with and particular reliance on a few chosen weapons persisted, but were still not easily captured by lists created for administrative or legal purposes. The fact that they eluded classification in many documents is an important piece of evidence about their unique value in contemporary eyes. The Earl of Leicester's will assumes that his friends and family know which is his best sword, we have noted. Turenne's inventory of two chateaus reveals many weapons but does not record the weapons and armor he took with him, into the fighting that killed him. Mézières's goods, in 1525, do record what he took with him because the belongings have been brought home, and left in their traveling trunks to be recorded; among them are two swords, sketchily described. No doubt Turenne's battle equipment would have included the same had they been recorded too.

Sometimes documents do reveal that the equipment that was most valued was kept close at hand. The chateau of Huguenot memoirist Pierre de Bourdeille, Sire de Brantôme, at the time of his death includes more than 150 books, but also, scattered in different chambers, more than thirty muskets and harquebuses as well as a handful of cannon and supplies of gunpowder.[33] Amid the many muskets and supplies of armor sufficient to outfit a dozen men are just two swords. But what is noteworthy about them is where they are: they are not stored with other arms but lie in the chamber where Brantôme died, along with his bedding, trunks with some of his clothing (the garderobe next door holds the rest), and some sixty of his books. We know that a trunk might hold goods just returned from or about to go out on a journey; chateaus' goods, in inventories, are often snapshots of belongings in motion. So, the location of his only swords near Brantôme's person when he died seems especially significant because Brantôme, we know, had retired from public life twenty-five years before his death. The swords are not in the trunk, packed away with other "wearing things," but their location close to his person suggests they were essential accoutrements to him.

Another glimpse comes from a will, that of the admiral of France Bernard de Nogaret, Sire de La Valette, dated January 1592. Again, we learn more than we otherwise might because the admiral has no living children. His jewels and most other "movables" are to be sold to pay for the construction of a convent and hospital, in addition to a new church where he and his wife will be buried. A few individual bequests follow, all of luxurious textiles: his late wife's dresses are given to various religious establishments "to make ornaments from them"; two cousins and two other friends each get a bed, that is, a set of covers and hangings. Finally, to one particular ally and friend, "all of my equipment for war, including horses and arms, *if they are to be found near me or in my control when I die.*"[34]

The will anticipates the circumstances that eventuated shortly thereafter: La Valette did die one month later, at the siege of Rocquebrune, in southern France, where he had been commanding royal troops against rebel forces opposed to Henry IV's rule. Thus, La Valette would die literally in harness, so his arms and war horses could pass to his friend *if* they were found near his person. Yet why did it matter that all this equipment be near him, in order to be bequeathed? I believe this document unwittingly sheds light on the unanswered question that other documents pose: what happens to all the arms—armor, horse trappings, swords—that are not mentioned in a document like this?

This provision in his will seems to anticipate that arms would easily disappear from a battlefield, if he died fighting, or might be subsumed into and hard to extract from larger assemblages of belongings otherwise. Again, this provision assumes that the friend will recognize La Valette's equipment when he sees it. More importantly, preserved here also is the assumption that connection to his person is important; it matters that La Valette not only used these things but had them in his possession, close to him, in his hands or on his body, at death. This is an echo of Blanche of Navarre's assurances, almost two hundred years before, that the ring she bequeaths had been worn by herself and her late husband King Philip. There is a determination in these cases that important items—rings, horses, or weapons—continue a man's legacy by being transferred intimately, from his body or at least from his sight to the hands of a close friend, in default of heirs. The authenticity of the belongings, their lineage, matters.

Thus, we note continuity, here, with the habits of prior generations. Luxurious clothing and precious metal plate are the first prestige items acquired and feature prominently among personal collections and as gifts at all ranks; armor is highly prized, exchanged as signature gifts and bequeathed very deliberately; heraldic signs, colors, and badges are gifted back and forth as emblems of affinity. As we have seen, there is even an actual market in these items: used weapons and armor and horse trappings are often snapped up when offered for sale to be repaired or refurbished or sold onward for the metal or the fabric; luxurious garments could be worn or remade into other "ornaments," including items bearing recognizable heraldic signs, which carry the identity of the donor into their new role.

Documents designed to track all these items do not spend as much ink and paper recording swords, except when the swords are sufficiently decorated to rise to the level of luxurious ornament or curious trinket and have been left behind in the guard of a retainer or must be inventoried for heirs. In those cases, they are treated like any other kind of item, dutifully recorded one by one. But the one or two swords most valued by each man are still kept in such close proximity to him that they rarely turn up in records of belongings left behind or otherwise in need of an accounting—except in (also rare) cases like that of the Sire de Mézières, whose trunkfuls of accoutrements return from the battlefield and are inventoried with the other household fixtures. Instead, we catch glimpses of swords when they are sent out to be repaired or are bequeathed to a friend. Though mostly out of our view, they are close at hand, known to familiars. Modest noblemen and gentry might still rely on only one or two swords, and so do the wealthy, even when they owned literally dozens more. These most valued weapons often evade list makers but they were emphatically *there*.

Their relative invisibility, in other words, is a sign of their importance. However, the glimpses we get should not tantalize us into fetishizing these weapons or to undervaluing the many other blades in warrior hands. First of all, the supposed contrast of battle swords versus decorative swords, useful versus ornamental, is an oversimplification. The presence of Turenne's collections of ornate "sets," not to mention Dinteville's elegant sword and dagger, reminds us that varieties of blades—some of which we arbitrarily conventionalize with the terms broadsword and rapier—coexisted from at least the first third of the century, quite apart from the many other blade types, like braquemarts, already available and amassed in individual hands. There was no transition, abrupt or otherwise, from one "kind" of sword to another, as though men were jettisoning their pasts. We see, in their mixed collections, that the life of swords in the sixteenth century could include a life as a wearable ornament, as collectible trophy, as an heirloom or ceremonial blade or prop for tourneys or duels, or as a battle-worthy weapon with strong personal associations. One kind of sword, or use of a sword, did not exclude or diminish the other and, together, the swords both made claims in the present and attached a warrior to his past.

We should also pause to imagine the saturating effect that accumulations of swords-as-accessories and individual swords-as-heirlooms had on their material environment. These other blades were gathered deliberately and often chosen as companions. Turenne had six sets of decorative swords and daggers with him in northern France; Mézières carried an inlaid sword "of antique design" to fighting in Italy, along with his other weapons. Indeed, we should think about these various weapons as different types with distinct roles, and also as sharing attributes and functions. While it is true that jewel-like swords were more suited to courtly self-presentation than to battle, they were nevertheless weapons ready for use when a confrontation spilled over into violence. Every sword included a blade, and thus none was "merely" decorative; the virtuosity of a potentially lethal blade was part of the artistry of the whole. A sword "of antique design," such as the one belonging to Mézières, could be both a trophy and a memento, representing a link to past family achievements. To believe that a warrior wielded a single "meaningful" weapon, which carried all his authority, identity, and honor with it, is nostalgia—and ignores the material record.

In fact, by the early sixteenth century elite men lived in a veritable sea of swords, above and beyond their own personal collections. Since the fifteenth century, more available steel enabled the manufacture of more and better armor but also more swords, which, we have seen, regularly found their way into the hands of modest fighters. Contemporary depictions of massacres and battles in the French religious wars after 1562 portray many fighters, even when contemporaries believed them to be common folk, wearing or wielding a sword. The images are all the more compelling as an effort at authenticity because the swords depicted vary in size and style. Some are short, some are long two-handed swords; grips and pommels are fashioned in diverse styles.

The proliferation of sword styles created opportunities for discrimination and distinction in expertise as well as ownership. The diversity of available bladed weapons, in turn, was reflected in the parallel availability of advice books for elite men on hand-to-hand staged combat as well as on the choice of blade for real self-defense, whether in battle or in a duel. One late fifteenth-century text was entirely devoted to instructions for one-on-one

FIGURE 4.3. Swords in action at midcentury. Several kinds of swords are depicted in this contemporary engraving of a famous massacre in 1562 that helped trigger decades of religious war in France. On the right, one soldier raises a single-edged curved braquemart; other soldiers use versions of the sharply pointed swords common since the fifteenth century. The commander, standing left center, wields a narrower blade, of more recent manufacture. Note, far right, the man shooting a harquebus is depicted also wearing sword and dagger. © RMN-Grand Palais / Art Resource, NY.

combat "whether for sport or in earnest" with a single-edged weapon, the braquemart; other late medieval manuals were virtual encyclopedias of technique—for standard long sword, for buckler (a small handheld shield) and knife, for poleax and so on.[35] The usefulness of different styles of swords was still debated at the end of the century—for example, in a 1599 manuscript dedicated to the Earl of Essex. The author of that work argues that short swords, rather than the lengthy, supple blades now popular, were better for both actual battle as well as for duels.[36] Multiple blade and hilt styles persisted through the century; dress swords, worn every day, were not always rapier-like (which, in any case, were routinely just called "swords" in documentation until the end of the century) and were certainly not the only blades with which dueling expertise might be perfected.

Supplementing the various swords now widespread in fighters' hands were the blades made in their hundreds for mock battles. For example, the accounts from one French aristocrat's household in 1514, the year of Louis XII's marriage to his second wife, the sister of Henry VIII, describe a staggering array of gifts of clothing to English peers, of horse trappings, and of festive garments for his own retinue, including newly made scabbards covered in white velvet and lengths of white taffeta for coordinating sword belts. But the accounts also list literally hundreds of weapons manufactured expressly for the celebratory jousts: more than fifteen hundred lances of various descriptions and almost four hundred swords—little ones, two-handed ones, arming swords are all included. The swords alone cost about 450 *livres tournois*. And this figure comes only from one account, designed to justify one man's expenditures, and does not necessarily represent the total outlay even by this one Frenchman, who happened to be François, Duke of Valois and Count of Angoulême, who became King Francis I when Louis died the following year.[37]

By the mid-fifteenth century, the kings of England had taken responsibility for substantial manufacture of ordnance, armor, and edged weapons. Henry VIII would make his mark—partly to counter royal rivals in Scotland and abroad—by improving the manufacture of armor in royal workshops. Known as "Greenwich armor," it became a fashionable and sought-after commodity. But royal smiths churned out edged weapons in great number to arm men for military expeditions and for spectacular entertainments, such as the massive tournament of sword fighting that was part of the staged meeting between Francis and Henry at the "field of the cloth of gold" in northern France in 1520.[38] By the end of the century, collections of armor housed in the Tower of London were being mounted for display; the collections mostly dated from the sixteenth century, though were assumed to be ancient in some cases.[39]

Assembling and displaying weapons was part of a larger impulse to collect and display marvels, especially new curiosities from around the world, and to enjoy the reflection of prestige such collections embodied.[40] What distinguishes the collection of swords and armor, however, is precisely the coincidence of the gathering and recording of worthy weapons with the explosion in the manufacture of swords and the diversity of weapons in individual warriors' hands. The care provided for Guy of Warwick's supposed sword is one example. Guy of Warwick was a fictional hero of Anglo-Norman romance, a champion of modest origin who proved his worth in various chivalric adventures, enough to win the hand of a lady. Tales about him began to appear in the early thirteenth century. By the end of the century, the actual Earl of Warwick had named his son and heir "Guy," who went on to win renown in an English victory over the Scots in 1298 and, later, for dispatching one of Edward II's hated favorites. Under Guy's grandson, the eleventh earl, in the 1390s, a new addition to the castle at Warwick was named "Guy's tower," and further confusion of romantic hero and heroic ancestor ensued, particularly as relics accumulated there.[41] By the early sixteenth century, the title was extinct, yet in 1509 Henry VIII authorized the appointment of one William Hoogeson to be "Keeper of Guy of Warwick's sword." Near the end of the century, the aged adviser to Elizabeth I, Lord Burghley, writes to authorize payment to one Thomas Atkinson who had been granted the office of "keeping of the sworde called Guy of Warwick's sword within the castle of Warwick" by the recently deceased earl (the title had been revived in midcentury for members of the Dudley family). The annual payment of 60s/10d had stopped with the earl's death some four years before, but Burghley writes "methinks it ffit that the said yearlie fee should be allowed unto the said Atkinson with the arrerages, synce the payement to him hath been discontinued." In authorizing the payment of the annual pension, plus arrears, Burghley refers to a prior guardian who had enjoyed the yearly pension for the duration of his life "by a former patent," and argued that Atkinson should enjoy the same rights, despite the earl's (rather inconvenient) death. So, the earl had named the keepers but the crown now paid the bill; maintenance of this legendary sword was a project in which the crown took a leading role.[42]

French kings had meanwhile begun their own collection of noteworthy arms and armor. That is what the list of venerable and supposedly enchanted weapons from 1499 represents, which I introduced at the outset of this study. It claims to be a list of weapons saved "in the guard of" past kings, "de tout temps . . . jusques à present"; thus its significance, and the meaning of the weapons included, lies partly in its supposed historical veracity. The list claims to preserve history, not myth, and celebrates the authority of the crown to control the artifacts, that is, remove them from circulation, and to establish their authenticity. The contrast with elites' scanty documentation of their most precious swords could not be greater; here, the crown seeks to determine which objects will be demarcated as worthy and to control access to their legendary pasts.[43]

Like all the lists I have discussed, however, this one rewards close scrutiny. The first thing that strikes the reader when comparing it to other lists of its day is the greater precision with which each object is described: each item comes with a story, or at least a name, but first, a description of its distinctive features that is much more standardized, from entry to entry, than is typical in an inventory of belongings. In a more routine inventory, composed for a single need in time, the descriptions of many objects reveal that the inventory maker did not know what he was looking at. He might know he was looking at a high-quality garment and be able to describe the fabric, but not always for what occasion it had been fashioned, or in the case of an old sword, where it came from and what it represented. And he might not describe all the objects in equal detail.

In contrast, almost every object in this royal inventory is carefully described by its principal features, then identified by its name or origin or by the feat it once accomplished in a remote past. For example, one entry reads, "an arming sword, the grip garnished with white silk cord, and on the pommel an Our Lady on one side and a sun on the other, called the sword of victory," while another reads "a sword with a white scabbard, a grip garnished with wood, on the pommel an Our Lady on one side and a Saint Martin on the other, called the sword of the Pope, which he sent to King Louis." The axes on the list, grouped together, are not rendered in quite as much detail as the swords, since they are less likely to be embellished. One, however, is decorated with three diamonds, "called the axe of Bertrand du Guesclin," and another was "previously enameled with *fleurs de lys*," one of two that "belonged to Saint Louis." Another ax dates from an even more remote past; it is described as "worked," that is, embellished in some unspecified way, and it "is called the axe of King Clovis, the first king."[44]

How do they know? How do the inventory makers know that two of these axes belonged to Saint Louis, or that the pope had sent the recent Louis XI that particular sword? The question is not, for the moment, did that ax really date from the sixth century, really belong to Clovis, or even whether the fourteenth-century constable, Bertrand du Guesclin, in fact had wielded that particular ax. What, quite literally, were they looking at, as they assembled this inventory, and why did these literal-minded inventory makers duly report this information?

This inventory would have been impossible to assemble without resort to some prior document. We must imagine either that the clerks were consulting an earlier list, dutifully matching each object to the prior record of it, or, more likely, that each sword, ax, or dagger came with a label attached to it. Indeed, if an earlier inventory was available, that inventory, or any preceding it, would have relied on labels, and newer objects, such as a sword from Louis XI (d. 1483), must have been catalogued in that way also. These labels would have resembled the small titulae that were attached to saints' relics to document their authenticity. Reliquaries containing relics from multiple saints, which were very common, generally identified each relic with a tiny inscribed slip, usually of parchment, with the saint's name. These slips could be wrapped around tiny bone fragments, or sewn onto the same cloth where bones were displayed in framed panels, say, over an altar, or fixed in some other way inside the containers that held the relics. Or they could simply be tied to the bone with a silk or linen or hemp cord, which might rot away over time, but be replaced, as could the titulae themselves, if they were in danger of crumbling or becoming illegible.

But if we assume that a label was affixed to each of the weapons in this list from 1499, allowing the inventory makers to record the provenance of each weapon, we still need to account for the character of these texts, these snippets of information. In many cases, what we have are encapsulated stories that capture action, not merely possession or origin. Telling examples are the entries for two most recently acquired swords that belonged to Charles VIII (d. 1498). Both are remembered as having taken part in the battle of Fornovo, a French victory of 1495, fought near Parma, over Italian resistance to his ambitions to rule in Naples; one of the swords "he had on the pommel of his saddle on the day of Fornovo." Its only distinguishing feature beyond its role on the day, mentioned in the list, was its black velvet scabbard. Right afterward comes the notation of the second sword, equally in a (matching?) black velvet scabbard, "which the said late King Charles VIIIᵉ had *in his hand on* the said day of Fornovo."[45] So we have a vignette of action, and the sketch of a well-drawn tableau; we can picture Charles on horseback brandishing one sword while another awaits in its scabbard. Neither the recently deceased king nor the event at Fornovo need much more by way of introduction since they are readily accessible in living memory.

But the memory of some other kings and great men, and of their belongings, would not have been as fresh. One arming sword, carefully described as having an Our Lady on one side of the pommel and a sun on the other, is "called the sword of the king who founded St. Denis." Would that be Dagobert (d. 637), who refounded as a Benedictine abbey the earliest church on the site holding St. Denis's remains, and who erected an elaborate shrine there for the saint? Or was it Pepin or Charlemagne who later rebuilt the basilica—if so, surely that pedigree would be claimed here—or perhaps Louis VI (d. 1137) under whose reign the now extant Gothic church was begun by the innovative abbot, Suger?[46] Immediately following that sword in the list is another arming sword, duly described in its turn; it has a pommel displaying Our Lady on one side and Saint Michael on the other, and "is called the sword of the king of France, which took arms against a giant in Paris and conquered him."[47] Here again, the king in question is unnamed, though we have a vignette of battle; we are told exactly what feat this sword once accomplished for him. Nine entries later, we come across a sword decorated with red leather and a long pommel "called the sword of the giant who was conquered by a king of France on the island of Notre Dame [île de la Cité] in Paris." A trophy, perhaps, from the same encounter where "the sword of the king of France" was victorious? The list records but does not reassemble or collate its tales.

Thus, the inventory makers are dutifully entering not only descriptions of the objects, one by one, but also the information about past action, briskly recorded at some prior time, on their labels or in a prior list. These abbreviated stories of origin represent the residue of longer, more complete accounts, stories that once were the product of and remained anchored in largely oral tradition and transmission. In the case of the encounter between king and giant, the specific king has been lost but the action has not. And it is revealing that both incidents are characterized in the same terms: the giant is "conquered" in both cases.

Scholars of oral cultures that have persisted into modern times report that tale-tellers—for example, Serbian "singers of stories" in the early twentieth century—explained to researchers at the time that "words," to them, meant units of storytelling. To use our terms: a "word," in traditional storytelling, means a phrase, a segment of action if not an actual sentence, that is the basic unit of oral storytelling. These phrase units not only serve as mnemonic devices for oral composition, they also are building blocks of meaning in that they become a series of what we, today, would call intertextual possibilities, whose variations can create new resonances of meaning within one composition.[48] Thus an entry in the 1499 list of weapons is like a mnemonic to retrieve an entire sequence of action.

But the entries in this document no longer work that way because they are too far removed from their stories of origin. We are seeing just the spare remains of those tales here—what J. R. R. Tolkien would call an echo, and a distant one at that. The story of the king who vanquished a giant near Notre Dame remains in three fragments unconnected by the inventory makers who mechanically record object after object and transcribe information from labels. The identity of the victorious king can no longer be retrieved, and the weapons are not reunited: the very form of list making works against that possibility.

The list betrays its distance from the origin tales in other ways. We can see the echoes of the past in the repetition, in entry after entry, of the sword's names, culled most likely from labels: the arming sword *"called* the sword of victory," or, "the sword of Charles VII[e] [d. 1461] that he *called* the well-loved" (my emphasis). A piece of paper records a name; we can learn what a sword was once called, but not why. The distance of the inventory writers from the origin of the objects is revealed also by the way the list is organized: it is divided by type of arms—swords first, then axes, then remnants of armor. Given that inventories were virtually always made in a manner that follows the gaze of the clerks—they do not abstractly organize items as they create a list—it is likely that the objects were viewed in the order the list preserves, which is largely a random one within these three major divisions. The objects within each category are not grouped by their supposed date of origin, when that could be guessed. The long-distant Clovis's alleged ax appears in the middle of the list of axes, several entries after two belonging to Saint Louis and just before the bejeweled ax wielded by the fourteenth-century constable, Bertrand du Guesclin. Embedded also, in this section of the list, is another wondrous weapon, perhaps from the confrontation with the giant near Notre Dame: this time, an ax from a giant himself who wielded it—but it stands alone, like the two swords, each also standing alone, from this or another encounter between king and giant in the list above. It is possible that the king's giant-killer sword, and the giant's own, as well as the giant's ax, echo two distinct stories that circulated in the Middle Ages about vanquished giants, set in the ninth and tenth centuries, respectively. In one, none other than William of Orange, companion to Charlemagne and hero of twelfth-century tales, kills a menacing giant. In the other, a count of Anjou fights a giant (who has arrived with invading Danes) on behalf of Lothair, the last Carolingian ruler of west Francia (d. 986). These tales were still repeated in sixteenth-century histories, but if they were the remote origins of the supposed fame of these blades, they are detached from the weapons here, in this royal list. Over time, in addition, bravely facing the giant has become the work of (unnamed) kings themselves, and the giant himself is connected to neither event.[49] Oddly interspersed with all these older weapons (or at least whose origins were obviously remote from the list makers) are several items that belonged to the recently deceased Louis XI (d. 1483).

Some names and descriptions do seem easier to connect with their origin point. For example, the descriptions of Charles VIII's two swords from the battle of Fornovo are identified by action, or visual cues, only: one was on his saddle, the other in his hand. They are not *called* "the sword that did great deed X or belonged to august person Y." Interesting, also, is the fact that these two swords are the only objects listed that are completely out of place. They are not grouped with the other swords at all, but appear between the axes and the armor, suggesting they were recent additions to the collection and not captured in some prior list. Charles VIII's swords from the day at Fornovo had a resonance in living memory and were newly arrived when the inventory was compiled and copied. In addition, we may be looking, in this case, at the kind of word-as-phrase that is the building block of tales: the image of the sword on the pommel or the sword in the hand are stock vignettes, memorable because they are doubly familiar. The story is still circulating orally, and is further memorable because it can be envisioned: the tableau is not a unique scene in warrior experience. We can recall, for example, the English freelance captain David Holgrave, whose two swords, one poised on his saddle, were memorable enough to be recorded years after he was killed in battle. It can be truthful and also a narrative trope.

There are also two exceptions to the randomness within the firm organizational categories, and they may be revealing in another way. The first two items in the "swords" section are, by any measure, the most venerable and precious. The first is a dagger. It has a handle made of crystal, the inventory reports, and it is called "the dagger of Saint Charlemagne"; the next item is Lancelot's sword. Of course, the stories of Lancelot's feats were still circulating, as elites' book collections testify. And any member of the elite would know of the legendary Charlemagne. Many of the other items were no doubt attached to stories that are difficult to fully reconstruct or even guess at. For example, perhaps the compilers of this list could remember, or assumed their audience would know, why a "knife shaped like a scimitar" (one of only two bladed weapons that are neither a sword nor an ax) was "called the knife [of] Saint Pierre de Luxembourg." Pierre of Luxembourg was a fourteenth-century French cleric who had had to literally battle for his bishopric during the Great Schism against a candidate supported by the rival pope favored, in turn, by the emperor. Was his "knife" known for its role in the fighting? Here again, the distance from the story is betrayed by the phrase "*is called*." The text of the entry for Lancelot's sword follows this pattern, too. It reads, "A sword with an iron handle fashioned like a key, *called* the sword of Lancelot, *it is said* [that] it is fairy [sword.]" This formula is identical to the way Turenne's inventory makers described his relic of Notre Dame: "*it is said* that it is the shift [*chemise*] of Notre Dame" (my emphasis). The inventory makers record this information as claim, not as truth. The document is dutiful but ambivalent.

These inventory makers open with their own claim that these objects have been in the guard of past kings "through all time to the present." This claim might be true of some of the older pieces, insofar as they were in royal control from the moment they were deemed worthy, such as with Saint Louis's axes, but clearly is not true in regard to the recently deceased Louis's and Charles's effects. And we also know from other sources that not all valued relics of the past had been saved; for example, some eighty years before, Charles VI (d. 1422) had in his possession, at his death, "a knife with which St. Louis fought when he was taken," presumably referring to when Louis IX was captured in battle when on crusade in Egypt. The knife does not appear on this newer list.[50] (Charlemagne's alleged sword, meanwhile, is not on the list either; as coronation regalia, it was in the control of the monastery at St. Denis.) This list from the end of the fifteenth century was likely composed when the new king, Louis XII, chose to move the assembled treasures from Amboise to his favored residence of Blois.[51] It is an active collection whose lineage extends to a remote past that cannot, as the inventory makers well knew, be fully recovered. And that, in the present of 1499, is part of the point. Some of the labels identify an action the weapon once took, but cannot name who wielded it. Some of the weapons carry only a name, like the sword of victory, wholly detached, now, from its origins.

We are a long, long way from an imaginary world where a sword could not help but stir a personal connection, move a warrior to anger so powerfully that it is as if the sword could accomplish the action alone, an actor in its own right. But that was, even in the year 1000, a form of nostalgia. Here, nostalgia takes a different form. These objects *needed* labels, or a prior paper trail; they are not active in the world anymore as swords once were, *and that detachment from the world of action is what the document celebrates.* The idea of gathering them all in a central location removes them from circulation and tries to endow them with power in another way, from the historical knowledge the crown can claim—in short, a new kind of category of weapons. The importance of each weapon, in other words, comes from its inclusion in the collection, not from the lost stories that are so fleetingly glimpsed. The fact that, apart from Lancelot's and Charlemagne's pieces, the weapons are not organized according to some sort of index of "venerableness" is also part of the point: celebrated here is the power of the crown to extend its reach to any and all memorable weapons and attach them to its own historical continuity. That they are in the king's hands is what makes them noteworthy. The creation of this collection in fact and in writing is akin to the translation of saints' relics, which lost hold over the faithful when too many generations separated their placement in a shrine and the advertising of miracles. The king is gathering to himself these relics of royal authority. When gathered as a collection, they become more than the sum of their parts. Like later collections in the Tower of London, they are an invitation to an experience of awe, and to marvel at the instruments, the mysteries, of power removed from anyone else's reach.

Actual truth about the objects is not required because the weapons gain their power from each other and from the royal resources expended to record them and thus preserve them for the future. The clerks do not need to believe that Lancelot's sword was made by fairies, or that other people believed it, nor do they need to dispute it. They simply record that "it is said" that fairies made it. They are documenting legend, not belief. They also do not claim that this sword with a handle like a key actually belonged to Lancelot, only that *it is called* Lancelot's sword. Neither the legend about this sword or any other sword or ax or bit of armor on the list can now be further contested. If a king chooses in the future to "spend" the worth of one of these pieces, as Richard Lionheart once did with Excalibur, its value will not come from the resonance of the legend, much less from a connection to the original owner, like Lancelot or Charlemagne, but from the fact that the crown had maintained control over this relic of its authority. Ironically, then, this record of weapons from an unrecoverable past is in some ways the most forward looking of the documents I have considered here. At the same time, it relies on an impulse that was ubiquitous in elite circles: that of keeping distinctive, venerable heirlooms close at hand—particularly compelling in an era when other swords, and other weapons, proliferated. The blade that, in Burghley's document, "is called Guy of Warwick's sword" was an outsize single example of such an inclination. It, and these French weapons, constituted a category of weapon that was both familiar and intelligible yet also unique, irreplaceable, and increasingly remote, which was the work that "special" swords alone could do in royal hands, with meticulous documentation to help them.

The painted image of ambassador Jean de Dinteville, on the other hand, is an example of continuity, not change. Evidence suggests that Dinteville chose the clothing he is wearing in Holbein's painting; in striking a pose in such an impressive array he is adhering to established behaviors of his class. But he likely agreed to the choice of the other objects depicted around him as well, and acceded to the religious or spiritual message they conveyed. When he finally departed for France in November of 1533, Dinteville took the painting home to his chateau of Polisy, near the royal residence of Fontainebleau. There, it eventually was accompanied by another painting (by a now unknown artist) probably composed while Jean and his brother were out of favor at court, in effect in the political wilderness. It depicted Jean and his older brother, the bishop of Auxerre, as Moses and Aaron before the pharaoh, about to embark on their journey out of Egypt. Later on, around 1545, Dinteville sat for still another portrait: an individual likeness in which he is dressed in Roman armor as Saint George, seated next to a dragon's severed head.[52] By that point, Dinteville had weathered the temporary disgrace of his family. This likeness as Saint George, in fact, reflected the favor of one of the most powerful noblemen in the realm, the cardinal of Lorraine, who had commissioned the painting, despite the fact that, earlier, Dinteville and his brothers had been closely allied with Lorraine's rivals at court. Meanwhile Jean kept the artist, Francesco Primaticcio, busy with commissions for the remodeling of Polisy itself in the latest Renaissance style that Francis I had popularized. Jean de Dinteville, in short, was an assiduous patron and consumer of goods and of images and extremely attentive to the claims to status that his person, and all of his accoutrements, conveyed. No doubt he was especially attentive in part because his family had risen in just two generations from bureaucratic service—a common enough tale of origins but one that meant Dinteville needed to play the game of political preferment with especial skill.

While we may read the personal accoutrements as evidence of his commitment to cut a fashionable figure at court, the collection of other objects in *The Ambassadors* could be read—as some scholars have implied—as reflections of Dinteville's ability to ponder, even imagine distance from, that persona, particularly on his sense of the place he occupied in a complex and ephemeral world, suggested by the various instruments on the shelves next to him and above all by the distorted death's head stretched across the floor near his feet. He was a learned man by aristocratic standards of the day, and he would have appreciated Holbein's artful detail, including the strange distorted skull. His sword, however, has rated barely a mention in modern scholars' interpretation of the image. When it is noticed, the sword is imagined in tension with the other objects in the painting, as though Dinteville were not capable of encompassing books, scientific devices and the like in his vision of his own world.[53] I conclude, rather, that Dinteville's sword was perfectly compatible, in his own eyes, with any other artifacts and attributes of self that the portrait depicts. The sword has adapted well to the conditions of the sixteenth century: it is a weapon for a warrior, and also a piece of jewelry for a courtier, a trophy from an arcane foe, a remembrance of self to others, a memento of a mythic past—and still a weapon. It is not afraid to share the spotlight with other marks of status—with pistols and daggers, orders of chivalry, rare fabrics and furs, jewels and relics, books and time pieces. In fact, it is the dagger that draws the viewer's eye on Dinteville's person. His sword, on the other hand, is almost hidden from view. Holbein's skill positions the sword against the lynx fur, separated and distinct from other objects; all that can be glimpsed are the telltale, ornate hilt, and a sliver of the scabbard—and it is more than enough. Holbein can be playful with its visibility because his audience expects it to be there. The whole point of the sword is that it guarantees a place of status, come what may. The ambassador stares out at us, leaning on the edge of the buffet. He feels the weight of the sword at his side, an anchoring presence in a crowded world of things.

Conclusion

Recently, as I drove toward Appomattox National Historic Park from the modern town of Appomattox, Virginia, I passed a private museum tucked along the roadside. In an effort to snare tourists, the museum advertised, on an oversize sign on its wall: "Robert E. Lee's sword!" The boast seemed a gesture of desperation, given the competition from the National Park up ahead where Lee's surrender had actually happened, and the fact that so many artifacts from Lee's life have long been on view elsewhere in the state. It also seemed disturbing, given the context of the rethinking of Confederate monuments then under way: a last gasp of memorials to the revered leader of the "lost cause." Of course, I was particularly struck by the assumed power of the artifact itself: the assumption that tourists would stop because of a sword.

I did not stop. But I found that the museum at the National Park a few miles on also relied on the symbolism of swords. One of the glass cases displayed a sword and a sword belt that had belonged to a Union army captain who was an African American man. This exhibit, like others at many Civil War battlefields, had been reconfigured to acknowledge the deeper history of the period, including the work of enslaved peoples and the contributions of freed men and women to the fighting. And here was the sword to stand in, to represent, an African American captain to tourists' eyes. Nothing could have been more effective at demonstrating our continuing equation of the sword with authority, with the power of command, and with honor. The sword had been placed in the glass case to make this man a worthy warrior to modern eyes; he was now present, an actor rather than a victim or, worse, simply absent. His sword had enabled us convincingly to reinterpret the past.

In the lifetimes of General Lee and the Union army captain, and certainly in our own time in the twenty-first century, swords have endured as an artifact capable of signaling both authority and honor. The history of those recent centuries lies beyond the bounds of this study except insofar as our unexamined assumptions about swords impinge on our ability to interpret the roles swords played in past material contexts and in past warriors' lives. The private museum's noisy advertisement of Lee's sword as well as the display at Appomattox Court House relies on our current acceptance of the power of this artifact, the sword, and, above all, on our assumption of familiarity with its resonances. Both assume that we "know" what it means, and that that meaning is unvarying and recognizable across time. It has power over us because it feeds our desires. Those desires, as I sketched at the outset, include a longing for days gone by when the things surrounding us were not ephemeral, and when their presence could anchor us in our world. It also includes our enchantment with an object whose manufacture cannot be parsed nor its appeal made transparent. It also—and its power to "forgive" Lee for his decisions—relies in particular on a separate nostalgia for war that was honorable no matter the "cause," where one warrior and his individual choices could make a difference. Those same attachments have been at work in popular culture, in books and films and television programs from the Lord of the Rings, to Star Wars, to Harry Potter, to Game of Thrones, not to mention all the retold versions of King Arthur.

My goal here has been, in part, to uncover the earlier processes by which swords gained the power to create an identity, "honorable warrior," that would be beyond dispute. I have explored how swords were valued by warriors in France and England in the premodern centuries before war itself was transformed by gunpowder weapons and the rise of mass armies. Other recent scholars have explored how swords remained central to the self-conception of warriors through the intervening centuries, to our own. Roger Manning, for example, dubs the British officer class after 1600 "swordsmen," because reliance on the sword as a marker of privilege and on swordplay as a form of expertise enabled them to weather the changing demands of command and subordination to the crown.[1]

If swords remained firmly and richly expressive of warrior identity, it was in part because they had already served as a vehicle for change and adaptation through time. Throughout, the material characteristics of the sword were always central to its significance: it could carry fashionable or personal-ized designs on the hilt or scabbard; it could be both old, if needed, or new as elements could be added or renewed if worn; above all, the blade was a work of art and an especially good one could have a very long life. Thus, the construction of a sword meant it could convey immediate, personalized messages and yet have a longevity celebrated and recognized across genera-tions. Swords did not mean just one thing, ever, but they were always good for thinking with, good for representing the timelessness of warrior identity and the security of one warrior's stature, good for appealing to some imag-ined past for purposes of any present. Our own enchantment, standing apart from the warrior tradition in our present, is not the same as theirs; their fascination with swords—that of any of the subjects I have examined—was subtler, more grounded in symbolic needs of their day, more authentic and therefore more secure.

But it is important to realize that swords became a focal point for warrior identity only gradually, over time. As it developed its power in elite culture, "memory" of earlier times when swords were larger than life grew also. One turning point was the years around 1200 when the formal presentation of a sword in a dubbing ceremony created the identity of a knight. It was a historical moment underpinned by and reflecting economic expansion and political development such that the need for distinction and hierarchy was felt more urgently and could be enacted by new material means—which then quickly became insufficient to the status they had helped to create. As we have noted, invocation of a supposed past of legendary swords existed in a context of regional courts, the storytelling that prevailed there, and a histo-ricizing inclination to ground present claims as political power consolidated. It was sustained by expanding literacy, which also was reflected in the lists where we now find swords recorded.

Enchanted swords, too, developed in historical time; they do not just exist in an unrecoverable past from which we later retrieve them. The imagined pasts of swords in the twelfth and thirteenth centuries endowed swords with less power than earlier generations had assumed they might have. The *Beowulf* poet, whenever he lived, did not think he lived in that world of out-size heroes and artifacts any longer, but he could convincingly (so we posit) create the sensibilities of that world for his audience, a world where humans shared the stage with other sentient beings, including monsters and swords. And he admires, even regrets, the kind of heroism that prevailed in those pre-Christian days. As swords gained political potency, as they became the required means of defense and self-expression, they lost their independent lives. The recreated Curtana never was an actor in its own right and across multiple generations faded into a mere prop, as Excalibur would also have done. In the end, Richard Lionheart got the fullest possible value out of Excalibur by trading on it one time only. In a world of growing arrays of belongings and talismans—swords and belts and badges and daggers and cups and chalices and tapestries, not to mention armor—even the most durable artifact was fleeting in its impact. That was why John de Warenne's sword had to be old and rusty to accomplish its assigned task of claiming his rights against his sovereign.

In the late Middle Ages swords underwent another, different, transformation. The first significant change in blade design occurred to accommodate the development of plate armor. The greater availability of better-quality steel permitted more and better armor and, by the sixteenth century, further changes in sword blades. The malleability of swords did not become a liability, however. Warrior men in the sixteenth century commissioned all the ornamental blades they could afford while still guarding other, likely battle-worthy, weapons of various sorts close to them. They also kept collecting trophy blades and one-of-a-kind curiosities. Fighting with each of these weapons required unique skill and so became a new means of exclusion, increasingly celebrated in texts. What one blade did not accomplish in self-presentation, self-defense, or self-promotion, another blade could.

Amid all this variety, swords retained a special weight that carried resonances of earlier centuries. There was more to the sword of the average warrior in the fourteenth or fifteenth or sixteenth centuries than the symbolic work of sword-as-command authority, sword as status, sword as exclusive luxury. The documentary record suggests that men regarded their one or two most-used blades as an extension of their persons, capable of representing them with a kind of immediacy. Their swords are treated the least like "belongings" of any a warrior owned: less likely to be in a mundane list, less likely to be gathered for storage with other like objects, less likely to be offered as a gift, or lent out, or claimed back or regifted, as we have seen clothing and armor circulated. An elite warrior in the sixteenth century might have many swords as essential decoration—"dress" swords worn as part of an outfit—and these were not treated cavalierly either. And he would also still have a sword or two he kept close at hand and might be known by, which might be of any design. It is partly this same impulse at work in the description of Charles VIII's swords in the French collection from the turn of the sixteenth century. The description of the king's swords recalls a vignette from Charles's presence at a French victory six years before: he was there, with this sword in his hand, that sword on his saddle. I have already emphasized the way the document identifies the sword by capturing narrated action; here I highlight the parallel with other warriors' swords. The swords recall the event, but they memorialize Charles by being not only witnesses to his action, emblems of his resolve on the day, but also embodiments of his presence, there and since.

Historians of fashion argue that, particularly in periods of marked change, clothing can be considered an agent; in the case of women's dress after 1918, for example, it literally changed what was possible even as it also reflected change. Insofar as some swords became required ornament, part of the "clothes that made the man," swords remained agents in this way from about 1500 forward. But swords were more than one thing at the end of the Middle Ages, and through the sixteenth century they were not only required ornament. They were no longer the actors we saw in *Beowulf*, capable by themselves of moving humans to kill and grieve, but, in contemporaries' imaginations, they held on to some of their capacity to represent and convey the person, not merely guarantee his stature. This was an early modern warrior's own experience of nostalgia.

This attribute of a sword, its assumed power to represent a person, is what made them rare and signature bequests between elites and also part of what made them attractive to rulers. Throughout their history, swords in elites' hands existed on a continuum with and in relation to those in royal hands. Kings and emperors gradually added swords to their array of symbols of power that had been derived originally from Roman precedent and, later, from ecclesiastical symbolism. Through the late Middle Ages, rulers "discovered" iconic weapons such as Arthur's Excalibur or Roland's sword for their ceremonial and legitimating effect. They also collected the arms of their predecessors and of renowned warriors or vanquished enemies of prior days. Not all of these items were swords, of course: there were axes and daggers and armor, too, reflecting the usefulness, in the day, of these other weapons and the continued importance of armor, particularly, through the sixteenth century. The careful record of weapons in the French crown's hands in 1499 is not evidence of belief in magic or legend but a claim to the right to recognize great men and control the stories that the weapons embody. It is about royal power, not myth so much as mystique—power over the artifacts themselves and over the ongoing memory of them established in writing.

It is in collections such as this one that we can see the beginnings, not only of the kind of museum collections that surround us now, with their claim to authentication of objects, but also of our modern certainty that swords have a constant meaning through time, "de tout temps jusqu'à présent," as the French document claims. Swords are indeed an artifact whose attributes give it a unique allure, good for imagining with, which can masquerade as a timeless appeal. But we must appreciate the contingent, historical processes that enabled swords to become ubiquitous, multifaceted, and omnipresent in elite hands by the sixteenth century. This rich and ever-proliferating landscape of swords lay behind royal attempts to assemble definitive collections, and also enabled swords, as a symbol of warrior identity, to withstand this effort at cooptation.

As royal authority sought to control elite violence, elites advertised and protected their status with the apparel of swords that were both unique prestige objects and weapons at the ready. This constituted yet another inflection of elite identity: that of an honorable being that was, above all, refined and cultivated but which still embodied a menace of violence—a being adapted to a more powerful state, but secure in its status within it.[2] If the crown, through collections (such as in the 1499 list), was trying to preempt control of the narrative, and the fact, of martial achievement, the ubiquitous dress sword, already present in Holbein's painting in 1533, expressed resistance to that narrative by staging a kind of disinterested privilege and honor wholly inherent in the individual, detached from wider political contexts. The context from which their everyday, elegant swords and matching daggers derived their symbolic heft was their own wider collections of weaponry, especially swords of all types, as well as pistols, daggers, staff weapons, and the even wider array of armor, clothing, jewels, and precious metalware they amassed and circulated among themselves. Every instance of self-presentation represented a choice from the midst of their own, ever-shifting, collections, gathered in various locales or from relatives' and friends' hands, and captured in various written records.

I have explored the deep history behind these developments. In concluding, I will reemphasize the fact that the meticulous list created in 1499 was assembled before elite swords had any serious competition in battle from handheld firearms, the weapon that would help transform armies into tools of the state. Warrior culture, as it entered the sixteenth century, was thus well insulated by its material expressions. Like its swords, and by means of them, it was both malleable and resilient; it was capable of change, even while it purported to remain always the same—that is, always invulnerable to challenge. Insofar as warrior culture was defined by and propped up by the world of goods, particularly by the rich and varied accumulations of swords, there is a strong argument for slow transformation and effective adaptation, rather than crisis or rupture with the past.

❧ Abbreviations

AN	Archives nationales, Paris
BL	British Library, London
Add MS	Additional Manuscripts
Harley	Harley Roll
Stow	Stow Charters
BN	Bibliothèque nationale, Paris
Clair	Fonds Clairambault
Ms. Fr	Manuscrits français
NAF	Nouvelles acquisitions françaises
NA	National Archives, Kew

❦ NOTES

Introduction

1. AN, *1 AP 2081, Chartrier de Thouars, "Inventaire des biens meubles du chasteau de St. Fargeau," 4 January 1525; concerning the arrangement of furnishings in great noble chateaus, see Kristen B. Neuschel, "Noble Households in the Sixteenth Century: Material Settings and Human Communities," *French Historical Studies* 15, no. 4 (1988): 595–622.

2. Neuschel, "Noble Households," esp. 618. There is evidence that nobles took precious tableware when traveling to assume extended commands as governors of chateaus or towns; see "Inventaire fait au chateau de Folleville après le décès de Louis de Lannoy, seigneur de Morvillers, gouverneur de Boulogne," in *Recueil de documents inédits concernant la Picardie*, ed. Victor de Beauvillé, 4 vols. (Paris, 1880–82), 4:333–34.

3. AN, 90 AP 23, Dossier 2, 26 September 1576, "Inventaire des accoutremens et aultres hardes de Monseigneur [. . .] tirez de son cabinet de Paris pour emener en ce lieu de St. Fargeau."

4. Christoph Martin Vogtherr, "Director's Foreword," *The Noble Art of the Sword: Fashion and Fencing in Renaissance Europe, 1520–1630*, ed. Tobias Capwell (London: Paul Holberton, 2012), 6.

5. BN, Ms. Fr 22335, ff.111–19, "Meubles estans en l'armeurerie du chasteau d'Amboise en laquelle sont les anciennes armeures qui de tout temps ont este gardees et fait garder par les Roys deffuncts jusques a present extraictz sur ung inventaire fait a Amboise le XXIIIe jour de septembre 1499."

6. The inventory signals that it is a copy, and is included in a number of inventories of the household of Anne of Brittany (d. 1514), wife and queen to Charles VIII and, afterward, to Louis XII.

7. Susan M. Pearce, "Collecting Reconsidered," in *Interpreting Objects and Collections*, ed. Susan M. Pearce (London: Routledge, 1994), 193–204.

8. See especially Bill Brown, "Thing Theory," in *Things*, ed. Bill Brown (Chicago: University of Chicago Press, 2004), 1–16; and W. J. T. Mitchell, *What Do Pictures Want? The Lives and Loves of Images* (Chicago: University of Chicago Press, 2005), chaps. 2 and 3. I have not followed Brown in distinguishing between "objects" and "things"— the latter being a material entity that is "not yet interpreted." Its relationship to humans, according to Brown, is effaced momentarily by its alien thing-ness, such as a car, once a companion, now a broken-down machine, obvious in its "thingness."

9. The Wallace Collection, London, personal communication to author, September 10, 2012.

10. In addition to Brown, "Thing Theory," see Victor Buchli, introduction to *The Material Culture Reader*, ed. Victor Buchli (Oxford: Berg, 2002), 1–22; Daniel Miller, ed., *Material Cultures: Why Some Things Matter* (Chicago: University of Chicago Press,

1998); J. D. Richards, "An Archaeology of Anglo-Saxon England," in *After Empire: Towards an Ethnology of Europe's Barbarians*, ed. G. Ausenda (Woodbridge, Suffolk: Boydell, 1995), 51–63.

11. Ian Hodder, "This Is Not an Article about Material Culture as Text," *Journal of Anthropological Archaeology* 8 (1989): 250–69.

12. Hodder describes this process by saying that objects "impinge on conceptual categories." See ibid., 257. See also "Editorial," *Journal of Material Culture* 1, no. 1 (1996): 5–14.

13. Frans Theuws and Monika Alkemade, "A Kind of Mirror for Men: Sword Depositions in Late Antique Northern Gaul," in *Rituals of Power: From Late Antiquity to the Early Middle Ages*, ed. Frans Theuws and Janet L. Nelson (Leiden: Brill, 2000), 422.

14. Daniel Miller, introduction to *Material Cultures: Why Some Things Matter*, stresses the notion of *how* objects mean.

15. See Buchli, introduction to *Material Culture Reader*, 2–3.

16. The term "memory peg" originates with Elisabeth van Houts, *Memory and Gender in Medieval Europe, 900–1200* (Toronto: University of Toronto Press, 1999), chap. 5.

17. Shirley Ann Brown, "Cognate Imagery: The Bear, Harold and the Bayeux Tapestry," in *King Harold II and the Bayeux Tapestry*, ed. Gale R. Owen-Crocker (Woodbridge, Suffolk: Boydell, 2005), 153–60; Victor Buchli, in introduction to *Material Culture Reader*, 13–15, cautions that material culture does not "translate" well into texts, since much sensual experience is lost by those means.

18. The literature on the military revolution is vast. On the original debate regarding early modern armies, see Clifford J. Rogers, ed., *The Military Revolution Debate* (Boulder, CO: Westview, 1995); as well as Clifford J. Rogers, ed., *The Oxford Encyclopedia of Medieval Warfare and Military Technology* (New York: Oxford University Press, 2010). Since the original debate the term has been expanded to apply to modern armies and military practice. See for example MacGregor Knox and Williamson Murray, eds., *The Dynamics of Military Revolution, 1300–2050* (Cambridge: Cambridge University Press, 2001).

19. See the essays in John Brewer and Roy Porter, eds., *Consumption and the World of Goods* (London: Routledge, 1993), esp. Peter Burke, "*Res et verba*: Conspicuous Consumption in the Early Modern World," 148–61; more recent is Frank Trentmann, ed., *The Oxford Handbook of the History of Consumption* (Oxford: Oxford University Press, 2012); and Frank Trentmann, *Empire of Things* (New York: HarperCollins, 2016). Noteworthy in all these works is the limited attention to medieval society.

20. Buchli, introduction to *Material Culture Reader*, 12.

21. See Randall Styers, *Making Magic: Religion, Magic and Science in the Modern World* (Oxford: Oxford University Press, 2004); see esp. the introduction, for a survey of the history of the shifting category "magic."

22. Anne Savage, "The Grave, the Sword and the Lament," in *Laments for the Lost in Medieval Literature*, ed. Jane Tolmie and M. J. Toswell (Turnhout, Belgium: Brepols, 2010), 67.

23. Alan R. Williams, *The Sword and the Crucible: A History of the Metallurgy of European Swords up to the Sixteenth Century* (Leiden: Brill, 2012), esp. part 1.

24. Hilda Roderick Ellis Davidson, *The Sword in Anglo-Saxon England: Its Archaeology and Literature* (Woodbridge, Suffolk: Boydell, 1998), 216.

25. Alfred Gell, "The Technology of Enchantment and the Enchantment of Technology," in *Anthropology, Art and Aesthetics*, ed. Jeremy Coote and Anthony Shelton (Oxford: Clarendon, 1994), esp. 49 and 56. Gell is particularly interested in art, but argues that art and technology are the same because they "enchant" in the same way. Contemporary objects such as smartphones and tablets are wonders of both technology and design, cultural critics note; like swords, they are made of components that no single worker can accomplish, and the vast majority of people cannot understand. In use, each individual machine or program has glitches that no IT expert can resolve. Jesse B. Williams, personal communication, August 31, 2014.

26. Hans Ulrich Gumbrecht, *Production of Presence: What Meaning Cannot Convey* (Stanford, CA: Stanford University Press, 2004).

27. Brigitte Miriam Bedos-Rezak, "Medieval Identity: A Sign and a Concept," *American Historical Review* 105, no. 5 (2000): 1516; Ann Marie Rasmussen, *Medieval Badges: Visual Communication and the Formation of Community* (Philadelphia: University of Pennsylvania Press, forthcoming). I thank Professor Rasmussen for sharing her work in manuscript.

28. A compelling description of these conditions appears in Andrew Cowell, "Swords, Clubs, and Relics: Performance, Identity, and the Sacred," *Yale French Studies* 110 (2006): esp. 9–10.

29. D. Miller, introduction to *Material Cultures*, 9; Gumbrecht argues that people in premodern Europe generally were more open to "presence effects" than those living after the Renaissance, but posits that both interpretation and experience of presence exist in all cultures, including our present. See *Production of Presence*, 24–32.

30. Hodder, "This Is Not an Article about Material Culture as Text," 261.

Chapter 1. Swords and Oral Culture in the Early Middle Ages

1. J. R. R. Tolkien, "*Beowulf*: The Monsters and the Critics," in "*Beowulf*": A *Verse Translation*, ed. Daniel Donoghue, trans. Seamus Heaney (New York: W. W. Norton, 2002), 103–30. Tolkien's essay, reprinted in other modern anthologies of criticism, was originally delivered as a Sir Israel Gollanz Memorial Lecture at the British Academy in 1936.

2. Ibid., 116.

3. Modern criticism of *Beowulf* is vast. On the dating of poem and manuscript, one should supplement Colin Chase, ed., *The Dating of "Beowulf"* (Toronto: University of Toronto Press, 1981), with Roberta Frank, "A Scandal in Toronto: The Dating of 'Beowulf' a Quarter Century On," *Speculum* 82, no. 4 (2007): 843–64; Roy Michael Liuzza, "On the Dating of *Beowulf*," in *The "Beowulf" Reader*, ed. Peter S. Baker (New York: Garland, 2000), 281–303; Andy Orchard, *A Critical Companion to "Beowulf"* (Woodbridge, Suffolk: D. S. Brewer, 2003).

4. Bonnie Effros, *Merovingian Mortuary Archaeology and the Making of the Early Middle Ages* (Berkeley: University of California Press, 2003), esp. chap. 3.

5. See, for example, Daniel Lord Smail, "Introduction: History and the Telescoping of Time; A Disciplinary Forum," and Carol Symes, "The Middle Ages between Nationalism and Colonialism," *French Historical Studies* 34, no. 1 (Winter 2011): 1–6 and 37–46.

6. See Andrew Taylor, "Was There a Song of Roland?," *Speculum* 76, no. 1 (January 2001): 28–65, concerning how the manuscript discovered in the Bodleian Library in Oxford became a French national treasure and the "song" created as a founding myth.

7. Anne Savage, "The Grave, the Sword and the Lament," in *Laments for the Lost in Medieval Literature*, ed. Jane Tolmie and M. J. Toswell (Turnhout, Belgium: Brepols, 2010), 80.

8. On the notion of rift, see Allan Megill, *Historical Knowledge, Historical Error* (Chicago: University of Chicago Press, 2007), 213.

9. Steven Walton, "Words of Technological Virtue: 'The Battle of Brunanburh' and Anglo-Saxon Sword Manufacture," *Technology and Culture* 36 (1995): 998. The rich descriptive language around swords in Anglo-Saxon literature is explored by Hilda Roderick Ellis Davidson, *The Sword in Anglo-Saxon England: Its Archaeology and Literature* (Oxford: Clarendon, 1962; corr. repr. Woodbridge, Suffolk: Boydell, 1998), 121–58.

10. Chris Caple points out that the first uses of metallurgy may have been for personal adornments and only over time were worked metals appreciated for their possibilities as weapons. See his *Objects: Reluctant Witnesses to the Past* (London: Routledge, 2006), 110.

11. Davidson, *Sword in Anglo-Saxon England*, 71.

12. This discussion is based on Alan Williams, *The Sword and the Crucible: A History of the Metallurgy of European Swords up to the Sixteenth Century* (Leiden: Brill, 2012), part 2.

13. Sonia Chadwick Hawkes, introduction to *Weapons and Warfare in Anglo-Saxon England*, ed. Sonia Chadwick Hawkes (Oxford: Oxford University Committee for Archaeology, 1989), 6.

14. Walton, "Words of Technological Virtue," 987–89. Interestingly, the particular style of the Saxons' weapons may have indicated that they came from somewhere in France, 996.

15. Frans Theuws and Monika Alkemade discuss swords as composite artifacts in "A Kind of Mirror for Men: Sword Depositions in Late Antique Northern Gaul," in *Rituals of Power: From Late Antiquity to the Early Middle Ages*, ed. Frans Theuws and Janet L. Nelson (Leiden: Brill, 2000), esp. 424–25. On the Abingdon sword, see Davidson, *Sword in Anglo-Saxon England*, 69, as well as fig. 67 and the cover illustration of the 1998 edition.

16. Theuws and Alkemade, "Mirror for Men," 420–22.

17. See the review of historiography and archaeological work by Guy Halsall, *Cemeteries and Society in Merovingian Gaul* (Leiden: Brill, 2010), esp. part 1.

18. Theuws and Alkemade, "Mirror for Men," 427–61, for the distribution and typologies of swords in Merovingian regions; and Guy Halsall, "The Origins of the *Reihengräberzivilization*: Forty Years On," in *Fifth-Century Gaul: A Crisis of Identity?*, ed. John Drinkwater and Hugh Elton (Cambridge: Cambridge University Press, 1992), 196–207.

19. Heinrich Härke, "Early Saxon Weapon Burials: Frequencies, Distributions and Weapon Combinations," in Hawkes, *Weapons and Warfare*, 49–59.

20. Heinrich Härke, "Material Culture as Myth: Weapons in Anglo-Saxon Graves," in *Burial and Society: The Chronological and Social Analysis of Archaeological*

Burial Data, ed. Claus Kjeld Jensen and Karen Høilund Nielsen (Aarhus, Denmark: Aarhus University Press, 1997), 119–25.

21. Caple, *Objects*, 120–21.

22. For example, the various versions of the Anglo-Saxon Chronicle postdate the phases of conquest and burial which Härke interprets partly by means of the Chronicle.

23. Theuws and Alkemade, "Mirror for Men," 454, 456–61.

24. Martin Carver, *Sutton Hoo: Burial Ground of Kings?* (Philadelphia: University of Pennsylvania Press, 1998) is the indispensable source from the lead archaeologist on the site. On the relations between southern England and the Merovingians, see Ian Wood, *The Merovingian North Sea* (Alingsås, Sweden: Viktoria, 1983), 12–18, cited by Susan Kelly, "Anglo-Saxon Lay Society and the Written Word," in *The Uses of Literacy in Early Mediaeval Europe*, ed. Rosamond McKitterick (Cambridge: Cambridge University Press, 1990), 41.

25. Savage, "Grave, Sword, and Lament," 68–69.

26. Carver, *Sutton Hoo*, 125. Nicholas Brooks notes the ceremonial, as opposed to military, function of helmets of this epoch: "Helmets [of this type] are used in the earliest king-making rituals, before the use of crowns, and are worn on important public occasions." "The Staffordshire Hoard and the Mercian Royal Court," Staffordshire Hoard Symposium, British Museum, London, March 2010, accessed September 28, 2014, http://finds.org.uk/staffshoardsymposium/papers/nicholasbrooks.

27. Martin Carver, "Burial as Poetry: The Context of Treasure in Anglo-Saxon Graves," in *Treasure in the Medieval West*, ed. Elizabeth M. Tyler (Woodbridge, Suffolk: York Medieval, 2000), 47–48.

28. Theuws and Alkemade, "Mirror for Men," emphasizes the importance of the burial ritual and the rhetorical richness of such acts. See also their discussion about whether "unsettled" should be construed as competition or perhaps tension, rather than meaning just uncertainty, 452–53.

29. Heinrich Härke, "The Circulation of Goods in Anglo-Saxon Society," in Theuws and Nelson, *Rituals of Power*, 393.

30. Theuws and Alkemade, "Mirror for Men," 464n153 and 469–70.

31. Some scholars argue that the circulation of goods in literature is constructed for fictional purposes, rather than reflecting actual practices. For example, see Leslie Webster, "Ideal and Reality: Versions of Treasure in the Early Anglo-Saxon World," in Tyler, *Treasure in the Medieval West*, esp. 58–59; other scholars assume that literature captures prior practice faithfully enough to be useful to the historian, for example, Härke, "Circulation," 378.

32. Dorothy Whitelock, ed., *Anglo-Saxon Wills* (Cambridge: Cambridge University Press, 1930), 56–62.

33. Härke, "Circulation," 393.

34. Jos Bazelmans, "Beyond Power: Ceremonial Exchanges in *Beowulf*," in Theuws and Nelson, *Rituals of Power*, 362–63.

35. Bazelmans draws attention to the process in *Beowulf* by which certain objects belonging to the king are destroyed (or, in other cases, buried) which helps free the successor to accede to power. Ibid., 367.

36. Timothy Reuter, "You Can't Take It with You: Testaments, Hoards and Movable Wealth in Europe: 600–1100," in Tyler, *Treasure in the Medieval West*, 13–14.

Reuter agrees with Martin Carver that even very rich graves, like Sutton Hoo, represented only a deliberate selection of objects, not the totality of a man's wealth.

37. Theuws and Alkemade, "Mirror for Men," 413.

38. Carver, "Context of Treasure," 37.

39. Brooks, "Staffordshire Hoard."

40. Whitelock, *Anglo-Saxon Wills*, 88–92 and 201. Internal evidence in the will dates it between 1052 and 1066.

41. Ibid., 6–9 and 103–8.

42. Nicholas Brooks believed the hoard represented materiel from the king's armorer: "Staffordshire Hoard."

43. On the survival and characteristics of early medieval wills, see Reuter, "You Can't Take It with You," 20–22; Härke, "Circulation," 378; Christina La Rocca and Luigi Provero, "The Dead and Their Gifts," in Theuws and Nelson, *Rituals of Power*, 225–33.

44. La Rocca and Provero, "Dead and Their Gifts," 231–32.

45. Reuter, "You Can't Take It with You," 23–24. For the notion of keeping while giving, see Annette B. Weiner, *Inalienable Possessions: The Paradox of Keeping-While-Giving* (Berkeley: University of California Press, 1992).

46. La Rocca and Provero, "Dead and Their Gifts," 251.

47. Ibid., 252.

48. Einhard and Notker the Stammerer, *Two Lives of Charlemagne*, trans., with an introduction and notes by Lewis Thorpe (London: Penguin Books, 1976), 77.

49. For the details of this ninth-century will, see La Rocca and Provero, "Dead and Their Gifts," esp. 240–59.

50. Reuter, "You Can't Take It with You," 19–24, discusses the process by which individual treasures became institutional ones.

51. Nicholas Brooks, "Weapons and Armour in the *Battle of Maldon*," chap. 8 in *Communities and Warfare, 700–1400* (London: Hambledon, 2000), esp. 174.

52. George Clark, "Maldon: History, Poetry and Truth," in *De Gustibus: Essays for Alain Renoir*, ed. John Miles Foley (New York: Garland, 1992), 84.

53. Gale R. Owen-Crocker, "Hawks and Horse-Trappings: The Insignia of Rank," in *The Battle of Maldon, AD 991*, ed. Donald Scragg (Oxford: Blackwell, 1991), 229–33.

54. On expectations regarding heriots, see Nicholas Brooks, "Weapons and Armour in the *Battle of Maldon*," chap. 8, and "Arms, Status and Warfare in Late-Saxon England," chap. 7 in *Communities and Warfare*.

55. See, for example, Savage, "Grave, Sword, and Lament," 67–70 and 75–77.

56. Liuzza, "On the Dating of *Beowulf*," 285–95.

57. On this point see Roberta Frank, "Skaldic Verse and the Date of *Beowulf*," in Chase, *Dating of "Beowulf*," esp. 129; Frank, "Scandal in Toronto"; see also Liuzza, "On the Dating of *Beowulf*," esp. 285.

58. My thanks to Professor Ann Marie Rasmussen for discussing these points with me.

59. C. R. Dodwell, *Anglo-Saxon Art: A New Perspective* (Ithaca, NY: Cornell University Press, 1982), 25, cited by Gillian Overing, "Swords and Signs: A Semiotic Perspective on *Beowulf*," *American Journal of Semiotics* 5, no. 1 (1987): 39.

60. Eric John, "*Beowulf* and the Margins of Literacy," in Baker, *"Beowulf" Reader*, esp. 65–67. John terms this a focus on loot or treasure while other scholars argue that objects serve as narrative devices in the story.

61. Overing, "Swords and Signs," 40, draws attention to this example; see also Lewis E. Nicholson, "Hunlafing and the Point of the Sword," in *Anglo-Saxon Poetry: Essays in Appreciation, for John C. McGalliard*, ed. Lewis E. Nicholson and Dolores Warwick Frese (Notre Dame, IN: University of Notre Dame Press, 1975), 50–61.

62. On the interlace structure of the poem, see John Leyerle, "The Interlace Structure of *Beowulf*," *University of Toronto Quarterly* 37 (1967): 1–17, reprinted in Donoghue, *"Beowulf": A Verse Translation*, 130–52; on the persistence of oral communication despite increasing use of written records, see Kelly, "Anglo-Saxon Lay Society," 61.

63. See the differing opinions of Phyllis Portnoy, "*Laf*-Craft in Five Old English Riddles," *Neophilologus* 97 (2013): 555–79; Nicholson, "Hunlafing," esp. 52–53.

64. Nicholson, "Hunlafing," 56–61, concerning swords carrying their pasts with them.

65. On the varying interpretations of Hrothgar's "reading," see Seth Lerer, *Literacy and Power in Anglo-Saxon Literature* (Lincoln: University of Nebraska Press, 1991), chap. 5; James Paz, "Aeschere's Head, Grendel's Mother and the Sword That Isn't a Sword: Unreadable Things in *Beowulf*," *Exemplaria* 25, no. 3 (Fall 2013): esp. 233–34. Regarding the archaisms in language in the poem, phrases that "might have sounded northern and darkly heathen to the Anglo-Saxon ear," see Frank, "Skaldic Verse," 134.

66. Colin Chase, "Saints' Lives, Royal Lives and the Date of *Beowulf*," in Chase, *Dating of "Beowulf*," 161–71. Chase argues that the evident Christianity of the poem reflects an earlier date of composition (ninth century) than is now accepted, since, had it been composed later, there would have been more comfort and ease in the twin identities of hero and Christian.

67. Kelly, "Anglo-Saxon Lay Society," 46.

68. There is agreement among scholars on this point, if not about whether the runes, in the story, are legible by the characters. See A. J. Frantzen, "Writing the Unreadable *Beowulf*: 'Writan' and 'Forwritan,' the Pen and the Sword," *Exemplaria* 3 (1991): 327–57; Paz, "Aeschere's Head"; Lerer, *Literacy and Power*.

69. It is interesting that Tolkien's *Lord of the Rings* epic repeats these moves. His story of Frodo and the ring is given a deep past, and a sword, as well as the rings, bridges the two epochs. On the work as literature, see T. A. Shippey, *J. R. R. Tolkien: Author of the Century* (Boston: Houghton Mifflin, 2000).

70. John Miles Foley, *Traditional Oral Epic: "The Odyssey," "Beowulf" and the Serbo-Croatian Return Song* (Berkeley: University of California Press, 1990), 33.

71. My thanks to Professor Ruth Morse for elucidation of this point and for sharing pertinent material from her forthcoming study *Imagined Histories: Fictions of the Past from "Beowulf" to Shakespeare*. Foley, it should be noted, asserts that "we cannot rule out . . . a *Beowulf*-poet who memorized great chunks of his poem, partially fixing it in rote memory even before it was written down." See John Miles Foley, *How to Read an Oral Poem* (Urbana: University of Illinois Press, 2002), 46.

72. On the mimicking of oral performance (and modern romanticizing of them) in written texts, see Taylor, "Song of Roland," esp. 36–41 and 61–64.

73. John, "*Beowulf* and the Margins of Literacy," 74.

74. Foley, *Traditional Oral Epic*, 34. See also Foley, *How to Read an Oral Poem*, especially 69–72 and 102–8. Here and throughout his work, Foley cautions against the

presumption of interpreting a work like *Beowulf* in the absence of its linguistic context and argues we cannot fully retrieve the sense of the immersive experience of an oral performance in its day.

75. I thus agree with Roberta Frank who argues that the poem was a "late culturally charged repetition, imaginatively reconciling its audience to new realities." Frank, "Scandal in Toronto," 863.

Chapter 2. Swords and Chivalric Culture in the High Middle Ages

1. Emma Mason, "The Hero's Invincible Weapon: An Aspect of Angevin Propaganda," in *The Ideals and Practice of Medieval Knighthood III: Papers from the Fourth Strawberry Hill Conference, 1988*, ed. Christopher Harper-Bill and Ruth Harvey (Woodbridge, Suffolk: Boydell, 1990), 130; John Gillingham, "Richard I and the Science of War in the Middle Ages," in *War and Government in the Middle Ages*, ed. John Gillingham and James Clarke Holt (Cambridge: Boydell, 1984), 90–91.

2. David Alban Hinton, *Gold and Gilt, Pots and Pins: Possessions and People in Medieval Britain*, Medieval History and Archaeology (Oxford: Oxford University Press, 2005), 197.

3. Thomas Hahn, "Gawain and Popular Romance in Britain," in *The Cambridge Companion to Medieval Romance*, ed. Roberta L. Krueger (Cambridge: Cambridge University Press, 2000), 218.

4. Jim Bradbury, "Geoffrey V of Anjou, Count and Knight," in Harper-Bill and Harvey, *Ideals and Practice of Medieval Knighthood III*, 32; Mason, "Hero's Invincible Weapon," 129.

5. On this process, see Amy G. Remensnyder, "Legendary Treasure at Conques: Reliquaries and Imaginative Memory," *Speculum* 71, no. 3 (July 1996): 884–906.

6. Mason, "Hero's Invincible Weapon," esp. 126–27.

7. The term "imaginative memory" is Remensnyder's. She sees such processes as instances of what Igor Kopytoff calls the "singularization" of objects, by which he means the withdrawal of a commodity from circulation with other like objects. See Igor Kopytoff, "The Cultural Biography of Things: Commoditization as Process," in *The Social Life of Things: Commodities in Cultural Perspective*, ed. Arjun Appadurai (Cambridge: Cambridge University Press, 1986), 73–77; Remensnyder, "Legendary Treasure," 885. See also the extensive discussion of categories of sameness and difference in medieval thought by Brigitte Miriam Bedos-Rezak, "Medieval Identity: A Sign and a Concept," *American Historical Review* 105, no. 5 (2000): 1489–1533.

8. Alan R. Williams, *The Sword and the Crucible: A History of the Metallurgy of European Swords up to the Sixteenth Century* (Leiden: Brill, 2012), chap. 13. See also Ian Peirce, "The Development of the Medieval Sword, c. 850–1300," in Harper-Bill and Harvey, *Ideals and Practice of Medieval Knighthood III*, 139–58.

9. Cited by John Gillingham, "Conquering the Barbarians: War and Chivalry in Twelfth-Century Britain," *Haskins Society Journal* 4 (1993), 78.

10. Ibid., 79–81; Matthew Strickland, *War and Chivalry: The Conduct and Perception of War in England and Normandy, 1066–1217* (New York: Cambridge University Press, 1996), chaps. 1 and 2.

11. For a discussion of the continuation of local feuding see Stephen D. White, "Feuding and Peace-Making in the Touraine around the Year 1100," *Traditio* 42 (1986): 195–263.

12. Matthew Strickland, "Arms and the Men: War, Loyalty and Lordship in Jordan Fantosme's Chronicle," in *The Ideals and Practice of Medieval Knighthood IV: Papers from the Fifth Strawberry Hill Conference, 1990*, ed. Christopher Harper-Bill and Ruth Harvey (Woodbridge, Suffolk: Boydell, 1992), 202.

13. Charles Coulson, *Castles in Medieval Society: Fortresses in England, France, and Ireland in the Central Middle Ages* (Oxford: Oxford University Press, 2003), esp. chap. 2, argues convincingly (if somewhat contentiously) that we have overvalued the military-strategic features of castles (indeed we have overlooked other features, as well as misidentified or misinterpreted defensive features) partly because we have not examined how the sites and the buildings were actually used as administrative centers, not simply as garrisoned military encampments. André Debord, *Aristocratie et pouvoir: Le rôle du château dans la France médiévale* (Paris: Picard, 2000), also emphasizes the role of the castle as administrative/economic center and agrees that their military function was delimited by varying developments in political history. See also Oliver Hamilton Creighton, *Castles and Landscapes: Power, Community and Fortification in Medieval England* (London: Equinox, 2002), on the distorted view we now have of the medieval landscape based on misinterpretation of surviving iconic sites. Castles were not routinely staffed with a garrison, which would be necessary for defense. Those built by crusading Europeans in the Holy Land were exceptions that proved the rule: in fact, they were crucial militarily for Europeans' hold on the land and were vulnerable because they were not adequately garrisoned.

14. David Crouch, *Tournament* (London: Hambledon and London, 2005), 96–98.

15. The scholarly debate concerning the evolution of political organization as the Carolingian empire declined and whether feudalism should be understood as an antithesis of the state is reviewed by Charles West, *Reframing the Feudal Revolution: Political and Social Transformation between Marne and Moselle, c. 800–c. 1100* (Cambridge: Cambridge University Press, 2013), introduction. The notion that western Europe at the outset of the central Middle Ages was prey to rampant "feudal anarchy" is outdated. Scholarship in military history has proceeded largely independent of this debate and typically presumes a period of greater violence and "anarchy" preceding the eleventh and twelfth centuries.

16. On this point and the spread of heraldry generally, see Adrian Ailes, "The Knight, Heraldry and Armour: The Role of Recognition and the Origins of Heraldry," in Harper-Bill and Harvey, *Ideals and Practice of Medieval Knighthood IV*, 1–22.

17. Hinton, *Gold and Gilt*, 201–2; Laurent Hablot, "'Ubi armae ibi princeps': Medieval Emblematics as the Real Presence of the Prince," in *Absentee Authority across Medieval Europe*, ed. Frédérique Lachaud and Michael Penman (Woodbridge, Suffolk: Boydell, 2017), 39.

18. David Crouch, *The Image of Aristocracy in Britain, 1000–1300* (London: Routledge: 1993), 180–90.

19. David Crouch, *The Birth of Nobility: Constructing Aristocracy in England and France, 900–1300* (Harlow: Pearson/Longman, 2005), chap. 7. While the relationship of knighthood to nobility was different in the two realms, Crouch argues that the two polities had systems of recognition and social advancement that were not, in their social and political effects, greatly different.

20. Hinton notes that status-envy led even up-and-coming merchants to sport gilded spurs. See *Gold and Gilt*, 172. After the battle of Courtrai in 1302, a Flemish

townsmen's victory over French knights, dead French aristocrats' golden spurs were amassed and displayed in a church.

21. Crouch, *Image of Aristocracy*, 194–95.

22. The discovery and repurposing of staffs, lances, and banners, as well as swords are discussed by Philippe Buc, "Conversion of Objects: Suger of St. Denis and Meinwerk of Paderborn," *Viator* 28 (1997): 119–23; Olivier Bouzy, "Les armes symboles d'un pouvoir politique: L'épée du sacre, la Sainte Lance, l'Oriflamme aux VIIIᵉ–XIIᵉ siècles," *Francia* 22, no. 1 (1995): 46–48.

23. Bouzy, "Armes symboles," 49–52.

24. Jane Martindale, "The Sword on the Stone: Some Resonances of a Medieval Symbol of Power," *Anglo-Norman Studies* 15 (1992): 209–11, 219–20.

25. Kurt Bauch, *Das Mittelalterliche Grabbild* (Berlin: De Gruyter, 1976), 55–56, argues that the Fontevrault effigies may in turn have derived stylistically from the tombs of Eleanor of Aquitaine's ducal forebears, whose effigies, some of the earliest to survive, depict recumbent mailed knights, girded with sword belt and sheathed sword; like the Angevin kings and Eleanor herself, they lie on a platform of stone drapery, the most significant feature which ties them to the Fontevrault tombs.

26. Martindale, "Sword on the Stone," 240–41. John's burial reflected his rapprochement with the pope in several ways, including being buried near the shrine of St. Wulfstan in Worcester Cathedral. Wulfstan had just been canonized, in 1203, by Pope Innocent. Innocent and John had been political allies concerning the line of succession in the Holy Roman Empire but had had a falling-out capped by John's loss at the battle of Bouvines, 1214. John accepted (under duress) Innocent's candidate for the archbishopric of Canterbury, and in return Innocent declared Magna Carta null and void.

27. Buc, "Conversion of Objects," argues that had we written descriptions of actual events, they would be less true records and more efforts to shape the event in memory going forward; see especially 141. For a discussion of the reciprocal influences of English and continental liturgies for coronations, see P. L. Ward, "The Coronation Ceremony in Mediaeval England," *Speculum* 14, no. 2 (April 1939): 160–78.

28. Tessa Rose, *The Coronation Ceremony of the Kings and Queens of England* (London: H. M. Stationery Office, 1992), 10–12 and 38–39.

29. Ibid., 13.

30. Ibid., 103; see also Ward, "Coronation Ceremony," 164, n2.

31. Martin Aurell, "L'épée, l'autel et le perron," in *Armes et jeux militaires dans l'imaginaire*, ed. Catalina Girbea (Paris: Classiques Garnier, 2016), 39–44.

32. Jacques Le Goff, "A Coronation Program," in *Coronations: Medieval and Early Modern Monarchic Ritual*, ed. János M. Bak (Berkeley: University of California Press, 1990), 50–56.

33. Bouzy, "Armes symboles," 52.

34. See Ewart Oakeshott's meticulous typology of swords, especially regarding hilt designs, useful for dating surviving examples. R. Ewart Oakeshott, *Records of the Medieval Sword* (Rochester: Boydell, 1991).

35. Rose, *Coronation Ceremony*, 14.

36. Bouzy, "Armes symboles," 54–57.

37. Laurent Hablot, "The Sacralization of the Royal Coats of Arms in Medieval Europe," in *Political Theology in Medieval and Early Modern Europe*, ed. Montserrat

Herrero, Jaume Aurell, and Angela C. Miceli Stout (Turnhout, Belgium: Brepols, 2017), 314–36. In addition to Henry III's invocations of Edward the Confessor, his son Edward I played catch-up by adding imagery of St. George bestowing the royal coat of arms which, with its heraldic beasts, did not itself convey sacrality.

38. "Chrétien de Troyes" was likely a pen name; he was not necessarily a cleric, as has been long supposed. He might even have been a fictional author figure himself, which allowed the actual composer of the tale additional fictive and editorial license. See Sarah Kay, "Who Was Chrétien de Troyes?," *Arthurian Literature* 15 (1996): 1–35; Simon Gaunt, *Retelling the Tale: An Introduction to Medieval French Literature* (London: Duckworth, 2001), 94–98.

39. Maureen C. Miller, *Clothing the Clergy: Virtue and Power in Medieval Europe, c. 800–1200* (Ithaca, NY: Cornell University Press, 2014), analyzes the representations of clerical sanctity and claims to lordship embodied in their vestments, which were sponsored and even sewn by elite women.

40. Gabrielle M. Spiegel, *Romancing the Past: The Rise of Vernacular Prose Historiography in Thirteenth-Century France* (Berkeley: University of California Press, 1993), chap. 3.

41. On the origins and composition of the Roland manuscript, see Andrew Taylor, "Was There a Song of Roland?," *Speculum* 76, no. 1 (January 2001): 28–65.

42. Spiegel, *Romancing the Past*, 89.

43. Michelle R. Warren, *History on the Edge: Excalibur and the Borders of Britain, 1100–1300* (Minneapolis: University of Minnesota Press, 2000), chap. 2.

44. See the cases of the thirteenth-century cleric Robert of Gloucester's writing and of Wace's work as analyzed in ibid., chap. 4, esp. 123–27, and chap. 5.

45. Jean Flori, "L'épée de Lancelot: Adoubement et idéologie au début du XIIIème siècle," in *Lancelot-Lanzelet*, ed. Danielle Buschinger and Michel Zink (Greifswald: Reineke-Verlag, 1995), esp. 153.

46. Warren, *History on the Edge*; Flori, "L'épée de Lancelot," 149.

47. Jeff Rider, "The Other Worlds of Romance," in Krueger, *Medieval Romance*, 121.

48. Before we even get to romance, Excalibur is more than one thing, and in some cases, not the only thing. As Arthur's sword gains and loses potency in service to various authors' purposes, other arms and armor are created for him, or are given larger roles than Geoffrey imagined. See, for example, Flori, "L'épée de Lancelot," 153–54.

49. This discussion of coexistence of different genres draws on the work of Sarah Kay, *The chansons de geste in the Age of Romance: Political Fictions* (Oxford: Clarendon, 1995).

50. Brian Stock, *Listening for the Text: On the Uses of the Past* (Philadelphia: University of Pennsylvania Press, 1990), 37–38.

51. The term "two-way traffic" is Richard W. Kaeuper's in his *Chivalry and Violence in Medieval Europe* (Oxford: Oxford University Press, 1999), chap. 2. Among the many studies of the intersection of chivalric romance and warrior life, see Elspeth Kennedy, "The Knight as Reader of Arthurian Romance," in *Culture and the King: The Social Implications of the Arthurian Legend*, ed. Martin B. Shichtman and James P. Carley (Albany: State University of New York Press, 1994); David Crouch, *William Marshal: Knighthood, War and Chivalry, 1147–1219*, 2nd ed. (London: Longman, 2002); Gabrielle Spiegel also diagnoses the text-context problem in "History, Historicism and the Social Logic of the Text in the Middle Ages," *Speculum* 65 (1990): 59–86.

180   NOTES TO PAGES 83–88

52. It is important to note that "courtly" does not imply feminine or celibate. See Rider, "Worlds of Romance," 125.

53. In addition to literary studies of chivalric texts, the historical literature on chivalry is vast in its own right. In response to earlier studies which weighed the religious ethos present in chivalric values, such as in Maurice Keen, *Chivalry* (New Haven, CT: Yale University Press, 1984), some scholars emphasize what they regard as the underestimated importance of prowess and acceptance of violence as a value, particularly in earlier phases. See, for example, Crouch, *Birth of Nobility*; and Kaeuper, *Chivalry and Violence*. At the same time, they and others acknowledge that the value of "courtliness" preceded a fuller notion of chivalry, as the idea, per Crouch, that you have to learn to get along with your betters in public forums. This theme is most fully developed by C. Stephen Jaeger, *The Origins of Courtliness: Civilizing Trends and the Formation of Courtly Ideals, 939–1210* (Philadelphia: University of Pennsylvania Press, 1985). Chivalry as the identity of the knightly class is only fully articulated by about 1200; the word itself is first coined late in the twelfth century by Chrétien de Troyes.

54. Frederic Cheyette and Howell Chickering emphasize the complex and playful nature of these texts and of the presence of the author in them in "Love, Anger, and Peace: Social Practice and Poetic Play in the Ending of *Yvain*," *Speculum* 80, no. 1 (2005): 75–117.

55. Ibid., 109.

56. Bedos-Rezak, "Medieval Identity," 1528–33.

57. Hablot, "'Ubi armae ibi princeps,'" esp. 44–45.

58. Aurell, "L'épée," 59–60.

59. On the "fictional orality" of medieval romance, see Gaunt, *Retelling the Tale*, esp. 16–23 and 30–35.

60. See Spiegel, *Romancing the Past*, 64–69.

61. Stock, *Listening for the Text*, esp. 133; see also Brian Stock, *The Implications of Literacy: Written Language and Models of Interpretation in the Eleventh and Twelfth Centuries* (Princeton, NJ: Princeton University Press, 1987), 85.

62. M. T. Clanchy, *From Memory to Written Record, England 1066–1307*, 2nd ed. (Oxford: Blackwell, 1993), 35–42. Clanchy notes that the story is also fanciful in that brandishing a sword in a legal proceeding would not have been allowed.

63. For examples of the identification of past and present in narratives, which betray the residue of oral composition as late as the sixteenth century, see Kristen B. Neuschel, *Word of Honor: Interpreting Noble Culture in Sixteenth-Century France* (Ithaca, NY: Cornell University Press, 1989), 112–13. Clanchy emphasizes, in the Earl de Warenne story, the way an object rather than written words guarantees the earl's rights as evidence of what he calls "an evocation of dying oral culture," *Memory to Written Record*, 35.

64. Buc makes this point about signature objects embodying relationships, and representing them in memory: "Conversion of Objects," 107.

65. On this concept, see Annette B. Weiner, *Inalienable Possessions: The Paradox of Keeping-While-Giving* (Berkeley: University of California Press, 1992), 6–8.

66. Andrew Cowell, "Swords, Clubs, and Relics: Performance, Identity, and the Sacred," *Yale French Studies* 110 (2006): 9–10.

67. Ibid., 15. The legendary hero is probably the result of a combination of legends arising from a number of different historical Williams, though a trusted relation of Charlemagne by that name did exist.

68. Curtana is named in treasury records from Edward III's reign in NA, E101/333/28, "Indenture and Inventory of Items in the Treasury," 28 November 1356, and is listed in almost exactly the same terms in treasury records for Richard II in 1377 in E101/335/2; for Richard III's coronation see NA, LC9/50, "Lord Chamberlain's Accounts and Memorabilia," 1483–1509; as well as W. H. St. John Hope, "The King's Coronation Ornaments," *Ancestor* 1 (1902): 127–59; and Anne F. Sutton and P. W. Hammond, eds., *The Coronation of Richard III: The Extant Documents* (Gloucester: Alan Sutton, 1983).

69. Saints' relics, too, had to be "rediscovered" and ceremonially rehoused periodically to ensure their efficacy in the public's mind. See Patrick Geary, "Sacred Commodities: The Circulation of Medieval Relics," in Appadurai, *Social Life of Things*, 169–91.

Chapter 3. Swords, Clothing, and Armor in the Late Middle Ages

1. A. Lecoy de La Marche, ed., *Extraits de comptes et mémoriaux du roi René* (Paris: Picard, 1873), 178–80.

2. For recent comparative studies of René's administration in the context of other aristocrats and princes, see Jean-Michel Matz and Noël-Yves Tonnerre, eds., *René d'Anjou, 1409–1480: Pouvoirs et gouvernement* (Rennes: Presses universitaires de Rennes, 2011). A basic survey is Jean Favier, *Le roi René* (Paris: Librairie Arthème Fayard, 2008).

3. It is our own retroactive privileging of the nation state as it evolved in the early modern centuries, and a consequent failure to appreciate the degree of war and violence in its name, which lead us to see these "late medieval" centuries as particularly chaotic and violent, a kind of political and cultural dead end. This historiography is reviewed by John Watts, *The Making of Polities: Europe, 1300–1500* (Cambridge: Cambridge University Press, 2009), introduction.

4. Susan Crane, *The Performance of Self: Ritual, Clothing, and Identity during the Hundred Years' War* (Philadelphia: University of Pennsylvania Press, 2002), chap. 1; see also Stella Mary Newton, *Fashion in the Age of the Black Prince* (Woodbridge, Suffolk: Boydell, 1980), esp. 1–13.

5. Odile Blanc, *Parades et parures: L'invention du corps de mode à la fin du Moyen Âge* (Paris: Gallimard, 1997), 191–200.

6. Young men and squires continued to wear short doublets and tight hose alone, thus signifying their dependent status. Raymond van Uytven, "Showing Off One's Rank," in *Showing Status: Representation of Social Positions in the Late Middle Ages*, ed. Wim Blockmans and Antheun Janse (Turnhout, Belgium: Brepols, 1999), 31–32.

7. Odile Blanc, "From Battlefield to Court: The Invention of Fashion in the Fourteenth Century," in *Encountering Medieval Textiles and Dress: Objects, Texts, Images*, ed. Désirée G. Koslin and Janet E. Snyder (New York: Palgrave Macmillan, 2002), 159.

8. Quoted in E. Amanda McVitty, "False Knights and True Men: Contesting Chivalric Masculinity in English Treason Trials, 1388–1415," *Journal of Medieval History* 40, no. 4 (2014): 474. A surviving muster roll of English infantry from 1457 records that 64 of the 201 men at the muster carried a dagger: Graeme Rimer, "Weapons," in *Blood Red Roses: The Archaeology of a Mass Grave from the Battle of Towton, 1461*, ed.

Veronica Fiorato, Anthea Boylston, and Christopher Knüsel, 2nd ed. (Oxford: Oxbow Books, 2007), 122–23.

9. A nineteenth-century drawing of the effigy of the fourth Earl of Hereford in Hereford Cathedral shows the earl with a jeweled sword belt, a sword at his side, but most obviously a ballock dagger, with its distinctive balls on the pommel positioned directly over his genitals. For other examples, see the reproductions in Nigel Saul, *Death, Art, and Memory in Medieval England: The Cobham Family and Their Monuments, 1300–1500* (Oxford: Oxford University Press, 2001).

10. AN, KK 268A, "Inventaires de la maison d'Orléans," December 1408–January 1409, ff. 23v and 25.

11. AN, KK 51, "Comptes de l'argenterie du Roy," ff. 9v–70v.

12. AN, KK 7, "Comptes de Nicolas Braque de la tresorerie du duc de Normandie et Guyenne," January–November, 1349. For a general discussion of accumulations of goods, see Jules Guiffrey, *Inventaires de Jean, duc de Berry*, 2 vols. (Paris, 1894–96), vol. 1, introduction.

13. AN, KK 8, "Comptes de l'argenterie de Jean le Bon," fragments, n.d., f. 130; Nicholas H. Nicolas, *Privy Purse Expenses of Elizabeth of York: Wardrobe Accounts of Edward the Fourth* (London: W. Pickering, 1830), esp. 156–62.

14. AN, KK 348, "Inventaire des biens meubles de Philippe d'Orléans, comte de Vertus," 1420, f. 34v.

15. This discussion of the image of King Charles is drawn from Crane, *Performance of Self*, 16–17.

16. Michel Pastoureau, "Le rabot médiéval: De l'outil à l'emblème," in *Armes et outils*, ed. Christiane Raynaud, Cahiers du Léopard d'Or, ed. Michel Pastoreau, vol. 14 (Paris: Le Léopard d'Or, 2012), 31–36. Pastoureau notes that some of the resonance of these devices came from the fact that they were repurposed mundane objects, such as workers' tools or primitive weapons like a club. It is the honor of an aristocrat, such as John the Fearless, that can transform a lowly object into a signature device.

17. Crane, *Performance of Self*, esp. 17–20.

18. For example, AN, KK 8, "Comptes [. . .] de Jean le Bon," f. 52.

19. AN, KK 51, "Comptes de l'argenterie du Roy," 1458–59, ff. 69–72.

20. Andrew Cowell, "Swords, Clubs, and Relics: Performance, Identity, and the Sacred," *Yale French Studies* 110 (2006): 15.

21. Benjamin L. Wild, "Emblems and Enigmas: Revisiting the 'Sword' Belt of Fernando de la Cerda," *Journal of Medieval History* 37, no. 4 (2011): esp. 390–96. For other examples of belts in elite collections, see AN, KK 8, "Comptes [. . .] de Jean le Bon," f. 106; NA, E101/335/5, "Indenture as to the Delivery of Certain Jewels, Plate and Goods for the King's Use," 20 November 1399, 1.

22. On Blanche's goods, see Marguerite Keane, "Most Beautiful and the Next Best: Value in the Collection of a Medieval Queen," *Journal of Medieval History* 34, no. 4 (2008): 360–73.

23. Alan R. Williams, *The Knight and the Blast Furnace: A History of the Metallurgy of Armour in the Middle Ages and the Early Modern Period* (Leiden: Brill, 2003), esp. 43, 55, 204. See also Thom Richardson, "Armour in England," *Journal of Medieval History* 37, no. 3 (2011): 304–20; Claude Gaier, *L'industrie et le commerce des armes dans les anciennes principautés belges du XIIIme à la fin du XVme siècle*, Bibliothèque de la Faculté de Philosophie et Lettres de l'Université de Liège, fasc. 202 (Paris: Les Belles Lettres,

1973). There is continuing controversy about when the English longbow came into use, and whether new armor represented a response to it as well as to crossbows. See Clifford J. Rogers, "The Development of the Longbow in Late Medieval England and 'Technological Determinism,'" *Journal of Medieval History* 37, no. 3 (2011): 321–41.

24. One example is noted in G. G. Astill, "An Early Inventory of a Leicestershire Knight," *Midland History* 2 (1974): 274–83.

25. A. R. Myers, "The Wealth of Richard Lyons," in *Essays in Medieval History Presented to Bertie Wilkinson*, ed. T. A. Sandquist and M. R. Powicke (Toronto: University of Toronto Press, 1969), 73–77.

26. AN, KK 348, "Inventaire [. . .] de Philippe d'Orléans," 1420, f. 16; Desmond Seward, *The Hundred Years War: The English in France, 1337–1453* (New York: Penguin, 1999), 130.

27. BL, Stow 622, "Testament of Sir Fouk de Pennebrugge," 1325, Tong. Inventories and accounts, such as AN, KK 348, "Inventaire [. . .] de Philippe d'Orléans," can reveal gifts and exchanges of important items that occurred before death or by other means not captured in wills, while wills were in some sense a performance of awareness of impending death more than they were careful dispersals of goods. Hence, a meticulous dispersal as in Fulk's will is all the more compelling. See Philippa Maddern, "Friends of the Dead: Executors, Wills and Family Strategy in Fifteenth-Century Norfolk," in *Rulers and Ruled in Late Medieval England: Essays Presented to Gerald Harris*, ed. Rowena E. Archer and Simon Walker (London: Hambledon, 1995), 155–74.

28. NA, Patent Rolls 33 Henry VI; Nicolas, *Privy Purse Expenses*, 156–62; one wardrobe account for Thomas, Duke of Clarence (d. 1421) mentions monies given to a seamstress for silk garnishments for his vambraces and rerebraces—the armor covering his arms: Christopher M. Woolgar, ed., *Household Accounts from Medieval England*, 2 vols. (Oxford: British Academy, 1992–93), 2:636. See also the examples cited by Juliet R. V. Barker, *The Tournament in England* (Woodbridge, Suffolk: Boydell, 1986), 169–70.

29. T. H. Turner, "The Will of Humphrey de Bohun, Earl of Hereford and Essex, with Extracts from the Inventory of His Effects, 1319–1322," *Archaeological Journal* 2 (1846): 339–49; see also Melville M. Bigelow, "The Bohun Wills," *American Historical Review* 1, no. 3 (1896): 414–35 and 1, no. 4 (1896): 631–49. It was hard to decorate mail itself, though Thomas of Woodstock's hauberk, the will tells us, "had the mark of the cross." As full pieces of plate armor became more common, over the fifteenth century, individual pieces of armor themselves became sites for decorative statements: shoulder or shin guards engraved and gilded, a coronet fashioned for a helmet. The connection to textiles and the identity markers they could convey was never fully severed, however.

30. AN, KK 7, "Comptes [. . .] du duc de Normandie [. . .]," ff. 46v–47r.

31. Laurent Hablot, "'Ubi armae ibi princeps': Medieval Emblematics as the Real Presence of the Prince," in *Absentee Authority across Medieval Europe*, ed. Frédérique Lachaud and Michael Penman (Woodbridge, Suffolk: Boydell, 2017), 52–53.

32. Christiane Raynaud, "Le poête, l'arme et l'outil d'après l'oeuvre complète d'Eustache Deschamps," in Raynaud, *Armes et outils*, 89–119. The falchion, for example, was often indistinguishable from the braquemart: both were wide curved single-edged weapons.

33. Christopher Knüsel and Anthea Boylston, "How Has the Towton Project Contributed to Our Knowledge of Medieval Warfare?," in Fiorato, Boylston, and Knüsel, *Blood Red Roses*, 178–80. Comparisons of injuries sustained at Towton, 1461, and at Visby, one hundred years earlier, as well as other earlier combat victims, reveal the greater incidence of blunt-force trauma in the later Middle Ages.

34. Jean de Wavrin, *Recueil des croniques et anchiennes istories de la Grant Bretaigne*, cited by Seward, *Hundred Years War*, 200.

35. It is important to note that men of the companies freely chose "sides" in these other ventures—English captains even allied with French nobles they had fought against previously. See Kenneth A. Fowler, *Medieval Mercenaries*, vol. 1, *The Great Companies* (Oxford: Blackwell, 2001).

36. The battle was at Towton, England, in 1461, and was a decisive encounter in the so-called War of the Roses. Shannon A. Novak, "Battle-Related Trauma," in Fiorato, Boylston, and Knüsel, *Blood Red Roses*, 90–101. Novak speculates that men wounded in the early stages of the battles would have received more arrow wounds than this small sample of the dead; had they been on horseback, they would have displayed leg wounds. It is also possible that men had been caught by pursuing mounted fighters when running away from the battle, and had jettisoned or lost their heavy helmets, if they had had them, in flight. See also Thom Richardson, "Armour," ibid., 137–47.

37. On the sparse remains of clothing and gear, see Andrea Burgess, "The Excavation and Finds," in Fiorato, Boylston, and Knüsel, *Blood Red Roses*, 29–35; and Tim Sutherland, "The Archaeological Investigation of the Towton Battlefield," ibid., 167.

38. Christiane Raynaud, introduction to *Armes et outils*, 17.

39. Christine de Pisan, *The Book of Fayttes of Armes and of Chyvalrye*, trans. William Caxton, ed. A. T. P. Byles (London: Oxford University Press, 1932), book 3, chap. 12.

40. Quoted in David Green, *The Hundred Years War: A People's History* (New Haven, CT: Yale University Press, 2014), 198.

41. Germain Butaud, "L'armement des citadins et des villageois à la fin du Moyen Âge: L'exemple de la Provence et du Comtat Venaissin," in Raynaud, *Armes et outils*, 224–25.

42. Rimer, "Weapons," 121.

43. Sir Thomas Grey, *Scalacronica*, ed. and trans. Andy King (Woodbridge, Suffolk: Boydell, 2005), 157.

44. This point is made by Fowler, *Mercenaries*, 106–7.

45. A. M. Chazaud, ed., *Chronique du bon duc Loys de Bourbon* (Paris: Renouard, 1876), 85.

46. AN, KK 500, no. 5, Inventaires des ducs d'Orléans, 5 May 1417.

47. AN, KK 8, "Comptes [. . .] de Jean le Bon," f. 107r.

48. NA, E101/335/5, "Indenture [. . .] of goods [. . .]," 20 November 1399, 1.

49. In 1399, Henry, Richard II's first cousin, had deposed and imprisoned him, first in the Tower of London and later at one of Henry's castles, Pontefract, where Richard died soon after in mysterious circumstances.

50. AN, KK 268A, "Inventaires de la maison d'Orléans," f. 23v.

51. Turner, "Will of Humphrey de Bohun."

52. The infant's blanket might be explained as a memento mori for one of his two eldest sons, both of whom had died in infancy. It is also possible all of Humphrey's

goods had been rifled through, and the drinking cups, reliquaries, pieces of armor without distinctive markings, or other easily pawned or repurposed items taken as booty.

53. Lecoy de La Marche, *Comptes* [. . .] *du roi René*, 218–25.

54. NA, E101/390/7, 1345. This is a list of armor, jewels, and other articles delivered by one keeper of the wardrobe to his successor.

55. Butaud, "L'armement des citadins," 244.

56. "Inventory of Effects Formerly Belonging to Sir John Fastolfe," *Archaeologia* 21 (1827): 272.

57. J. Payne Collier, ed., *The Household Books of John Duke of Norfolk and Thomas Earl of Surrey* (London, 1844), 420–21.

58. For what follows, see Henri Bresc, ed., *Le Livre de raison de Paul de Sade, Avignon, 1390–94* (Paris: Comité des travaux historiques et scientifiques, 2013).

59. Ibid., 56n85.

60. Ibid., 45.

61. David Crouch, *Tournament* (London: Hambledon and London, 2005), surveys the origins and development of tournament practices. While one can argue that the term "tournament," as opposed to "joust," should only be applied to the era when true melees were part of the event, late medieval and sixteenth-century contemporaries spoke of "tourneying," whatever actually was included in the event, hence my use of the term across time.

62. For example, "Account of Expenses of John, Duke of Brabant and Henry and Thomas of Lancaster, 1292–93," *Camden Miscellany* 2 (1852–53). It is important to note that royal interest in fostering tournaments waxed and waned according to their political needs. See Catalina Girbea, "Rapport introductif: L'imaginaire du tournoi," in *Armes et jeux militaires dans l'imaginaire: XIIe–XVe siècles*, ed. Catalina Girbea (Paris: Classiques Garnier, 2016), 7–33.

63. Michael Camille, *Mirror in Parchment: The Luttrell Psalter and the Making of Medieval England* (Chicago: University of Chicago Press, 1998), 51–56, applies this analysis to the image in the Luttrell Psalter.

64. Richard Barber, *Edward III and the Triumph of England: The Battle of Crécy and the Company of the Garter* (London: Allen Lane, 2013), chaps. 2–4.

65. It is difficult even for an analyst as astute as Barber to avoid talking about eventual English success as resulting partly from "stubbornly refusing knightly glory" (ibid., 148).

66. Fowler, *Mercenaries*, 295.

67. Pisan, *Book of Fayttes of Armes*, part 1, chap. 23. Pisan envisions a role for cavalry in battle, and imagines men-at-arms fighting on foot—that is, elites like those on horseback—as an essential constituent of battle formations. She argues for their role in the coherence of forces when she says that in case "yf [common foot soldiers] wolde flee they might be kepte in style [that is, in their ranks] by the men at armes," 81.

68. Green, *Hundred Years War*, 41.

69. On Verneuil, see M. K. Jones, "Battle of Verneuil," *War in History* 9 (2002): 379–411.

70. Malcolm Vale, *War and Chivalry: Warfare and Aristocratic Culture in England, France, and Burgundy at the End of the Middle Ages* (Athens: University of Georgia Press, 1981), esp. chap. 4. Vale argues that the use of the lance persisted until the last quarter of the sixteenth century.

71. See the records of tournament combat in G. A. Lester, *Sir John Paston's "Grete Boke": A Descriptive Catalogue, with an Introduction, of British Library MS Lansdowne 285* (Cambridge: D. S. Brewer, 1984), a modern summary and commentary on the original manuscript (BL, Lansdowne 285).

72. AN, KK 7, "Comptes [. . .] du duc de Normandie [. . .]," f. 41.

73. See the "complete harness" for the Duke of Norfolk, put on board ship for his expedition to Scotland in 1481: Collier, *Household Books of John Duke of Norfolk*, 275.

74. NA, E101/390/7, 1345. This is a list of armor, jewels, and other articles delivered by one keeper of the wardrobe to his successor.

75. Woolgar, *Household Accounts*, 2:595.

76. BL, Add MS 34393, "An Inventory of the Goods of Late Syr Rychard Cromwell, Knyght," n.d. f. 12. Internal evidence dates the manuscript to the first third of the sixteenth century.

77. See the facsimile edition: Alexandra Sinclair, ed. *The Beauchamp Pageant* (Donington, Lincolnshire: Paul Watkins, 2003).

78. René's book, *Triacte de la forme de devis d'un tournoi*, was probably produced in the 1460s at Angers; it purports to be a history of tournament practice as well as a sort of instruction manual.

79. BL, Lansdowne 285, f. 9v. On the origins of the material in the manuscript and Paston's lending of his book, see Lester, *Sir John Paston's "Grete Boke,"* 46–64.

80. Jacqueline Jenkins and Julie Sanders, introduction to *Editing, Performance, Texts: New Practices in Medieval and Early Modern English Drama*, ed. Jacqueline Jenkins and Julie Sanders (New York: Palgrave Macmillan, 2014), 5.

81. See Girbea, "Rapport introductif," who makes the case of the "imaginaire du tournoi."

82. BL, Stow 622, "Testament of Sir Fouk de Pennebrugge."

83. Bigelow, "Bohun Wills."

84. This is an elaboration of the point made by M. T. Clanchy regarding documents standing as tokens in themselves in his *From Memory to Written Record, England 1066–1307*, 2nd ed. (Oxford: Blackwell, 1993).

Chapter 4. Swords and Documents in the Sixteenth Century

1. This interpretation of the objects is argued by John North, *The Ambassadors' Secret: Holbein and the World of the Renaissance* (London: Hambledon and London, 2002), part 3.

2. Hats mattered: since their introduction as elements of fashion in the fourteenth century, the latest models were sought after by elites, as their correspondence reveals. See, for example, the comparable velvet hat with gold brooch worn by a newly created English baron ten years before Dinteville's portrait: BL, Add MS 25460, "Inventory after Death of Edward Stanley, First Baron Mounteagle," 20 April 1523, Hornby, f. 8v.

3. Dinteville's dress (doublet, furred cloak, etc.) almost exactly replicates that worn by members of the Order of Saint Michel in an illustration of the 1530 statutes of the order, save for the fact that, here, his badge hangs from a hefty but simple gold chain, not from the initially mandated collar fashioned in the form of scallop shells. North, *Ambassadors' Secret*, 144–49, argues that the structure of the composition

also forces our attention on the medallion. On the depiction of individual items like the tassel and Dinteville's silk shirt, see Susan Foister, Asok Roy, and Martin Wyld, *Holbein's Ambassadors* (London: National Gallery, 1997), 80, 85–86.

4. This point is made by North, *Ambassadors' Secret*, 78.

5. Bert S. Hall, *Weapons and Warfare in Renaissance Europe: Gunpowder, Technology, and Tactics* (Baltimore: Johns Hopkins University Press, 1997), 140–46, 190–96. Hall notes that gunpowder weapons—smaller than cannon but not as manageable as harquebuses—had been used by townspeople in the Low Countries against attacking armies, often from improvised defensive positions. It was not until the sixteenth century that handheld guns were deployed in sufficient number among infantry to affect the outcome of open battle.

6. The earliest use of the two terms in any aristocratic inventory I have encountered is in a 1613 list of apparel belonging to Henry Percy, Earl of Northumberland. G. R. Batho, ed., *The Household Papers of Henry Percy, Ninth Earl of Northumberland* (London: Royal Historical Society, 1962), 108.

7. AN, *1 AP 2081, Chartrier de Thouars, "Inventaire des biens meubles du chasteau de St. Fargeau," 4 January 1525.

8. John Gough Nichols, ed., "Inventories of [. . .] Henry of Fitzroy, Duke of Richmond, and [. . .] Katherine, Princess Dowager," *Camden Miscellany* 3 (1855): 1–21.

9. BN, Ms. Fr 20465, 133–34.

10. BL, Add MS 24936, Will of Thomas Wriothesley, First Earl of Southampton, 21 July 1550. Along with the pairs of rivets, the inventory lists six "demilances," which could have referred either to poled weapons or to the light armor typically worn by the bearer of those shorter lances.

11. NA, E154/3/16, "A True Inventory of the Armour and Household Stuffe and Goods Remainynge and Beinge in the Castell [. . .] of Arundel Taken the 20th of April 1589," ff. 3v–4.

12. BL, Add MS 34393, f. 7 "Goods of [. . .] Sir Rychard Cromwelle," ff. 26r–v and 29r–30v.

13. NA, E199/43/2, "Inventory of William Shelley," 24 March 1586.

14. Jousting remained popular through much of the century; it was no longer royally sponsored in France after the 1559 mortal wounding of Henry II in a joust, but remained a popular entertainment among idle fighting men nonetheless, and was still staged by the English crown through the century. See the discussion in Philip Benedict, Lawrence P. Bryant, and Kristen B. Neuschel, "Graphic History: What Readers Knew and Were Taught in the *Quarante tableaux* of Perrissin and Tortorel," *French Historical Studies* 28 (Spring 2005): 206–10.

15. BL, Add MS 34393, f. 7 "Goods of [. . .] Sir Rychard Cromwelle."

16. BN, Ms. Fr 4682 f. 103, Baptême de Catherine de Clèves.

17. AN, R² 49, Liasse 2 No 4, "Inventaire des biens meubles trouves au chasteau de Joze baille a Monsieur de Champietres," 10 June 1558 (my emphasis).

18. BN, Ms. Fr 3187, ff. 88–99v, "Etats des dons et pieces envoiez par le Roy a Monseigneur d'Humieres, chevalier de l'ordre du Roy, capitaine de 50 homme d'armes, gouverneur de Peronne, Montdidier et Roye, pour estre distribue aux personnes cy apres nommes selon et ainsy qu'il s'ensuit."

19. For example, from the presumptive heir to the French throne to both French and English nobles at the time of the marriage of Henry VII's sister to the French

king in 1514: AN, KK 240, "Comptes de Pierre Barbace, argentier du duc de Valois et comte d'Angouleme," January–December 1514.

20. BL, Add MS 25463, which includes two wills of Edward Stanley, first Baron Mounteagle, redacted at different times before his death in 1523. Bequests include only monies for the Church and rich items of clothing to be given to peers; see also BL, Add MS 34393, ff. 3r and 7, "An Inventory of the Goods of the Late Sir Rychard Cromwelle, Knyght," where one Lady Denny is allowed to have her pickings of the stores of clothing as thanks for her kindness to Sir Richard's minor children. The executor of the will gave "to diverse persons" twenty pounds' worth of clothing.

21. The only example I have found are belongings of Prince Henry, son of James I, including gifts of swords: "A sword all set with diamonds" that had been a gift of the queen, his mother; a rapier and dagger set presented by his grandfather, the king of Denmark; and a third sword set with diamonds presented by John, Lord Harrington. William Bray, "An Account of the Revenue, the Expenses, and Jewels of Prince Henry (d. 1612)," *Archaeologia* 15 (1806): 13–26.

22. BL, Add MS 28213, f. 6, Will of Sir John Scrope of Castlecombe, January 1517.

23. BL, Add MS 4140 ff. 174r–175v., Will of Sir Robert Wingfield, 1541 (fragment).

24. BL, Add MS 24936, Will [. . .] 1st Earl of Southampton, 21 July 1550.

25. BL, Harley D35, Inventory and Will of Robert Dudley, Earl of Leicester, no date.

26. For discussion of gift exchange, see Natalie Zemon Davis, *The Gift in Six-teenth-Century France* (Madison: University of Wisconsin Press, 2000); Kristen B. Neuschel, *Word of Honor: Interpreting Noble Culture in Sixteenth-Century France* (Ithaca, NY: Cornell University Press, 1989), esp. 72–74 and 167–68.

27. See for example, NA, E154/2/5, "Inventory of the Goods of Sir William Stanley," ca. 1495, in his several houses. Armor and arms, including elegant horse trappings, body armor, bows, and artillery, are included, but few clothes and no swords at all. Gentry households' collections reveal abundant plate and napery or textiles before anything else, and then arms and armor, but many inventories of manor houses reveal no swords at all. Such is the case, for example, with the sixteenth-century inventories in Malcolm Wanklyn, ed., *Inventories of Worcestershire Landed Gentry, 1537–1786* (Worcester: Worcestershire Historical Society, 1998).

28. "Armory" as conceptual category, including goods in many different locations, captured in one inventory, is found for example in NA, E154/6/42, "Such goods as Were the Erle of Warwick's at His Apprehension at Cambridge," 22 July 1533, f. 1v. It is important to note that, to contemporaries, "arms" could also mean coats of arms, that is, heraldry.

29. E. M. Thompson, "The Will and Inventory of Robert Morton, AD 1486–1488," *Journal of the British Archaeological Association* 33 (1877): 308–20.

30. Daniel Gurney, "Extracts from the Household and Privy Purse Accounts of the Lestranges of Hunstanton, 1519–1578," *Archaeologia* 25 (1834): 449–50.

31. AN, *1 AP 2081, Chartrier de Thouars, "Inventaire [. . .] du chasteau de St. Fargeau," 4 January 1525; Nichols, "Inventories of [. . .] Henry of Fitzroy, Duke of Richmond," 1–21.

32. AN, R² 49, Liasse 2 No 4, "Inventaire des biens meubles [. . .]," 10 June 1558.

33. BN, NAF 6891, ff. 1–18v. 7 July 1614, copy.

34. BL, Add MS 30526, ff. 135–38 (my emphasis).

35. The warning that his instructions hold for fighting "whether in sport or in earnest" is repeated many times by Hans Lecküchner, in his *The Art of Swordsmanship*, trans. Jeffrey L. Forgeng (Woodbridge, Suffolk: Boydell and Brewer, 2015). A contemporary manual for fencing with diverse weaponry is Hans Talhoffer's *Fechtbuch* or "fighting book," published in a modern edition as Hans Talhoffer, *Medieval Combat: A Fifteenth-Century Illustrated Manual of Sword-Fighting and Close-Quarter Combat*, trans. and ed. Mark Rector (London: Greenhill Books, 2000).

36. BL, Add MS 34192, G. Silver, "Paradoxes of Defense," 1599.

37. AN, KK 240, "Comptes [. . .] du duc de Valois et comte d'Angouleme."

38. NA E36/9, "Account of Sir Edward Guildford, Master of the King's Armory," includes monies for more than 2,400 swords of different dimensions for the various tournaments staged at the Field of the Cloth of Gold. See also Alan R. Young, *Tudor and Jacobean Tournaments* (Dobbs Ferry, NY: Sheridan House, 1987), 58–66.

39. One hundred years later, the collections purportedly included late medieval pieces, such as John of Gaunt's helmet. Charles J. ffoulkes, *Inventory and Survey of the Armouries of the Tower of London*, 2 vols. (London: H. M. Stationery Office, 1916), 1:19, 87.

40. For perspectives on early modern collecting, see Susan M. Pearce, ed., *Interpreting Objects and Collections* (London: Routledge, 1994); Paula Findlen, *Possessing Nature: Museums, Collecting, and Scientific Culture in Early Modern Italy* (Berkeley: University of California Press, 1994).

41. On the legend, see Velma Bourgeois Richmond, *The Legend of Guy of Warwick* (New York: Garland, 1996).

42. *Letters and Papers, Foreign and Domestic, Henry VIII*, vol. 1, *1509–1514* (London: H. M. Stationery Office, 1920), 37. For Burghley's authorization, see NA, E101/632/6, William Cecil to Auditors and Receivers of the County of Warwick, 30 December 1595.

43. This parallels what Laurent Hablot identifies as royal efforts to control the creation of aristocratic emblems. See his "'Ubi armae ibi princeps': Medieval Emblematics as the Real Presence of the Prince," in *Absentee Authority across Medieval Europe*, ed. Frédérique Lachaud and Michael Penman (Woodbridge, Suffolk: Boydell, 2017), 52–55.

44. BN, Ms. Fr 22335, ff. 111–19, "Meubles estans en l'armeurerie du chasteau d'Amboise en laquelle sont les anciennes armeures qui de tout temps ont este gardees et fait garder par les Roys deffuncts jusques a present extraictz sur ung inventaire fait à Amboise le XXIIIᵉ jour de septembre 1499."

45. Ibid., f. 117 (my emphasis).

46. Antoine Le Roux de Lincy argued that of all the ancient weapons, such as that attributed to Clovis, Dagobert's was the most likely to have been extant. See "Inventaire des vieilles armes conservées dans le château d'Amboise du temps de Louis XII, (septembre 1499)," *Bibliothèque de l'École des Chartes* 9 (1848): 413–14.

47. BN, Ms. Fr 22335, f. 113, "Meubles estans en l'armeurerie du chasteau d'Amboise."

48. John Miles Foley, *Traditional Oral Epic: "The Odyssey," "Beowulf," and the Serbo-Croatian Return Song* (Berkeley: University of California Press, 1990), chaps. 1 and 5; John Miles Foley, *How to Read an Oral Poem* (Urbana: University of Illinois Press, 2002), esp. 11–21, 125–45.

49. Le Roux de Lincy, "Inventaire," 412–13, identifies the sixteenth-century history that purports to record these encounters.

50. BN, Clair 834, "Inventaire après décès de Charles VI," 1422, p. 69.

51. This is Le Roux de Lincy's suggestion in "Inventaire," 418–19.

52. Foister, Roy, and Wyld, *Holbein's Ambassadors*, 23–24. The authors note that Dinteville had already been sketched by François Clouet at the French court, probably in 1532.

53. North, *Ambassadors' Secret*, 51; Stephen Greenblatt, *Renaissance Self-Fashioning, from More to Shakespeare*, with a new preface (Chicago: University of Chicago Press, 2005), 18.

Conclusion

1. Roger B. Manning, *Swordsmen: The Martial Ethos in the Three Kingdoms* (Oxford: Oxford University Press, 2003).

2. See the argument regarding this evolving identity by Markku Peltonen, *The Duel in Early Modern England: Civility, Politeness and Honour* (Cambridge: Cambridge University Press, 2003). On dueling, see also François Billacois, *Le duel dans la société française du XVIᵉ–XVIIᵉ siècles* (Paris: École des hautes études en sciences sociales, 1986). Dueling in the sense of staged face-to-face combat with chosen weapons had been a subject of instruction since the earliest manuals in the fourteenth century, but dueling became a special preoccupation of ever-armed, privileged men by the end of the sixteenth century and, not surprisingly, was sternly contested by royal power.

BIBLIOGRAPHY

Manuscript Sources

France

ARCHIVES NATIONALES

Série AP (Archives privées)

Série K (Monuments historiques)

Série R (Papiers de princes)

BIBLIOTHÈQUE NATIONALE

Fonds Clairambault

Manuscrits français

Nouvelles acquisitions françaises

United Kingdom

BRITISH LIBRARY

Additional Manuscripts

Harley Manuscripts

Lansdowne Manuscripts

Stowe Manuscripts

NATIONAL ARCHIVES

Patent Rolls

Series E (Exchequer)

Published Sources

"Account of expenses of John, Duke of Brabant and Henry and Thomas of Lancaster, 1292–93." *Camden Miscellany* 2 (1852–53): 1–18.

"Apparel for the Field of Henry, Earl of Northumberland." *Archaeologia* 26 (1836): 395–405.

Batho, G. R., ed. *The Household Papers of Henry Percy, Ninth Earl of Northumberland.* London: Royal Historical Society, 1962.

Beauvillé, Victor de, ed. *Recueil de documents inédits concernant la Picardie.* 4 vols. Paris, 1880–82.

Bellaguet, L., ed. *Chronique du religieux de Saint-Denys.* Vol. 1. Paris: Imprimerie de Crapelet, 1839.

Bresc, Henri, ed. *Le Livre de raison de Paul de Sade, Avignon, 1390–94.* Paris: Comité des travaux historiques et scientifiques, 2013.

Chazaud, A. M., ed. *Chronique du bon duc Loys de Bourbon.* Paris: Renouard, 1876.

Collier, J. Payne, ed. *The Household Books of John Duke of Norfolk and Thomas Earl of Surrey.* London, 1844.

Dillon-Lee, Harold Arthur, and W. H. St. John Hope. "Inventory of the Goods and Chattels Belonging to Thomas, Duke of Gloucester, and Seized at His Castle at Pleshy, Co. Essex, 21 Richard II. (1397) with Their Values, as Shown in the Escheator's Accounts." *Archaeological Journal* 54 (1897): 275–308.

Douët-d'Arcq, L. *Choix de pièces inédites relatives au règne de Charles VI.* Paris: Renouard, 1863.

——. *Comptes de l'argenterie des rois de France au XIVe siècle.* Société de l'histoire de France 64. New York: Johnson Reprint, 1966.

——. *Comptes de l'hôtel des rois de France aux XIVe et XVe siècles.* Paris: Renouard, 1865.

——. *Nouveau recueil de comptes de l'argenterie des rois de France.* Paris: Renouard, 1874.

Einhard and Notker the Stammerer. *Two Lives of Charlemagne.* Translated, with an introduction and notes by Lewis Thorpe. London: Penguin Books, 1976.

Grey, Sir Thomas. *Scalacronica.* Edited and translated by Andy King. Woodbridge, Suffolk: Boydell, 2005.

Guiffrey, Jules. *Inventaires de Jean, duc de Berry.* 2 vols. Paris, 1894–96.

Gurney, Daniel. "Extracts from the Household and Privy Purse Accounts of the Lestranges of Hunstanton, 1519–1578." *Archaeologia* 25 (1834): 411–569.

Hope, W. H. St. John. "The King's Coronation Ornaments." *Ancestor* 1 (1902): 127–59.

——. "The Last Will and Testament of John de Veer, Thirteenth Earl of Oxford." *Archaeologia* 66 (1915): 275–348.

"Inventory of Effects Formerly Belonging to Sir John Fastolfe." *Archaeologia* 21 (1827): 232–80.

Lecküchner, Hans. *The Art of Swordsmanship.* Translated and with an introduction by Jeffrey L. Forgeng. Woodbridge, Suffolk: Boydell and Brewer, 2015.

Lecoy de La Marche, A., ed. *Extraits des comptes et mémoriaux du roi René pour servir à l'histoire des arts au XVe siècle.* Paris: Picard, 1873.

Le Roux de Lincy, Antoine. "Inventaire des vieilles armes conservées dans le château d'Amboise du temps de Louis XII." *Bibliothèque de l'École des Chartes* 9 (1848): 412–22.

Letters and Papers, Foreign and Domestic, Henry VIII, vol. 1, *1509–1514.* London: H. M. Stationery Office, 1920.

Nichols, John Gough, ed. "Inventories of [. . .] Henry of Fitzroy, Duke of Richmond and [. . .] Katharine, Princess Dowager." *Camden Miscellany* 3 (1855): 1–21.

Nicolas, Nicholas H. *Privy Purse Expenses of Elizabeth of York: Wardrobe Accounts of Edward the Fourth.* London: W. Pickering, 1830.

Pisan, Christine de. *The Book of Fayttes of Armes and of Chyvalrye.* Translated by William Caxton. Edited by A. T. P. Byles. London: Oxford University Press, 1932.

Sutton, Anne F., and P. W. Hammond, eds. *The Coronation of Richard III: The Extant Documents*. Gloucester: Alan Sutton, 1983.

Talhoffer, Hans. *Medieval Combat: A Fifteenth-Century Illustrated Manual of Sword-Fighting and Close-Quarter Combat*. Translated and edited by Mark Rector. London: Greenhill Books, 2000.

Thompson, E. M. "The Will and Inventory of Robert Morton, AD 1486–1488." *Journal of the British Archaeological Association* 33 (1877): 308–20.

Turner, T. H. "The Will of Humphrey de Bohun, Earl of Hereford and Essex, with Extracts from the Inventory of His Effects, 1319–1322." *Archaeological Journal* 2 (1846): 339–49.

Wanklyn, Malcolm, ed. *Inventories of Worcestershire Landed Gentry, 1537–1786*. Worcester: Worcestershire Historical Society, 1998.

Whitelock, Dorothy, ed. *Anglo-Saxon Wills*. Cambridge: Cambridge University Press, 1930.

Woolgar, Christopher M., ed. *Household Accounts from Medieval England*. 2 vols. Oxford: British Academy, 1992–93.

Secondary Sources

Aberth, John. *A Knight at the Movies: Medieval History on Film*. New York: Routledge, 2003.

Abulafia, David. "The Norman Kingdom of Africa and the Norman Expeditions to Majorca and the Muslim Mediterranean." *Anglo-Norman Studies* 7 (1984): 26–49.

Addington, Larry H. *The Patterns of War through the Eighteenth Century*. Bloomington: Indiana University Press, 1990.

Aers, David. "New Historicism and the Eucharist." *Journal of Medieval and Early Modern Studies* 33 (2003): 231–60.

Ailes, Adrian. "The Knight, Heraldry and Armour: The Role of Recognition and the Origins of Heraldry." In Harper-Bill and Harvey, *Ideals and Practice of Medieval Knighthood IV*, 1–22.

Ainsworth, Peter F. *Jean Froissart and the Fabric of History: Truth, Myth, and Fiction in the Chroniques*. Oxford: Clarendon, 1990.

Alexander, Michael. *Medievalism: The Middle Ages in Modern England*. New Haven, CT: Yale University Press, 2007.

Allmand, C. T. *Power, Culture, and Religion in France, c.1350–c.1550*. Woodbridge, Suffolk: Boydell, 1989.

———. *War, Government and Power in Late Medieval France*. Liverpool: Liverpool University Press, 2000.

Allmand, C. T., and George William Coopland. *War, Literature, and Politics in the Late Middle Ages*. New York: Barnes and Noble, 1976.

Althoff, Gerd, Johannes Fried, Patrick J. Geary, and German Historical Institute (Washington, DC). *Medieval Concepts of the Past: Ritual, Memory, Historiography*. Cambridge: Cambridge University Press, 2002.

Amtower, Laurel. *Engaging Words: The Culture of Reading in the Later Middle Ages*. The New Middle Ages. New York: Palgrave, 2000.

Anglo, Sydney. *Chivalry in the Renaissance*. Woodbridge, Suffolk: Boydell, 1990.

——. "How to Win at Tournaments: The Technique of Chivalric Combat." *Antiquaries Journal* 68 (1988): 248–64.

Appadurai, Arjun, ed. *The Social Life of Things: Commodities in Cultural Perspective*. Cambridge: Cambridge University Press, 1986.

Apter, Emily S., and William Pietz. *Fetishism as Cultural Discourse*. Ithaca, NY: Cornell University Press, 1993.

Archer, Rowena E., and Simon Walker, eds. *Rulers and Ruled in Late Medieval England: Essays Presented to Gerald Harris*. London: Hambledon, 1995.

Arnold, Thomas F., and John Keegan. *The Renaissance at War*. London: Cassell, 2001.

Arthur, Ross Gilbert. *Medieval Sign Theory and "Sir Gawain and the Green Knight."* Toronto: University of Toronto Press, 1987.

Arthur, Ross Gilbert, and Noël Lynn Corbett, eds. *The Knight of the Two Swords: A Thirteenth-Century Arthurian Romance*. Gainesville: University Press of Florida, 1996.

Astill, G. G. "An Early Inventory of a Leicestershire Knight." *Midland History* 2 (1974): 274–83.

Aurell, Martin. "L'épée, l'autel et le perron." In *Armes et jeux militaires dans l'imaginaire*, edited by Catalina Girbea. Paris: Classiques Garnier, 2016.

Ayton, Andrew. *Knights and Warhorses: Military Service and the English Aristocracy under Edward III*. Woodbridge, Suffolk: Boydell, 1994.

Ayton, Andrew, and J. L. Price. Introduction to *The Medieval Military Revolution: State, Society and Military Change in Medieval and Early Modern Europe*, edited by Andrew Ayton and J. L. Price. London: I. B. Tauris, 1995.

Bachrach, Bernard S. "Charles Martel, Mounted Shock Combat, the Stirrup and Feudalism." In *Armies and Politics in the Early Medieval West*. Aldershot, Hampshire: Variorum, 1993.

——. *Merovingian Military Organization, 481–751*. Minneapolis: University of Minnesota Press, 1972.

Bainton, Henry. "Literate Sociability and Historical Writing in Later Twelfth-Century England." *Anglo-Norman Studies* 34 (2012): 23–40.

Bak, János M., ed. *Coronations: Medieval and Early Modern Monarchic Ritual*. Berkeley: University of California Press, 1990.

Baker, Peter S., ed. *The "Beowulf" Reader*. New York: Garland, 2000.

Balard, Michel, ed. *Le combattant au Moyen Âge*. Paris: Publications de la Sorbonne, 1995.

——. *Les princes et le pouvoir au Moyen Âge*. Paris: Publications de la Sorbonne, 1993.

Barber, Richard W. *Edward III and the Triumph of England: The Battle of Crécy and the Company of the Garter*. London: Allen Lane, 2013.

Barber, Richard W., and Juliet R. V. Barker. *Tournaments: Jousts, Chivalry and Pageants in the Middle Ages*. Woodbridge, Suffolk: Boydell, 1989.

Barker, Juliet R. V. *The Tournament in England*. Woodbridge, Suffolk: Boydell, 1986.

Barnie, John. *War in Medieval English Society: Social Values in the Hundred Years War, 1337–99*. Ithaca, NY: Cornell University Press, 1974.

Barrow, Julia, and Andrew Wareham, eds. *Myth, Rulership, Church and Charters: Essays in Honour of Nicholas Brooks*. Aldershot, Hampshire: Ashgate, 2008.

Bassett, Steven. *The Origins of Anglo-Saxon Kingdoms*. London: Leicester University Press, 1989.

Bauch, Kurt. *Das Mittelalterliche Grabbild*. Berlin: De Gruyter, 1976.

Baumgartner, Frederic J. *From Spear to Flintlock: A History of War in Europe and the Middle East to the French Revolution*. New York: Praeger, 1991.

Baüml, Franz H. "Varieties and Consequences of Medieval Literacy and Illiteracy." *Speculum* 55, no. 2 (1980): 237–65.

Bazelmans, Jos. "Beyond Power: Ceremonial Exchanges in *Beowulf*." In *Rituals of Power: From Late Antiquity to the Early Middle Ages*, edited by Frans Theuws and Janet L. Nelson. Leiden: Brill, 2000.

——. *By Weapons Made Worthy: Lords, Retainers, and Their Relationship in "Beowulf."* Amsterdam: Amsterdam University Press, 1999.

Beaune, Colette. *Naissance de la nation: France*. Paris: Gallimard, 1985.

Bedos-Rezak, Brigitte Miriam. "Medieval Identity: A Sign and a Concept." *American Historical Review* 105, no. 5 (2000): 1489–1533.

——. *When Ego Was Imago*. Leiden: Brill, 2011.

Bell, Adrian R., Anne Curry, Andy King, and David Simpkin, eds. *The Soldier in Later Medieval England*. Oxford: Oxford University Press, 2013.

Belozerskaya, Marina. *Luxury Arts of the Renaissance*. London: Thames and Hudson, 2005.

Benedict, Philip, Kristen Brooke Neuschel, and Lawrence M. Bryant. "Graphic History: What Readers Knew and Were Taught in the *Quarante tableaux* of Perrissin and Tortorel." *French Historical Studies* 28 (Spring 2005): 175–229.

Bennett, Matthew. *Agincourt, 1415*. Oxford: Osprey, 1991.

——. "The Development of Battle Tactics in the Hundred Years War." In *Arms, Armies, and Fortifications in the Hundred Years War*, edited by Anne Curry and Michael Hughes. Woodbridge, Suffolk: Boydell, 1994.

——. "The Medieval Warhorse Reconsidered." In *Medieval Knighthood V: Papers from the Sixth Strawberry Hill Conference, 1994*, edited by Stephen Church and Ruth Harvey. Woodbridge, Suffolk: Boydell, 1995.

——. "The Myth of the Military Supremacy of Knightly Cavalry." In *Armies, Chivalry and Warfare in Medieval Britain and France: Proceedings of the 1995 Harlaxton Symposium*, edited by Matthew Strickland. Stamford, Lincolnshire: Paul Watkins, 1998.

——. "Poetry as History? The 'Roman de Rou' of Wace as a Source for the Norman Conquest." *Anglo-Norman Studies* 5 (1982): 21–39.

——. "Violence in Eleventh-Century Normandy: Feud, Warfare, Politics." In *Violence and Society in the Early Medieval West*, edited by Guy Halsall, 126–40. Woodbridge, Suffolk: Boydell, 1998.

Benson, Larry Dean, and John Leyerle, eds. *Chivalric Literature: Essays on Relations between Literature and Life in the Later Middle Ages*. Kalamazoo, MI: Medieval Institute Publications, 1980.

Bever, Edward, and Randall Styers, eds. *Magic in the Modern World: Strategies of Repression and Legitimization*. University Park: Pennsylvania State University Press, 2017.

Biernoff, Suzannah. *Sight and Embodiment in the Middle Ages*. New York: Palgrave Macmillan, 2002.

Bigelow, Melville M. "The Bohun Wills." *American Historical Review* 1, no. 3 (1896): 414–35 and 1, no. 4 (1896): 631–49.

Billacois, François. *Le duel dans la société française du XVIe–XVIIe siècles*. Paris: École des hautes études en sciences sociales, 1986.

Black, Jeremy. *Rethinking Military History*. London: Routledge, 2004.

Blackman, Susan A. "A Pictorial Synopsis of Arthurian Episodes for Jacques d'Armagnac, Duke of Nemours." In *Word and Image in Arthurian Literature*, edited by Keith Busby. New York: Garland, 1996.

Blanc, Odile. "From Battlefield to Court: The Invention of Fashion in the Fourteenth Century." In *Encountering Medieval Textiles and Dress: Objects, Texts, Images*, edited by Désirée G. Koslin and Janet E. Snyder, 157–72. New York: Palgrave Macmillan, 2002.

——. *Parades et parures: L'invention du corps de mode à la fin du Moyen Âge*. Paris: Gallimard, 1997.

Blockmans, Wim, and Antheun Janse, eds. *Showing Status: Representation of Social Positions in the Late Middle Ages*. Turnhout, Belgium: Brepols, 1999.

Bone, Peter. "The Development of Anglo-Saxon Swords from the Fifth to the Eleventh Century." In *Weapons and Warfare in Anglo-Saxon England*, edited by Sonia Chadwick Hawkes. Oxford: Oxford University Committee for Archaeology, 1989.

Bothwell, James. *Edward III and the English Peerage: Royal Patronage, Social Mobility, and Political Control in Fourteenth-Century England*. Woodbridge, Suffolk: Boydell, 2004.

Bouchard, Constance Brittain. *Strong of Body, Brave and Noble: Chivalry and Society in Medieval France*. Ithaca, NY: Cornell University Press, 1998.

——. *Sword, Miter, and Cloister: Nobility and the Church in Burgundy, 980–1198*. Ithaca, NY: Cornell University Press, 1987.

Bouzy, Olivier. "Les armes symboles d'un pouvoir politique: L'épée du sacre, la Sainte Lance, l'Oriflamme aux VIIIe–XIIe siècles." *Francia* 22, no. 1 (1995): 45–57.

Boyarin, Jonathan. "The Cultural Construction of Reading in Anglo-Saxon England." In *The Ethnography of Reading*, edited by Jonathan Boyarin. Berkeley: University of California Press, 1993.

Bradbury, Jim. "Geoffrey V of Anjou, Count and Knight." In Harper-Bill and Harvey, *Ideals and Practice of Medieval Knighthood III*, 32.

——. *The Medieval Archer*. New York: St. Martin's, 1985.

Bradley, Richard. *The Passage of Arms: An Archaeological Analysis of Prehistoric Hoards and Votive Deposits*. Cambridge: Cambridge University Press, 1990.

Bray, William. "An Account of the Revenue, the Expenses, and Jewels of Prince Henry (d.1612)." *Archaeologia* 15 (1806): 13–26.

Brewer, John, and Roy Porter, eds. *Consumption and the World of Goods*. London: Routledge, 1993.

Britnell, R. H. *The Closing of the Middle Ages? England, 1471–1529*. Oxford: Blackwell, 1997.

Brodsky, G. W. Stephen. *Gentlemen of the Blade: A Social and Literary History of the British Army since 1660*. New York: Greenwood, 1988.

Brooks, Nicholas. "Arms, Status and Warfare in Late-Saxon England." In *Communities and Warfare, 700–1400*, 138–61. London: Hambledon, 2000.

——. "Weapons and Armour in the *Battle of Maldon*." In *Communities and Warfare, 700–1400*, 162–74. London: Hambledon, 2000.

Brown, Bill, ed. *Things*. Chicago: University of Chicago Press, 2004.

——. "Thing Theory." In Brown, *Things*, 1–16.

Brown, Shirley Ann. "Cognate Imagery: The Bear, Harold and the Bayeux Tapestry." In *King Harold II and the Bayeux Tapestry*, edited by Gale R. Owen-Crocker, 153–60. Woodbridge, Suffolk: Boydell, 2005.

Brownlee, Kevin, Marina Scordilis Brownlee, and Stephen G. Nichols. *The New Medievalism*. Baltimore: Johns Hopkins University Press, 1991.

Bryant, Lawrence M. *Ritual, Ceremony and the Changing Monarchy in France, 1350–1789*. Farnham, Surrey: Ashgate/Variorum, 2010.

Bryson, Anna. *From Courtesy to Civility: Changing Codes of Conduct in Early Modern England*. Oxford Studies in Social History. Oxford: Clarendon, 1998.

Buc, Philippe. "Conversion of Objects: Suger of St. Denis and Meinwerk of Paderborn." *Viator* 28 (1997): 99–143.

Buchli, Victor, ed. *The Material Culture Reader*. Oxford: Berg, 2002.

Bumke, Joachim. *Courtly Culture: Literature and Society in the High Middle Ages*. Translated by Thomas Dunlap. Woodstock, NY: Overlook, 2000.

Burgess, Andrea. "The Excavation and Finds." In Fiorato, Boylston, and Knüsel, *Blood Red Roses*, 29–35.

Burke, Peter. *The Fortunes of the "Courtier": The European Reception of Castiglione's "Cortegiano."* London: Polity, 1995.

——. "*Res et verba*: Conspicuous Consumption in the Early Modern World." In *Consumption and the World of Goods*, edited by John Brewer and Roy Porter, 148–61. London: Routledge, 1993.

Burland, Margaret, David LaGuardia, and Andrea Tarnowski. *Meaning and Its Objects: Material Culture in Medieval and Renaissance France*. Yale French Studies 110. New Haven, CT: Yale University Press, 2006.

Burns, E. Jane. *Bodytalk: When Women Speak in Old French Literature*. New Cultural Studies. Philadelphia: University of Pennsylvania Press, 1993.

Buschinger, Danielle, Wolfgang Spiewok, and Michel Zink, eds. *Lancelot, Lanzelet: Hier et aujourd'hui*. Greifswald: Reineke-Verlag, 1995.

Butaud, Germain. "L'armement des citadins et des villageois à la fin du Moyen Âge: L'exemple de la Provence et du Comtat Venaissin." In Raynaud, *Armes et outils*, 221–52.

Caferro, William. *John Hawkwood: An English Mercenary in Fourteenth-Century Italy*. Baltimore: Johns Hopkins University Press, 2006.

Camille, Michael. *Image on the Edge: The Margins of Medieval Art*. London: Reaktion Books, 1992.

——. *Mirror in Parchment: The Luttrell Psalter and the Making of Medieval England*. Chicago: University of Chicago Press, 1998.

Campbell, James. "England, ca. 991." In *The Battle of Maldon: Fiction and Fact*, edited by Janet Cooper, 1–17. London: Hambledon, 1993.

Caple, Chris. *Objects: Reluctant Witnesses to the Past*. London: Routledge, 2006.

Capwell, Tobias, ed. *The Noble Art of the Sword: Fashion and Fencing in Renaissance Europe, 1520–1630*. London: Paul Holberton, 2012.

Carroll, Stuart. *Blood and Violence in Early Modern France*. Oxford: Oxford University Press, 2006.

Carruthers, Mary. *The Book of Memory: A Study of Memory in Medieval Culture*. Cambridge: Cambridge University Press, 1990.

——. "Meditations on the 'Historical Present' and 'Collective Memory' in Chaucer and *Sir Gawain and the Green Knight.*" In *Time in the Medieval World*, edited by C. Humphrey and W. M. Ormrod, 137–55. York: York Medieval, 2001.

Carruthers, Mary, and Jan M. Ziolkowski. *The Medieval Craft of Memory: An Anthology of Texts and Pictures.* Philadelphia: University of Pennsylvania Press, 2002.

Carver, Martin. *The Age of Sutton Hoo: The Seventh Century in North-Western Europe.* Woodbridge, Suffolk: Boydell, 1992.

——. "Burial as Poetry: The Context of Treasure in Anglo-Saxon Graves." In Tyler, *Treasure in the Medieval West*, 25–48.

——. "Kingship and Material Culture in Early Anglo-Saxon East Anglia." In *The Origins of Anglo-Saxon Kingdoms*, edited by Steven Bassett. Leicester: Leicester University Press, 1989.

——. *Sutton Hoo: Burial Ground of Kings?* Philadelphia: University of Pennsylvania Press, 1998.

Carver, Martin, and Angela Care Evans. *Sutton Hoo: A Seventh-Century Princely Burial Ground and Its Context.* London: British Museum, 2005.

Charters, David, Marc Milner, and J. Brent Wilson. *Military History and the Military Profession.* Westport, CT: Praeger, 1992.

Chase, Colin, ed. *The Dating of "Beowulf."* Toronto: University of Toronto Press, 1981.

——. "Saints' Lives, Royal Lives and the Date of *Beowulf.*" In Chase, *Dating of "Beowulf,"* 161–71.

Cheyette, Frederic, and Howell Chickering. "Love, Anger, and Peace: Social Practice and Poetic Play in the Ending of *Yvain.*" *Speculum* 80, no. 1 (2005): 75–117.

Chickering, Howell D., and Thomas H. Seiler. *The Study of Chivalry: Resources and Approaches.* Kalamazoo: Medieval Institute Publications of Western Michigan University, 1988.

Chilton, Elizabeth S. *Material Meanings: Critical Approaches to the Interpretation of Material Culture.* Salt Lake City: University of Utah Press, 1999.

Church, Stephen, and Ruth Harvey, eds. *Medieval Knighthood V: Papers from the Sixth Strawberry Hill Conference, 1994.* Woodbridge, Suffolk: Boydell, 1995.

Clanchy, M. T. *From Memory to Written Record, England 1066–1307.* 2nd ed. Oxford: Blackwell, 1993.

Clark, George. "Maldon: History, Poetry and Truth." In *De Gustibus: Essays for Alain Renoir*, edited by John Miles Foley. New York: Garland, 1992.

Clark, John. "A Sword of about 1500 from the Thames." *Transactions of the London and Middlesex Archaeological Society* 24 (1973): 159–61.

Clifford, James. *The Predicament of Culture: Twentieth-Century Ethnography, Literature, and Art.* Cambridge, MA: Harvard University Press, 1988.

Cline, Ruth Huff. "The Influence of Romances on Tournaments of the Middle Ages." *Speculum* 20, no. 2 (1945): 204–11.

Cohen, Jeffrey Jerome. *Medieval Identity Machines.* Minneapolis: University of Minnesota Press, 2003.

Cohn, Samuel Kline. *Lust for Liberty: The Politics of Social Revolt in Medieval Europe, 1200–1425; Italy, France, and Flanders.* Cambridge, MA: Harvard University Press, 2006.

Coleman, Janet. *Ancient and Medieval Memories: Studies in the Reconstruction of the Past.* Cambridge: Cambridge University Press, 1992.

Coleman, Joyce. *Public Reading and the Reading Public in Late Medieval England and France*. Cambridge: Cambridge University Press, 1996.

Contamine, Philippe. *Guerre, état et société à la fin du Moyen Âge: Études sur les armées des rois de France, 1337–1494*. Paris: Mouton, 1972.

——. "Les Tournois en France à la fin du Moyen Âge." In *Das ritterliche Turnier im Mittelalter: Beiträge zu einer vergleichenden Formen-und Verhaltensgeschichte des Rittertums*, edited by Josef Fleckenstein. Göttingen: Vandenhoeck and Ruprecht, 1985.

——. *Pages d'histoire militaire médiévale: XIVᵉ–XVᵉ siècles*. Paris: Boccard, 2005.

——. *War in the Middle Ages*. New York: Blackwell, 1984.

Cooper, Helen. *The English Romance in Time: Transforming Motifs from Geoffrey of Monmouth to the Death of Shakespeare*. Oxford: Oxford University Press, 2004.

Cooper, Janet. *The Battle of Maldon: Fiction and Fact*. London: Hambledon, 1993.

Cooper, Lisa H., and Andrea Denny-Brown, eds. *Lydgate Matters: Poetry and Material Culture in the Fifteenth Century*. New York: Palgrave Macmillan, 2008.

Coss, Peter R., and Maurice Keen, eds. *Heraldry, Pageantry, and Social Display in Medieval England*. Woodbridge, Suffolk: Boydell, 2002.

Coss, Peter R., and Christopher Tyerman, eds. *Soldiers, Nobles and Gentleman: Essays in Honour of Maurice Keen*. Woodbridge, Suffolk: Boydell, 2009.

Coulson, Charles. *Castles in Medieval Society: Fortresses in England, France, and Ireland in the Central Middle Ages*. Oxford: Oxford University Press, 2003.

——. "Valois Powers over Fortresses on the Eve of the Hundred Years War." In *Armies, Chivalry and Warfare in Medieval Britain and France: Proceedings of the 1995 Harlaxton Symposium*, edited by Matthew Strickland. Stamford, Lincolnshire: Paul Watkins, 1998.

Coupland, Simon. "Carolingian Arms and Armor in the Ninth Century." *Viator* 21 (1990): 29–50.

Cowell, Andrew. *The Medieval Warrior Aristocracy: Gifts, Violence, Performance, and the Sacred*. Woodbridge, Suffolk: D. S. Brewer, 2007.

——. "Swords, Clubs, and Relics: Performance, Identity, and the Sacred." *Yale French Studies* 110 (2006): 7–18.

Crane, Susan. *Insular Romance: Politics, Faith, and Culture in Anglo-Norman and Middle English Literature*. Berkeley: University of California Press, 1986.

——. *The Performance of Self: Ritual, Clothing, and Identity during the Hundred Years' War*. Philadelphia: University of Pennsylvania Press, 2002.

Creighton, Oliver Hamilton. *Castles and Landscapes: Power, Community and Fortification in Medieval England*. London: Equinox, 2002.

Cripps-Day, Francis Henry. *The History of the Tournament in England and France*. New York: AMS, 1982.

Cronan, Dennis. "The Rescuing Sword." *Neophilologus* 77, no. 3 (1993): 467–78.

Crouch, David. *The Birth of Nobility: Constructing Aristocracy in England and France, 900–1300*. Harlow: Pearson/Longman, 2005.

——. *The Image of Aristocracy in Britain, 1000–1300*. London: Routledge, 1993.

——. *Tournament*. London: Hambledon and London, 2005.

——. *William Marshal: Knighthood, War and Chivalry, 1147–1219*. 2nd ed. London: Longman, 2002.

Crouzet, Denis. *Les guerriers de dieu: La violence au temps des troubles de religion, vers 1525–vers 1610*. 2 vols. Seyssel: Champ Vallon, 1990.

Curry, Anne. *Agincourt, 1415: Henry V, Sir Thomas Erpingham and the Triumph of the English Archers.* Stroud, Gloucestershire: Tempus, 2000.

——. *The Hundred Years' War.* New York: St. Martin's, 1993.

Curry, Anne, and Michael Hughes, eds. *Arms, Armies, and Fortifications in the Hundred Years War.* Woodbridge, Suffolk: Boydell, 1994.

Davidson, Hilda Roderick Ellis. *The Sword in Anglo-Saxon England: Its Archaeology and Literature.* Oxford: Clarendon, 1962. Corrected reprint. Woodbridge, Suffolk: Boydell, 1998.

Davis, Kathleen. "Sovereign Subjects, Feudal Law and the Writing of History." *Journal of Medieval and Early Modern Studies* 36, no. 2 (2006): 223–62.

Davis, Natalie Zemon. *The Gift in Sixteenth-Century France.* Madison: University of Wisconsin Press, 2000.

Davis, Norman, ed. *Paston Letters and Papers of the Fifteenth Century.* 2 vols. Oxford: Clarendon, 1971–1976.

Debord, André. *Aristocratie et pouvoir: Le rôle du château dans la France médiévale.* Paris: Picard, 2000.

De Grazia, Margreta, Maureen Quilligan, and Peter Stallybrass. *Subject and Object in Renaissance Culture.* Cambridge: Cambridge University Press, 1996.

DeMarrais, Elizabeth, Chris Gosden, and Colin Renfrew. *Rethinking Materiality: The Engagement of Mind with the Material World.* Cambridge: McDonald Institute for Archaeological Research, 2004.

Denholm-Young, N. "The Tournament in the 13th Century." In *Studies in Medieval History Presented to F. M. Powicke,* edited by Richard William Hunt. Oxford: Clarendon, 1948.

Dewald, Jonathan. *The European Nobility, 1400–1800.* Cambridge: Cambridge University Press, 1996.

Dodwell, C. R. *Anglo-Saxon Art: A New Perspective.* Ithaca, NY: Cornell University Press, 1982.

——. *Pictorial Arts of the West, 800–1200.* New Haven, CT: Yale University Press, 1993.

Donagan, Barbara. "Halcyon Days and the Literature of War: England's Military Education before 1642." *Past and Present* 147 (1995): 65–100.

Dufournet, Jean, and Nelly Andrieux-Reix. *La mort du roi Arthur, ou, le crépuscule de la chevalerie.* Paris: H. Champion, 1994.

Dugan, H. Holly. Review of *Materializing Gender in Early Modern English Literature and Culture,* by Will Fisher. *Renaissance Quarterly* 60, no. 2 (2007): 672–73.

Duggan, Anne. *Nobles and Nobility in Medieval Europe: Concepts, Origins, Transformations.* Woodbridge, Suffolk: Boydell, 2000.

Duindam, Jeroen Frans Jozef. *Myths of Power: Norbert Elias and the Early Modern European Court.* Amsterdam: Amsterdam University Press, 1994.

Dyer, Christopher. *Standards of Living in the Later Middle Ages: Social Change in England, c. 1200–1500.* Cambridge: Cambridge University Press, 1989.

Edgington, Susan, and Sarah Lambert. *Gendering the Crusades.* Cardiff: University of Wales Press, 2001.

Editorial. *Journal of Material Culture* 1, no. 1 (March 1996): 5–14.

Effros, Bonnie. *Merovingian Mortuary Archaeology and the Making of the Early Middle Ages.* Berkeley: University of California Press, 2003.

Epstein, Robert. "Eating Their Words: Food and Text in the Coronation Banquet of Henry VI." *Journal of Medieval and Early Modern Studies* 36, no. 2 (2006): 355–78.

Evans, Joan. *Dress in Mediaeval France*. Oxford: Clarendon, 1952.

Fahlander, Fredrik, and Terje Oestgaard. *Material Culture and Other Things*. Gothenburg: University of Gothenburg, Department of Archaeology, 2004.

Favier, Jean. *Le roi René*. Paris: Librairie Arthème Fayard, 2008.

Fenster, Thelma S., and Clare A. Lees, eds. *Gender in Debate from the Early Middle Ages to the Renaissance*. New York: Palgrave, 2002.

Fentress, James, and Chris Wickham. *Social Memory*. Cambridge, MA: Blackwell, 1992.

Ferguson, R. Brian, ed. *Warfare, Culture, and Environment*. Orlando, FL: Academic Press, 1984.

ffoulkes, Charles J. *Inventory and Survey of the Armouries of the Tower of London*. 2 vols. London: H. M. Stationery Office, 1916.

Findlen, Paula, ed. *Early Modern Things*. New York: Routledge, 2012.

———. *Possessing Nature: Museums, Collecting, and Scientific Culture in Early Modern Italy*. Berkeley: University of California Press, 1994.

Fiorato, Veronica, Anthea Boylston, and Christopher Knüsel, eds. *Blood Red Roses: The Archaeology of a Mass Grave from the Battle of Towton, 1461*. 2nd rev. ed. Oxford: Oxbow Books, 2007.

Flori, Jean. "L'épée de Lancelot: Adoubement et idéologie au début du XIIIème siècle." In *Lancelot-Lanzelet*, edited by Danielle Buschinger and Michel Zink. Greifswald: Reineke-Verlag, 1995.

Foister, Susan, Asok Roy, and Martin Wyld. *Holbein's Ambassadors*. London: National Gallery, 1997.

Foley, John Miles. *How to Read an Oral Poem*. Urbana: University of Illinois Press, 2002.

———. *Traditional Oral Epic: "The Odyssey," "Beowulf," and the Serbo-Croatian Return Song*. Berkeley: University of California Press, 1990.

Fowler, Kenneth A. *Medieval Mercenaries*. Vol. 1. Oxford: Blackwell, 2001.

Fox, Adam, and D. R. Woolf. *The Spoken Word: Oral Culture in Britain, 1500–1850*. Manchester: Manchester University Press, 2002.

Fradenburg, L. O. *City, Marriage, Tournament: Arts of Rule in Late Medieval Scotland*. Madison: University of Wisconsin Press, 1991.

Frank, Roberta. "A Scandal in Toronto: *The Dating of 'Beowulf'* a Quarter Century On." *Speculum* 82, no. 4 (2007): 843–64.

———. "Skaldic Verse and the Date of *Beowulf*." In *The Dating of "Beowulf*," edited by Colin Chase. Toronto: University of Toronto Press, 1981.

Frantzen, A. "Writing the Unreadable *Beowulf*: 'Writan' and 'Forwritan,' the Pen and the Sword." *Exemplaria* 3 (1991): 327–57.

Freedman, Paul H. *Out of the East: Spices and the Medieval Imagination*. New Haven, CT: Yale University Press, 2008.

Freedman, Paul H., and Gabrielle Spiegel. "Medievalisms Old and New: The Rediscovery of Alterity in North American Medieval Studies." *American Historical Review* 103 (1998): 677–704.

Gaier, Claude. *L'industrie et le commerce des armes dans les anciennes principautés belges du XIIIme à la fin du XVme siècle*. Bibliothèque de la Faculté de Philosophie et Lettres de l'Université de Liège, fasc. 202. Paris: Les Belles Lettres, 1973.

Gameson, Richard. *The Study of the Bayeux Tapestry*. Woodbridge, Suffolk: Boydell, 1997.

Garnett, George, and John Hudson, eds. *Law and Government in Medieval England and Normandy: Essays in Honour of Sir James Holt*. Cambridge: Cambridge University Press, 1994.

Gaunt, Simon. *Retelling the Tale: An Introduction to Medieval French Literature*. London: Duckworth, 2001.

Geary, Patrick J. *Phantoms of Remembrance: Memory and Oblivion at the End of the First Millennium*. Princeton, NJ: Princeton University Press, 1994.

——. "Sacred Commodities: The Circulation of Medieval Relics." In *The Social Life of Things: Commodities in Cultural Perspective*, edited by Arjun Appadurai, 169–91. Cambridge: Cambridge University Press, 1986.

Gell, Alfred. *Art and Agency: An Anthropological Theory*. Oxford: Clarendon, 1998.

——. "The Technology of Enchantment and the Enchantment of Technology." In *Anthropology, Art and Aesthetics*, edited by Jeremy Coote and Anthony Shelton, 40–66. Oxford: Clarendon, 1994.

Gellner, Ernest. *Plough, Sword, and Book: The Structure of Human History*. Chicago: University of Chicago Press, 1989.

Gerritsen, Anne, and Giorgio Riello, eds. *Writing Material Culture History*. London: Bloomsbury Academic, 2015.

Gilchrist, Roberta. *Gender and Archaeology: Contesting the Past*. London: Routledge, 1999.

Gillingham, John. "Conquering the Barbarians: War and Chivalry in Twelfth-Century Britain." *Haskins Society Journal* 4 (1993): 67–84.

——. *The English in the Twelfth Century: Imperialism, National Identity, and Political Values*. Woodbridge, Suffolk: Boydell, 2000.

——. "Fontenoy and After: Pursuing Enemies to the Death in France between the Ninth and the Eleventh Centuries." In *Frankland: The Franks and the World of the Early Middle Ages*, edited by Paul Fouracre and David Ganz. Manchester: Manchester University Press, 2008.

——. "Kingship, Chivalry and Love: Political and Cultural Values in the Earliest History Written in French; Geoffrey Gaimar's *Estoire des Engleis*." In *Anglo-Norman Political Culture and the Twelfth-Century Renaissance*, edited by C. Warren Hollister. Woodbridge, Suffolk: D. S. Brewer, 1997.

——. "Richard I and the Science of War in the Middle Ages." In *War and Government in the Middle Ages*, edited by John Gillingham and James Clarke Holt. Woodbridge, Suffolk: Boydell, 1984.

——. "1066 and the Introduction of Chivalry into England." In *Law and Government in Medieval England and Normandy: Essays in Honour of Sir James Holt*, edited by George Garnett and John Hudson. Cambridge: Cambridge University Press, 2002.

——. "War and Chivalry in the *History of William the Marshal*." In *Proceedings of the Newcastle upon Tyne Conference, 1987*, edited by Peter R. Coss. Woodbridge, Suffolk: Boydell, 1988.

Gillingham, John, and James Clarke Holt, eds. *War and Government in the Middle Ages: Essays in Honour of J. O. Prestwich*. Cambridge: Boydell, 1984.

Girbea, Catalina, ed. *Armes et jeux militaires dans l'imaginaire: XIIe–XVe siècles*. Paris: Classiques Garnier, 2016.

Girbea, Catalina, Laurent Hablot, and Raluca Radulescu, eds. *Marqueurs d'identité dans la littérature médiévale: Mettre en signe l'individu et la famille (XIIe–XVe siècles)*. Turnhout, Belgium: Brepols, 2014.

Godden, Malcolm, and Michael Lapidge. *The Cambridge Companion to Old English Literature*. Cambridge: Cambridge University Press, 1991.

Goffart, Walter A. *Barbarian Tides: The Migration Age and the Later Roman Empire*. Philadelphia: University of Pennsylvania Press, 2006.

Grafton, Anthony, and Ann Blair. *The Transmission of Culture in Early Modern Europe*. Philadelphia: University of Pennsylvania Press, 1990.

Graves, Donald E. "'Naked Truths for the Asking': Twentieth-Century Military Historians and the Battlefield Narrative." In *Military History and the Military Profession*, edited by David A. Charters, Marc Milner, and J. Brent Wilson. Westport, CT: Praeger, 1992.

Green, David. *The Hundred Years War: A People's History*. New Haven, CT: Yale University Press, 2014.

Green, Richard Firth. *Elf Queens and Holy Friars: Fairy Beliefs and the Medieval Church*. Philadelphia: University of Pennsylvania Press, 2016.

Greenblatt, Stephen. *Renaissance Self-Fashioning, from More to Shakespeare*. With a new preface. Chicago: University of Chicago Press, 2005.

Grimbert, Joan T., and Norris J. Lacy, eds. *A Companion to Chrétien de Troyes*. Cambridge: D. S. Brewer, 2005.

Guenée, Bernard. *States and Rulers in Later Medieval Europe*. Oxford: Blackwell, 1985.

Gumbrecht, Hans Ulrich. *Production of Presence: What Meaning Cannot Convey*. Stanford, CA: Stanford University Press, 2004.

Gunn, S. J., Hans Cools, and David Grummitt. *War, State, and Society in England and the Netherlands, 1477–1559*. Oxford: Oxford University Press, 2007.

Hablot, Laurent. "The Sacralization of the Royal Coats of Arms in Medieval Europe." In *Political Theology in Medieval and Early Modern Europe: Discourses, Rites and Representations*, edited by Montserrat Herrero, Jaume Aurell, and Angela C. Miceli Stout. Turnhout, Belgium: Brepols, 2017.

——. "'Ubi armae ibi princeps': Medieval Emblematics as the Real Presence of the Prince." In *Absentee Authority across Medieval Europe*, edited by Frédérique Lachaud and Michael Penman. Woodbridge, Suffolk: Boydell, 2017.

Hadley, D. M. *Masculinity in Medieval Europe*. Women and Men in History. London: Longman, 1999.

Hahn, Thomas. "Gawain and Popular Romance in Britain." In *The Cambridge Companion to Medieval Romance*, edited by Roberta L. Krueger. Cambridge: Cambridge University Press, 2000.

Haidu, Peter. *The Subject of Violence: The Song of Roland and the Birth of the State*. Bloomington: Indiana University Press, 1993.

Hall, Bert S. *Weapons and Warfare in Renaissance Europe: Gunpowder, Technology, and Tactics*. Baltimore: Johns Hopkins University Press, 1997.

Hallam, Elizabeth M. "Monasteries as 'War Memorials': Battle Abbey and La Victoire." In *The Church and War*, edited by W. J. Sheils, 47–57. London: Basil Blackwell, 1983.

Hallam, Elizabeth M., and Jennifer Lorna Hockey. *Death, Memory, and Material Culture*. Oxford: Berg, 2001.

Halsall, Guy. "Anthropology and the Study of Pre-Conquest Warfare and Society: The Ritual War in Anglo-Saxon England." In *Weapons and Warfare in Anglo-Saxon England*, edited by Sonia Chadwick Hawkes, 155–77. Oxford: Oxford University Committee for Archaeology, 1989.

———. *Cemeteries and Society in Merovingian Gaul*. Leiden: Brill, 2010.

———. "Gender and the End of Empire." *Journal of Medieval and Early Modern Studies* 34, no. 1 (2004): 17–39.

———. "The Origins of the *Reihengräberzivilization*: Forty Years On." In *Fifth-Century Gaul: A Crisis of Identity?*, edited by John Drinkwater and Hugh Elton. Cambridge: Cambridge University Press, 1992.

———. *Warfare and Society in the Barbarian West, 450–900*. Warfare and History. London: Routledge, 2003.

Hamilakis, Yannis, Mark Pluciennik, and Sarah Tarlow. *Thinking through the Body: Archaeologies of Corporeality*. New York: Kluwer Academic / Plenum, 2002.

Harari, Yuval N. *Renaissance Military Memoirs: War, History, and Identity, 1450–1600*. Woodbridge, Suffolk: Boydell, 2004.

Härke, Heinrich. "Changing Symbols in a Changing Society: The Anglo-Saxon Burial Rite in the Seventh Century." In Carver, *Age of Sutton Hoo*, 149–65.

———. "The Circulation of Goods in Anglo-Saxon Society." In *Rituals of Power from Late Antiquity to the Early Middle Ages*, edited by Franz Theuws and Janet L. Nelson, 377–99. Leiden: Brill, 2000.

———. "Early Saxon Weapon Burials: Frequencies, Distributions and Weapon Combinations." In *Weapons and Warfare in Anglo-Saxon England*, edited by Sonia Chadwick Hawkes. Oxford: Oxford University Committee for Archaeology, 1989.

———. "Knives in Early Saxon Burials: Blade Length and Age at Death." *Medieval Archaeology* 33 (1989): 144–48.

———. "Material Culture as Myth: Weapons in Anglo-Saxon Graves." In *Burial and Society: The Chronological and Social Analysis of Archaeological Burial Data*, edited by Claus Kjeld Jensen and Karen Høilund Nielsen, 119–25. Aarhus, Denmark: Aarhus University Press, 1997.

———. "Swords, Warrior Graves and Anglo-Saxon Warfare." *Current Archaeology* 16 (2004): 556–61.

———. "Warrior Graves? The Background of the Anglo-Saxon Weapon Burial Rite." *Past and Present* 126 (1990): 22–43.

Harper-Bill, Christopher, and Ruth Harvey, eds. *The Ideals and Practice of Medieval Knighthood: Papers from the First and Second Strawberry Hill Conferences*. Woodbridge, Suffolk: Boydell, 1986.

———. *The Ideals and Practice of Medieval Knighthood II: Papers from the Third Strawberry Hill Conference, 1986*. Woodbridge, Suffolk: Boydell, 1988.

———. *The Ideals and Practice of Medieval Knighthood III: Papers from the Fourth Strawberry Hill Conference, 1988*. Woodbridge, Suffolk: Boydell, 1990.

———. *The Ideals and Practice of Medieval Knighthood IV: Papers from the Fifth Strawberry Hill Conference, 1990*. Woodbridge, Suffolk: Boydell, 1992.

Hawkes, Sonia Chadwick, ed. *Weapons and Warfare in Anglo-Saxon England*. Oxford: Oxford University Committee for Archaeology, 1989.

Hays, Michael L. *Shakespearean Tragedy as Chivalric Romance: Rethinking "Macbeth," "Hamlet," "Othello," and "King Lear."* Cambridge: D. S. Brewer, 2003.

Hayward, Maria. *The 1542 Inventory of Whitehall: The Palace and Its Keeper.* London: Society of Antiquaries of London, 2004.

Hedges, Chris. *War Is a Force That Gives Us Meaning.* New York: Public Affairs, 2002.

Herrero, Montserrat, Jaume Aurell, and Angela C. Miceli Stout, eds. *Political Theology in Medieval and Early Modern Europe: Discourses, Rites, Representations.* Turnhout, Belgium: Brepols, 2017.

Herrick, Samantha Kahn. *Imagining the Sacred Past: Hagiography and Power in Early Normandy.* Cambridge, MA: Harvard University Press, 2007.

Hicks, Carola, ed. *England in the Eleventh Century: Proceedings of the 1990 Harlaxton Symposium.* Stamford, Lincolnshire: Paul Watkins, 1992.

Hicks, M. A. *The Wars of the Roses.* New Haven, CT: Yale University Press, 2010.

Higate, Paul. *Military Masculinities: Identity and the State.* Westport, CT: Praeger, 2003.

Hindman, Sandra. *Sealed in Parchment: Rereadings of Knighthood in the Illuminated Manuscripts of Chrétien de Troyes.* Chicago: University of Chicago Press, 1994.

Hinton, David Alban. *Gold and Gilt, Pots and Pins: Possessions and People in Medieval Britain.* Medieval History and Archaeology. Oxford: Oxford University Press, 2005.

Hodder, Ian, ed. *The Meanings of Things: Material Culture and Symbolic Expression.* London: Unwin Hyman, 1989.

——. "This Is Not an Article about Material Culture as Text." *Journal of Anthropological Archaeology* 8 (1989): 250–69.

Hodder, Ian, and Scott Hutson. *Reading the Past: Current Approaches to Interpretation in Archaeology.* Cambridge: Cambridge University Press, 2003.

Hodges, Kenneth L. *Forging Chivalric Communities in Malory's "Le Morte Darthur."* New York: Palgrave Macmillan, 2005.

Holdsworth, Christopher. "'An Airier Aristocracy': The Saints at War." *Transactions of the Royal Historical Society* 6 (1996): 103–22.

Hooper, Nicholas. "The Anglo-Saxons at War." In *Weapons and Warfare in Anglo-Saxon England*, edited by Sonia Chadwick Hawkes, 191–201. Oxford: Oxford University Committee for Archaeology, 1989.

Hooper, Nicolas, and Matthew Bennett. *The Cambridge Illustrated Atlas of Warfare: The Middle Ages, 732–1487.* Cambridge: Cambridge University Press, 1996.

Horrox, Rosemary, and W. M. Ormrod. *A Social History of England, 1200–1500.* Cambridge: Cambridge University Press, 2006.

Huizinga, Johan. *The Autumn of the Middle Ages.* Chicago: University of Chicago Press, 1996.

——. *Homo Ludens: A Study of the Play Element in Culture.* International Library of Sociology. London: Routledge and K. Paul, 1980.

Humphrey, Chris, and W. M. Ormrod. *Time in the Medieval World.* Rochester, NY: York Medieval, 2001.

Hunt, Alice. *The Drama of Coronation: Medieval Ceremony in Early Modern England.* Cambridge: Cambridge University Press, 2008.

Jackson, Richard A. *Vive le Roi! A History of the French Coronation from Charles V to Charles X*. Chapel Hill: University of North Carolina Press, 1984.

Jacquot, Jean, and Elie Konigson, eds. *Les fêtes de la Renaissance*. Paris: Centre national de la recherche scientifique, 1956.

Jaeger, C. Stephen. *Ennobling Love: In Search of a Lost Sensibility*. Philadelphia: University of Pennsylvania Press, 1999.

———. *The Origins of Courtliness: Civilizing Trends and the Formation of Courtly Ideals, 939–1210*. Philadelphia: University of Pennsylvania Press, 1985.

James, Edward. "Royal Burials among the Franks." In Carver, *Age of Sutton Hoo*, 243–54.

Jardine, Lisa. *Worldly Goods: A New History of the Renaissance*. New York: Nan A. Talese, 1996.

Jarman, Neil. "Material of Culture, Fabric of Identity." In *Material Cultures: Why Some Things Matter*, edited by Daniel Miller. Chicago: University of Chicago Press, 1998.

Jenkins, Jacqueline, and Julie Sanders, eds. *Editing, Performance, Texts: New Practices in Medieval and Early Modern English Drama*. New York: Palgrave Macmillan, 2014.

Jensen, Claus Kjeld. *Burial and Society: The Chronological and Social Analysis of Archaeological Burial Data*. Aarhus, Denmark: Aarhus University Press, 1997.

John, Eric. "*Beowulf* and the Margins of Literacy." In *The "Beowulf" Reader*, edited by Peter S. Baker. New York: Garland, 2000.

Johnston, Michael. *Romance and the Gentry in Late Medieval England*. Oxford: Oxford University Press, 2014.

Jones, Ann Rosalind, and Peter Stallybrass. *Renaissance Clothing and the Materials of Memory*. Cambridge Studies in Renaissance Literature and Culture. Cambridge: Cambridge University Press, 2000.

Jones, M. K. "Battle of Verneuil." *War in History* 9 (2002): 379–411.

Jones, Robert W. *Bloodied Banners: Martial Display on the Medieval Battlefield*. Warfare in History. Woodbridge, Suffolk: Boydell, 2010.

Kaeuper, Richard W. *Chivalry and Violence in Medieval Europe*. Oxford: Oxford University Press, 1999.

Kaeuper, Richard W., and Elspeth Kennedy. *The "Book of Chivalry" of Geoffroi de Charny: Text, Context, and Translation*. Philadelphia: University of Pennsylvania Press, 1996.

Kagay, Donald J., and L. J. Andrew Villalon. *The Circle of War in the Middle Ages: Essays on Medieval Military and Naval History*. Woodbridge, Suffolk, Boydell, 1999.

Karras, Ruth Mazo. *From Boys to Men: Formations of Masculinity in Late Medieval Europe*. Philadelphia: University of Pennsylvania Press, 2003.

Kay, Sarah. *The chansons de geste in the Age of Romance: Political Fictions*. Oxford: Clarendon, 1995.

———. "Who Was Chrétien de Troyes?" *Arthurian Literature* 15 (1996): 1–35.

Keane, Marguerite. "Most Beautiful and the Next Best: Value in the Collection of a Medieval Queen." *Journal of Medieval History* 34, no. 4 (2008): 360–73.

Keen, Maurice Hugh. *Chivalry*. New Haven, CT: Yale University Press, 1984.

———. "Chivalry, Nobility and the Laws of Arms." In *War, Literature, and Politics in the Late Middle Ages*, edited by C. T. Allmand and George William Coopland. New York: Barnes and Noble Books, 1976.

——. "English Military Experience and the Court of Chivalry: The Case of Grey v. Hastings." In *Guerre et société en France, en Angleterre et en Bourgogne, XIVe–XVe siècle*, edited by Philippe Contamine, Charles Giry-Deloison, and Maurice H. Keen. Villeneuve d'Ascq: Université Charles de Gaulle Lille III, 1991.

——. "Gadifer de La Salle: A Late Medieval Knight Errant." In *The Ideals and Practice of Medieval Knighthood: Papers from the First and Second Strawberry Hill Conferences*, edited by Christopher Harper-Bill and Ruth Harvey. Woodbridge, Suffolk: Boydell, 1986.

——. *The Laws of War in the Late Middle Ages*. London: Routledge and K. Paul, 1965.

Kelly, Susan. "Anglo-Saxon Lay Society and the Written Word." In *The Uses of Literacy in Early Mediaeval Europe*, edited by Rosamond McKitterick. Cambridge: Cambridge University Press, 1990.

Kendall, Calvin B., and Peter S. Wells, eds. *Voyage to the Other World: The Legacy of Sutton Hoo*. Minneapolis: University of Minnesota Press, 1992.

Kennedy, Elspeth. "The Knight as Reader of Arthurian Romance." In *Culture and the King: The Social Implications of the Arthurian Legend*, edited by Martin B. Shichtman and James P. Carley. Albany: State University of New York Press, 1994.

Kieckhefer, Richard. *Magic in the Middle Ages*. Cambridge Medieval Textbooks. Cambridge: Cambridge University Press, 1989.

Kim, Hyonjin. *The Knight without the Sword: A Social Landscape of Malorian Chivalry*. Woodbridge, Suffolk: D. S. Brewer, 2000.

Kingery, W. D. *Learning from Things: Method and Theory of Material Culture Studies*. Washington, DC: Smithsonian Institution, 1996.

Knecht, R. J. *The French Renaissance Court, 1483–1589*. New Haven, CT: Yale University Press, 2008.

Knox, MacGregor, and Williamson Murray, eds. *The Dynamics of Military Revolution, 1300–2050*. Cambridge: Cambridge University Press, 2001.

Knüsel, Christopher, and Anthea Boylston. "How Has the Towton Project Contributed to Our Knowledge of Medieval Warfare?" In Fiorato, Boylston, and Knüsel, *Blood Red Roses*, 169–88.

Kopytoff, Igor. "The Cultural Biography of Things: Commoditization as Process." In *The Social Life of Things: Commodities in Cultural Perspective*, edited by Arjun Appadurai. Cambridge: Cambridge University Press, 1986.

Koslin, Désirée G., and Janet Ellen Snyder. *Encountering Medieval Textiles and Dress: Objects, Texts, Images*. New York: Palgrave Macmillan, 2002.

Kristiansen, Kristian. "An Essay on Material Culture: Some Concluding Reflections." In *Material Culture and Other Things: Post-Disciplinary Studies in the 21st Century*, edited by Fredrik Fahlander and Terje Oestigaard. Gothenburg: University of Gothenburg Department of Archaeology, 2004.

Krueger, Roberta L., ed. *The Cambridge Companion to Medieval Romance*. Cambridge: Cambridge University Press, 2000.

Lachaud, Frédérique. "Armour and Military Dress in Fourteenth-Century England." In *Armies, Chivalry and Warfare in Medieval Britain and France*, edited by Matthew Strickland. Stamford, Lincolnshire: Paul Watkins, 1998.

Lachaud, Frédérique, and Michael Penman, eds. *Absentee Authority across Medieval Europe*. Woodbridge, Suffolk: Boydell, 2017.

Lang, Janet, and Barry Ager. "Swords of the Anglo-Saxon and Viking Periods in the British Museum: A Radiographic Study." In *Weapons and Warfare in Anglo-Saxon England*, edited by Sonia Chadwick Hawkes. Oxford: Oxford University Committee for Archaeology, 1989.

Laradji, Aline. *La Légende de Roland: De la genèse française à l'épuisement de la figure du héros en Italie.* Paris: Harmattan, 2008.

La Rocca, Christina, and Luigi Provero. "The Dead and their Gifts." In *Rituals of Power: From Late Antiquity to the Early Middle Ages*, edited by Frans Theuws and Janet L. Nelson. Leiden: Brill, 2000.

Lecoq, Anne-Marie. *François Ier imaginaire: Symbolique et politique à l'aube de la Renaissance française.* Paris: Macula, 1987.

Lees, Clare A. "Men and *Beowulf.*" In *Medieval Masculinities: Regarding Men in the Middle Ages*, edited by Clare A. Lees. Minneapolis: University of Minnesota Press, 1994.

Legg, L. G. Wickham, ed. *English Coronation Records.* Westminster: A. Constable, 1901.

Le Goff, Jacques. "A Coronation Program." In *Coronations: Medieval and Early Modern Monarchic Ritual*, edited by János M. Bak. Berkeley: University of California Press, 1990.

——. *Pour un autre Moyen Âge.* Paris: Gallimard, 1977.

Leitch, Megan G. *Romancing Treason: The Literature of the Wars of the Roses.* Oxford: Oxford University Press, 2015.

Lejeune, Rita, and Jacques Stiennon. *La légende de Roland dans l'art du Moyen Âge.* Brussels: Arcade, 1967.

Lemonnier, Pierre. *Technological Choices: Transformation in Material Cultures since the Neolithic.* London: Routledge, 1993.

Lerer, Seth. *Inventing English: A Portable History of the Language.* New York: Columbia University Press, 2007.

——. *Literacy and Power in Anglo-Saxon Literature.* Lincoln: University of Nebraska Press, 1991.

Lester, G. A. *Sir John Paston's "Grete Boke": A Descriptive Catalogue, with an Introduction, of British Library MS Lansdowne 285.* Cambridge: D. S. Brewer, 1984.

Lewis, Michael J., Gale R. Owen-Crocker, and Dan Terkla, eds. *The Bayeux Tapestry: New Approaches; Proceedings of a Conference at the British Museum.* Oxford: Oxbow Books, 2011.

Leyerle, John. "The Interlace Structure of *Beowulf.*" *University of Toronto Quarterly* 37 (1967): 1–17.

Leyser, Karl. "Early Medieval Warfare." Chap. 3 in *Communications and Power in Medieval Europe: The Carolingian and Ottonian Centuries.* Edited by Timothy Reuter. London: Hambledon, 1994.

——. "Ritual, Ceremony and Gesture: Ottonian Germany." Chap. 12 in *Communications and Power in Medieval Europe: The Carolingian and Ottonian Centuries.* Edited by Timothy Reuter. London: Hambledon, 1994.

Linehan, Peter, and Janet L. Nelson. *The Medieval World.* London: Routledge, 2001.

Liuzza, Roy Michael. "On the Dating of *Beowulf.*" In *The "Beowulf" Reader*, edited by Peter S. Baker, 281–303. New York: Garland, 2000.

Livingston, Michael, ed. *The Battle of Brunanburh: A Casebook.* Exeter: University of Exeter Press, 2011.

Lochrie, Karma, Peggy McCracken, and James A. Schultz. *Constructing Medieval Sexuality*. Minneapolis: University of Minnesota Press, 1997.

Lowenthal, David. *The Past Is a Foreign Country*. Cambridge: Cambridge University Press, 1985.

———. "The Value of Age and Decay." In *Durability and Change: The Science, Responsibility and Cost of Sustaining Cultural Heritage*, edited by W. E. Krumbein, P. Brimblecombe, D. E. Cosgrove, and S. Stanforth. Chichester, West Sussex: John Wiley and Sons, 1994.

Lubar, Steven D., and W. D. Kingery. *History from Things: Essays on Material Culture*. Washington, DC: Smithsonian Institution, 1993.

Maddern, Philippa. "Friends of the Dead: Executors, Wills and Family Strategy in Fifteenth-Century Norfolk." In *Rulers and Ruled in Late Medieval England: Essays Presented to Gerald Harris*, edited by Rowena E. Archer and Simon Walker, 155–74. London: Hambledon, 1995.

Maddox, Donald. *Fictions of Identity in Medieval France*. Cambridge: Cambridge University Press, 2000.

Manning, Roger B. *Swordsmen: The Martial Ethos in the Three Kingdoms*. Oxford: Oxford University Press, 2003.

Martindale, Jane. "The Sword on the Stone: Some Resonances of a Medieval Symbol of Power (The Tomb of King John in Worcester Cathedral)." *Anglo-Norman Studies* 15 (1992): 199–241.

Martines, Lauro. "The Renaissance and the Birth of Consumer Society." *Renaissance Quarterly* 51 (1998): 193–203.

Mason, Emma. "The Hero's Invincible Weapon: An Aspect of Angevin Propaganda." In *The Ideals and Practice of Medieval Knighthood III: Papers from the Fourth Strawberry Hill Conference, 1988*, edited by Christopher Harper-Bill and Ruth Harvey. Woodbridge, Suffolk: Boydell, 1990.

Matz, Jean-Michel, and Noël-Yves Tonnerre, eds. *René d'Anjou, 1409–1480: Pouvoirs et gouvernement*. Rennes: Presses universitaires de Rennes, 2011.

McCracken, Grant David. *Culture and Consumption: New Approaches to the Symbolic Character of Consumer Goods and Activities*. Bloomington: Indiana University Press, 1988.

McKitterick, Rosamond, ed. *The Uses of Literacy in Early Mediaeval Europe*. Cambridge: Cambridge University Press, 1990.

McVitty, E. Amanda. "False Knights and True Men: Contesting Chivalric Masculinity in English Treason Trials, 1388–1415." *Journal of Medieval History* 40, no. 4 (2014): 458–77.

Megill, Allan. *Historical Knowledge, Historical Error*. Chicago: University of Chicago Press, 2007.

Merrifield, Ralph. *The Archaeology of Ritual and Magic*. London: Batsford, 1987.

Mertes, Kate. *The English Noble Household, 1250 to 1600: Good Governance and Politic Rule*. Oxford: Blackwell, 1988.

Miller, Daniel. *Acknowledging Consumption: A Review of New Studies*. Material Cultures. London: Routledge, 1995.

———, ed. *Material Cultures: Why Some Things Matter*. Chicago: University of Chicago Press, 1998.

Miller, Maureen C. *Clothing the Clergy: Virtue and Power in Medieval Europe, c. 800–1200*. Ithaca, NY: Cornell University Press, 2014.

Mitchell, W. J. T. *What Do Pictures Want? The Lives and Loves of Images*. Chicago: University of Chicago Press, 2005.

Molloy, Barry, ed. *The Cutting Edge: Studies in Ancient and Medieval Combat*. Stroud, Gloucestershire: Tempus, 2007.

Muchembled, Robert, E. William Monter, and European Science Foundation. *Cultural Exchange in Early Modern Europe*. 4 vols. Cambridge: Cambridge University Press, 2006.

Mukerji, Chandra. *From Graven Images: Patterns of Modern Materialism*. New York: Columbia University Press, 1983.

Mulryne, J. R., and Margaret Shewring. *War, Literature and the Arts in Sixteenth-Century Europe*. New York: St. Martin's, 1989.

Myers, A. R. "The Wealth of Richard Lyons." In *Essays in Medieval History Presented to Bertie Wilkinson*, edited by T. A. Sandquist and M. R. Powicke. Toronto: University of Toronto Press, 1969.

Nall, Catherine. *Reading and War in Fifteenth-Century England: From Lydgate to Malory*. Cambridge: D. S. Brewer, 2012.

Nelson, Janet L. *Politics and Ritual in Early Medieval Europe*. London: Hambledon, 1986.

——. "Thematic Reviews: Gender, Memory and Social Power." In *Gendering the Middle Ages*, edited by Pauline Stafford and Anneke B. Mulder-Bakker. Oxford: Blackwell, 2001.

Nelson, Janet L., and F. Theuws, eds. *Rituals of Power: From Late Antiquity to the Early Middle Ages*. Leiden: Brill, 2000.

Neuschel, Kristen B. "From 'Written Record' to the Paper Chase? The Documentation of Noble Life in the Sixteenth Century." *Historical Reflections / Réflections historiques* 27 (2001): 201–18.

——. "Noble Households in the Sixteenth Century: Material Settings and Human Communities." *French Historical Studies* 15, no. 4 (1988): 595–622.

——. *Word of Honor: Interpreting Noble Culture in Sixteenth-Century France*. Ithaca, NY: Cornell University Press, 1989.

Newton, Stella Mary. *Fashion in the Age of the Black Prince*. Woodbridge, Suffolk: Boydell, 1980.

Nicholson, Lewis E. "Hunlafing and the Point of the Sword." In *Anglo-Saxon Poetry: Essays in Appreciation, for John C. McGalliard*, edited by Lewis E. Nicholson and Dolores Warwick Frese, 50–61. Notre Dame, IN: University of Notre Dame Press, 1975.

Nicolle, David. *Warriors and Their Weapons around the Time of the Crusades: Relationships between Byzantium, the West and the Islamic World*. Aldershot, Hampshire: Ashgate/Variorum, 2002.

Nordhaus, John. *Arma et litterae: The Education of the noblesse de race in Sixteenth-Century France*. Ann Arbor: University Microfilms, 1974.

Norris, Margot. *Writing War in the Twentieth Century*. Charlottesville: University Press of Virginia, 2000.

North, John. *The Ambassadors' Secret: Holbein and the World of the Renaissance*. London: Hambledon and London, 2002.

Novak, Shannon A. "Battle-Related Trauma." In Fiorato, Boylston, and Knüsel, *Blood Red Roses*, 90–101.

Oakeshott, R. Ewart. *European Weapons and Armor*. Woodbridge, Suffolk: Boydell, 1980.

——. *Records of the Medieval Sword*. Rochester: Boydell, 1991.

O'Meara, Carra Ferguson. *Monarchy and Consent: The Coronation Book of Charles V of France*. London: Harvey Miller, 2001.

Ong, Walter J. *Orality and Literacy: The Technologizing of the Word*. London: Routledge, 2002.

Orchard, Andy. *A Critical Companion to "Beowulf."* Woodbridge, Suffolk: D. S. Brewer, 2003.

——. *Pride and Prodigies: Studies in the Monsters in the "Beowulf" Manuscript*. Woodbridge, Suffolk: D. S. Brewer, 1995.

Ormrod, W. M. *Edward III*. New Haven, CT: Yale University Press, 2011.

Overing, Gillian. *Language, Sign and Gender in "Beowulf."* Carbondale: Southern Illinois University Press, 1990.

——. "Swords and Signs: A Semiotic Perspective on *Beowulf*." *American Journal of Semiotics* 5, no. 1 (1987): 35–54, 56–57.

Owen-Crocker, Gale R. *Dress in Anglo-Saxon England*. Woodbridge, Suffolk: Boydell, 2004.

——. *The Four Funerals in "Beowulf" and the Structure of the Poem*. Manchester: Manchester University Press, 2000.

——. "Hawks and Horse-Trappings: The Insignia of Rank." In *The Battle of Maldon, AD 991*, edited by Donald Scragg. Oxford: Blackwell, 1991.

——. *King Harold II and the Bayeux Tapestry*. Woodbridge, Suffolk: Boydell, 2005.

Parker, Geoffrey, ed. *The Cambridge History of Warfare*. Cambridge: Cambridge University Press, 2005.

Pastoureau, Michel. "Jouer aux chevaliers de la Table Ronde à la fin du Moyen Âge." In *Le Goût du lecteur à la fin du Moyen Âge*, edited by Danielle Bohler, 65–81. Cahiers du Léopard d'Or, vol. 11. Paris: Le Léopard d'Or, 2006.

——. "Le rabot médiéval: De l'outil à l'emblème." In Raynaud, *Armes et outils*, 27–36.

Paz, James. "Aeschere's Head, Grendel's Mother and the Sword That Isn't a Sword: Unreadable Things in *Beowulf*." *Exemplaria* 25, no. 3 (Fall 2013): 231–51.

Pearce, Susan M. "Collecting Reconsidered." In *Interpreting Objects and Collections*, ed. Susan M. Pearce. London: Routledge, 1994.

——, ed. *Interpreting Objects and Collections*. London: Routledge, 1994.

——. *Museums, Objects and Collections: A Cultural Study*. Leicester: Leicester University Press, 1992.

——. *On Collecting: An Investigation into Collecting in the European Tradition*. Collecting Cultures Series. London: Routledge, 1995.

Pearce, Susan M., Ken Arnold, Alexandra Bounia, and Paul Martin. *The Collector's Voice: Critical Readings in the Practice of Collecting*. 4 vols. Aldershot, Hampshire: Ashgate, 2000.

Peck, Linda Levy. *Consuming Splendor: Society and Culture in Seventeenth-Century England*. Cambridge: Cambridge University Press, 2005.

Peirce, Ian. "The Development of the Medieval Sword, c. 850–1300." In Harper-Bill and Harvey, *Ideals and Practice of Medieval Knighthood III*, 139–58.

Pellegram, Andrea. "The Message in Paper." In *Material Cultures: Why Some Things Matter*, edited by Daniel Miller. Chicago: University of Chicago Press, 1998.

Peltonen, Markku. *The Duel in Early Modern England: Civility, Politeness and Honour.* Cambridge: Cambridge University Press, 2003.

Perry, Curtis. *Material Culture and Cultural Materialisms in the Middle Ages and Renaissance.* Turnhout, Belgium: Brepols, 2001.

Pick, Daniel. *War Machine: The Rationalisation of Slaughter in the Modern Age.* New Haven, CT: Yale University Press, 1993.

Piponnier, Françoise, and Perrine Mane. *Dress in the Middle Ages.* New Haven, CT: Yale University Press, 1997.

Portnoy, Phyllis. "*Laf*-Craft in Five Old English Riddles." *Neophilologus* 97 (2013): 555–79.

Potter, David. *Renaissance France at War: Armies, Culture and Society, c.1480–1560.* Woodbridge, Suffolk: Boydell, 2008.

Prestwich, J. O., and Michael Prestwich. *The Place of War in English History, 1066–1214.* Woodbridge, Suffolk: Boydell, 2004.

Prestwich, Michael. *Armies and Warfare in the Middle Ages: The English Experience.* New Haven, CT: Yale University Press, 1996.

Rasmussen, Ann Marie. *Medieval Badges: Visual Communication and the Formation of Community.* Philadelphia: University of Pennsylvania Press, forthcoming.

Raynaud, Christiane, ed. *Armes et outils.* Cahiers du Léopard d'Or, ed. Michel Pastoreau, vol. 14. Paris: Le Léopard d'Or, 2012.

———. "Le poête, l'arme et l'outil d'après l'oeuvre complète d'Eustache Deschamps." In Raynaud, *Armes et outils,* 89–119.

Remensnyder, Amy G. "Legendary Treasure at Conques: Reliquaries and Imaginative Memory." *Speculum* 71, no. 3 (July 1996): 884–906.

———. *Remembering Kings Past: Monastic Foundation Legends in Medieval Southern France.* Ithaca, NY: Cornell University Press, 1995.

Renfrew, Colin, and Christopher Scarre. *Cognition and Material Culture: The Archaeology of Symbolic Storage.* Cambridge: McDonald Institute for Archaeological Research, 1998.

Reuter, Timothy. "Nobles and Others: The Social and Cultural Expression of Power Relations in the Middle Ages." In *Nobles and Nobility in Medieval Europe,* edited by Anne J. Duggan. Woodbridge, Suffolk: Boydell, 2000.

———. "Plunder and Tribute in the Carolingian Empire." *Transactions of the Royal Historical Society* 35 (1985): 75–94.

———. "You Can't Take It with You: Testaments, Hoards and Movable Wealth in Europe, 600–1100." In Tyler, *Treasure in the Medieval West,* 11–24.

Reynaud, Marcelle-Renée. *Le temps des princes: Louis II et Louis III d'Anjou-Provence, 1384–1434.* Lyon: Presses universitaires de Lyon, 2000.

Richards, J. D. "An Archaeology of Anglo-Saxon England." In *After Empire: Towards an Ethnology of Europe's Barbarians,* edited by G. Ausenda, 51–63. Woodbridge, Suffolk: Boydell, 1995.

Richardson, Thom. "Armour." In Fiorato, Boylston, and Knüsel, *Blood Red Roses,* 137–47.

———. "Armour in England." *Journal of Medieval History* 37, no. 3 (2011): 304–20.

Richmond, Velma Bourgeois. *The Legend of Guy of Warwick.* New York: Garland, 1996.

Rider, Jeff. "The Other Worlds of Romance." In Krueger, *Medieval Romance,* 115–31.

Rogers, Clifford J. "The Development of the Longbow in Late Medieval England and 'Technological Determinism.'" *Journal of Medieval History* 37, no. 3 (2011): 321–41.

——, ed. *The Military Revolution Debate: Readings on the Military Transformation of Early Modern Europe.* Boulder, CO: Westview, 1995.

——, ed. *The Oxford Encyclopedia of Medieval Warfare and Military Technology.* New York: Oxford University Press, 2010.

Rose, Tessa. *The Coronation Ceremony of the Kings and Queens of England.* London: H. M. Stationery Office, 1992.

Rosenthal, Joel Thomas. *Telling Tales: Sources and Narration in Late Medieval England.* University Park: Pennsylvania State University Press, 2003.

Rosenwein, Barbara H. *Anger's Past: The Social Uses of an Emotion in the Middle Ages.* Ithaca, NY: Cornell University Press, 1998.

Rubin, Miri, and Jacques Le Goff. *The Work of Jacques Le Goff and the Challenges of Medieval History.* Woodbridge, Suffolk: Boydell, 1997.

Sahlins, Marshall David. *How "Natives" Think: About Captain Cook, for Example.* Chicago: University of Chicago Press, 1995.

——. *Islands of History.* Chicago: University of Chicago Press, 1985.

Sandberg, Brian. *Warrior Pursuits: Noble Culture and Civil Conflict in Early Modern France.* Baltimore: Johns Hopkins University Press, 2010.

Saul, Nigel. *Death, Art, and Memory in Medieval England: The Cobham Family and Their Monuments, 1300–1500.* Oxford: Oxford University Press, 2001.

Savage, Anne. "The Grave, the Sword and the Lament." In *Laments for the Lost in Medieval Literature,* edited by Jane Tolmie and M. J. Toswell. Turnhout, Belgium: Brepols, 2010.

Sayer, Duncan, and Howard Williams, eds. *Mortuary Practices and Social Identities in the Middle Ages: Essays in Burial Archaeology in Honour of Heinrich Härke.* Exeter: University of Exeter Press, 2009.

Scaglione, Aldo D. *Knights at Court: Courtliness, Chivalry and Courtesy from Ottonian Germany to the Italian Renaissance.* Berkeley: University of California Press, 1991.

Schiffer, Michael B., and Andrea R. Miller. *The Material Life of Human Beings: Artifacts, Behavior, and Communication.* London: Routledge, 1999.

Scragg, Donald, ed. *The Battle of Maldon, AD 991.* Oxford: Basil Blackwell, 1991.

Searle, Eleanor. *Predatory Kinship and the Creation of Norman Power, 840–1066.* Berkeley: University of California Press, 1988.

Seward, Desmond. *The Hundred Years War: The English in France, 1337–1453.* New York: Penguin, 1999.

Sheehan, Michael M. *The Will in Medieval England, from the Conversion of the Anglo-Saxons to the End of the Thirteenth Century.* Toronto: Pontifical Institute of Mediaeval Studies, 1963.

Shichtman, Martin B., and James P. Carley. "Introduction: The Social Implications of the Arthurian Legend." In *Culture and the King: The Social Implications of the Arthurian Legend; Essays in Honor of Valerie M. Lagorio,* edited by Martin B. Shichtman and James P. Carley. Albany: State University of New York Press, 1994.

Shippey, T. A. *J. R. R. Tolkien: Author of the Century.* Boston: Houghton Mifflin, 2000.

Simpkin, David. *The English Aristocracy at War: From the Welsh Wars of Edward I to the Battle of Bannockburn.* Woodbridge, Suffolk: Boydell, 2008.

Sinclair, Alexandra, ed. *The Beauchamp Pageant.* Donington, Lincolnshire: Richard III and Yorkist History Trust in Association with Paul Watkins, 2003.

Smail, Daniel Lord. "Introduction: History and the Telescoping of Time; A Disciplinary Forum." *French Historical Studies* 34, no. 1 (Winter 2011): 1–6.

Small, Graeme. *Late Medieval France.* Basingstoke, Hampshire: Palgrave Macmillan, 2009.

Smith, Nicole Danielle. *Sartorial Strategies: Outfitting Aristocrats and Fashioning Conduct in Late Medieval Literature.* Notre Dame, IN: University of Notre Dame Press, 2012.

Spiegel, Gabrielle M. "History, Historicism, and the Social Logic of the Text in the Middle Ages." *Speculum* 65 (1990): 59–86.

——. *Romancing the Past: The Rise of Vernacular Prose Historiography in Thirteenth-Century France.* Berkeley: University of California Press, 1993.

Sponsler, Claire. "What the 'Beauchamp Pageant' Says about Medieval Plays." In *Editing, Performance, Texts: New Practices in Medieval and Early Modern English Drama,* edited by Jacqueline Jenkins and Julie Sanders. Basingstoke, Hampshire: Palgrave Macmillan, 2014.

Springer, Carolyn. *Armour and Masculinity in the Italian Renaissance.* Toronto: University of Toronto Press, 2010.

Spyer, Patricia, ed. *Border Fetishisms: Material Objects in Unstable Spaces.* Zones of Religion. New York: Routledge, 1998.

Staley, Lynn. *Languages of Power in the Age of Richard II.* University Park: Pennsylvania State University Press, 2005.

Stallybrass, Peter. "Marx's Coat." In *Border Fetishisms,* ed. Patricia Spyer, 183–207. New York: Routledge, 1998.

——. "Worn Worlds: Clothes, Mourning, and the Life of Things." *Yale Review* 81 (1993): 35–50.

Stallybrass, Peter, and Ann Rosalind Jones. "Fetishizing the Glove in Renaissance Europe." *Critical Inquiry* 28 (2001): 114–32.

Steer, Francis W. "A Medieval Household: The Urswick Inventory." *Essex Review* 63 (1954): 4–20.

Stern, Lesley. "'Paths That Wind through the Thicket of Things.'" In Brown, *Things,* 393–430.

Stewart, Susan. *On Longing: Narratives of the Miniature, the Gigantic, the Souvenir, the Collection.* Durham, NC: Duke University Press, 1993.

Stock, Brian. *The Implications of Literacy: Written Language and Models of Interpretation in the Eleventh and Twelfth Centuries.* Princeton, NJ: Princeton University Press, 1987.

——. *Listening for the Text: On the Uses of the Past.* Philadelphia: University of Pennsylvania Press, 1990.

Strathern, Marilyn. *The Gender of the Gift: Problems with Women and Problems with Society in Melanesia.* Studies in Melanesian Anthropology. Berkeley: University of California Press, 1988.

Stretton, Grace. "Some Aspects of Medieval Travel." *Transactions of the Royal Historical Society,* 4th ser., 7 (1924): 77–97.

——. "The Travelling Household in the Middle Ages." *Journal of the British Archaeo-logical Society* 40 (1935): 75–103.

Strickland, Matthew. *Anglo-Norman Warfare: Studies in Late Anglo-Saxon and Anglo-Norman Military Organization and Warfare.* Woodbridge, Suffolk: Boydell, 1992.

——. *Armies, Chivalry and Warfare in Medieval Britain and France: Proceedings of the 1995 Harlaxton Symposium.* Stamford, Lincolnshire: Paul Watkins, 1998.

——. "Arms and the Men: War, Loyalty and Lordship in Jordan Fantosme's Chron-icle." In *The Ideals and Practice of Medieval Knighthood IV: Papers from the Fifth Strawberry Hill Conference,* edited by Christopher Harper-Bill and Ruth Harvey. Woodbridge, Suffolk: Boydell, 1992.

——. "Slaughter, Slavery or Ransom: The Impact of the Conquest on Conduct in Warfare." In *England in the Eleventh Century: Proceedings of the 1990 Harlaxton Symposium,* edited by Carola Hicks. Stamford, Lincolnshire: Paul Watkins, 1992.

——. *War and Chivalry: The Conduct and Perception of War in England and Normandy, 1066–1217.* New York: Cambridge University Press, 1996.

Styers, Randall. *Making Magic: Religion, Magic and Science in the Modern World.* Oxford: Oxford University Press, 2004.

Sutton, Anne F., and P. W. Hammond. *The Coronation of Richard III: The Extant Docu-ments.* Gloucester: Sutton, 1983.

Symes, Carol. "The Middle Ages between Nationalism and Colonialism." *French His-torical Studies* 34, no. 1 (Winter 2011): 37–46.

Tamen, Miguel. *Friends of Interpretable Objects.* Cambridge, MA: Harvard University Press, 2001.

Taylor, Andrew. "Was There a Song of Roland?" *Speculum* 76, no. 1 (January 2001): 28–65.

Theuws, Frans. "Grave Goods, Ethnicity, and the Rhetoric of Burial Rights in Late Antique Northern Gaul." In *Ethnic Constructs in Antiquity,* edited by Ton Dersk and Nico Roymans. Amsterdam: Amsterdam University Press, 2009.

Theuws, Frans, and Monika Alkemade. "A Kind of Mirror for Men: Sword Deposi-tions in Late Antique Northern Gaul." In *Rituals of Power: From Late Antiquity to the Early Middle Ages,* edited by Frans Theuws and Janet L. Nelson. Leiden: Brill, 2000.

Theuws, Frans, and Janet L. Nelson, eds., *Rituals of Power: From Late Antiquity to the Early Middle Ages.* Leiden: Brill, 2000.

Tiffany, Daniel. "Lyric Substance: On Riddles, Materialism and Poetic Obscurity." In Brown, *Things,* 72–98.

Tilley, Christopher Y. *Metaphor and Material Culture.* Social Archaeology. Oxford: Blackwell, 1999.

Tilley, Christopher Y., Patricia Spyer, Webb Keane, Susanne Küchler, and Michael Rowlands. *Handbook of Material Culture.* London: Sage, 2006.

Tolkien, J. R. R. "*Beowulf:* The Monsters and the Critics." In "*Beowulf*": A Verse Trans-lation, edited by Daniel Donoghue, translated by Seamus Heaney. New York: W. W. Norton, 2002.

Tolmie, Jane, and M. J. Toswell, eds. *Laments for the Lost in Medieval Literature.* Turn-hout, Belgium: Brepols, 2010.

Trentmann, Frank. *Empire of Things.* New York: HarperCollins, 2016.

——, ed. *The Oxford Handbook of the History of Consumption*. Oxford: Oxford University Press, 2012.

Turrell, Denise, Martin Aurell, Christine Manigand, Jérôme Grévy, Laurent Hablot, and Catalina Girbea, eds. *Signes et couleurs des identités politiques: Du Moyen Âge à nos jours*. Rennes: Presses universitaires de Rennes, 2008.

Tyler, Elizabeth M. "'The Eyes of the Beholders Were Dazzled': Treasure and Artifice in the *Encomium Emmae Reginae*." *Early Medieval Europe* 8, no. 2 (1999): 247–70.

——. *Old English Poetics: The Aesthetics of the Familiar in Anglo-Saxon England*. Woodbridge, Suffolk: York Medieval Press in association with Boydell Press, 2006.

——. "Treasure and Convention in Old English Verse." *Notes and Queries* 43, no. 1 (1996): 2–13.

——, ed. *Treasure in the Medieval West*. Woodbridge, Suffolk: York Medieval, 2000.

Vale, Juliet. *Edward III and Chivalry: Chivalric Society and Its Context, 1270–1350*. Woodbridge, Suffolk: Boydell, 1982.

Vale, Malcolm. *The Princely Court: Medieval Courts and Culture in North-West Europe, 1270–1380*. Oxford: Oxford University Press, 2001.

——. *War and Chivalry: Warfare and Aristocratic Culture in England, France, and Burgundy at the End of the Middle Ages*. Athens: University of Georgia Press, 1981.

——. "Warfare and the Life of the French and Burgundian Nobility in the Late Middle Ages." In *Adelige Sachkultur des Spätmittelalters: Internationaler Kongress Krems an der Donau 22–25 September 1980*.Vienna: Verlag der Österreichischen Akademie der Wissenschaften, 1982.

Van Houts, Elisabeth M. C. *History and Family Traditions in England and the Continent, 1000–1200*. Aldershot: Ashgate, 1999.

——. *Memory and Gender in Medieval Europe, 900–1200*. Toronto: University of Toronto Press, 1999.

Van Uytven, Raymond. "Showing Off One's Rank." In *Showing Status: Representation of Social Positions in the Late Middle Ages*, edited by Wim Blockmans and Antheun Janse. Turnhout, Belgium: Brepols, 1999.

Venarde, Bruce L. *Women's Monasticism and Medieval Society: Nunneries in France and England, 890–1215*. Ithaca, NY: Cornell University Press, 1997.

Vernier, Richard. *The Flower of Chivalry: Bertrand du Guesclin and the Hundred Years War*. Woodbridge, Suffolk: D. S. Brewer, 2003.

Viswanathan, S. "On the Melting of the Sword: *Wael-Rapas* and the Engraving of the Sword-Hilt in *Beowulf*." *Philological Quarterly* 58, no. 3 (1979): 360–63.

Walker, John Albert, and Sarah Chaplin. *Visual Culture: An Introduction*. Manchester: Manchester University Press, 1997.

Walton, Steven. "Words of Technological Virtue: 'The Battle of Brunanburh' and Anglo-Saxon Sword Manufacture." *Technology and Culture* 36 (1995): 987–99.

Ward, P. L. "The Coronation Ceremony in Mediaeval England." *Speculum* 14, no. 2 (April 1939): 160–78.

Warren, Michelle R. *History on the Edge: Excalibur and the Borders of Britain, 1100–1300*. Minneapolis: University of Minnesota Press, 2000.

Watts, John. *The Making of Polities: Europe, 1300–1500*. Cambridge: Cambridge University Press, 2009.

Waugh, Robin, and James Weldon, eds. *The Hero Recovered: Essays on Medieval Heroism in Honor of George Clark*. Kalamazoo, MI: Medieval Institute, 2010.

Webster, Leslie. "Ideal and Reality: Versions of Treasure in the Early Anglo-Saxon World." In Tyler, *Treasure in the Medieval West.*

Weiner, Annette B. *Inalienable Possessions: The Paradox of Keeping-While-Giving.* Berkeley: University of California Press, 1992.

Welch, Evelyn S. *Shopping in the Renaissance: Consumer Cultures in Italy, 1400–1600.* New Haven, CT: Yale University Press, 2005.

West, Charles. *Reframing the Feudal Revolution: Political and Social Transformation between Marne and Moselle, c. 800–c. 1100.* Cambridge: Cambridge University Press, 2013.

White, Stephen D. "Feuding and Peace-Making in the Touraine around the Year 1100." *Traditio* 42 (1986): 195–263.

Wickham, Chris. *Framing the Early Middle Ages: Europe and the Mediterranean, 400–800.* Oxford: Oxford University Press, 2005.

Wild, Benjamin L. "Emblems and Enigmas: Revisiting the 'Sword' Belt of Fernando de la Cerda." *Journal of Medieval History* 37, no. 4 (2011): 378–96.

Williams, Alan R. *The Knight and the Blast Furnace: A History of the Metallurgy of Armour in the Middle Ages and the Early Modern Period.* Leiden: Brill, 2003.

———. *The Sword and the Crucible: A History of the Metallurgy of European Swords up to the Sixteenth Century.* Leiden: Brill, 2012.

Williams, Alan R., and Anthony de Reuck. *The Royal Armoury at Greenwich: A History of Its Technology.* London: Trustees of the Royal Armouries, 1995.

Williams, Howard. *Archaeologies of Remembrance: Death and Memory in Past Societies.* New York: Kluwer Academic / Plenum, 2003.

———. "Death, Memory and Time: A Consideration of Mortuary Practices at Sutton Hoo." In *Time in the Medieval World,* edited by C. Humphrey and W. M. Ormrod. York: York Medieval, 2001.

———. "Keeping the Dead at Arm's Length: Memory, Weaponry and Early Medieval Mortuary Practices." *Journal of Social Archaeology* 5, no. 2 (2005): 253–75.

———. "Material Culture as Memory: Combs and Cremation in Early Medieval Britain." *Early Medieval Europe* 12, no. 2 (2003): 89–128.

Woolgar, Christopher M. "Fast and Feast: Conspicuous Consumption and the Diet of the Nobility in the Fifteenth Century." In *Revolution and Consumption in Late Medieval England,* edited by M. A. Hicks, 7–26. Woodbridge, Suffolk: Boydell, 2001.

———. *The Great Household in Late Medieval England.* New Haven, CT: Yale University Press, 1999.

———. *The Senses in Late Medieval England.* New Haven, CT: Yale University Press, 2006.

Wright, Nicholas. *Knights and Peasants: The Hundred Years War in the French Countryside.* Warfare in History 4. Woodbridge, Suffolk: Boydell, 1998.

Young, Alan R. *Tudor and Jacobean Tournaments.* Dobbs Ferry, NY: Sheridan House, 1987.

Young, James Edward. *The Texture of Memory: Holocaust Memorials and Meaning.* New Haven, CT: Yale University Press, 1993.

Index